HANDBOOK
OF SPORTS
ECONOMICS
RESEARCH

HANDBOOK OF SPORTS ECONOMICS RESEARCH

EDITED BY JOHN FIZEL

M.E.Sharpe
Armonk, New York
London, England

Library of Congress Cataloging-in-Publication Data

Handbook of sports economics research / John Fizel, editor
   p. cm.
Includes bibliographical references and index.
  ISBN 0-7656-1594-0 (hardcover : alk. paper)
  1. Sports—Economic aspects—United States—Handbooks, manuals, etc.
2. Sports administration—Economic aspects—United States—Handbooks, manuals,
etc. 3. Professional sports—Economic aspects—United States—Handbooks,
manuals, etc. I. Title.

GV716.H36 2006
338.4'7796—dc22   2005018045

Printed in the United States of America

The paper used in this publication meets the minimum requirements of
American National Standard for Information Sciences
Permanence of Paper for Printed Library Materials,
ANSI Z 39.48-1984.

BM (c) 10   9   8   7   6   5   4   3   2   1

Contents

Part III: Issues Across the Sports Industry

Part IV: Econometrics and Theory in Sports Economics

List of Tables and Figures

Tables

Figures

Part I

Introduction

Handbook of
Sports Economics Research

An Overview

John Fizel

The *Handbook of Sports Economics Research* is a foray into an exciting and escalating market, the business of sports. In the past five years alone, there have been hundreds of academic sport-related publications, a plethora of new course offerings in sports economics, the development of new textbooks in sports economics, and a significant increase in the number of sessions at economic conferences devoted to economic analysis of sports.

Moreover, it is the business of sports that transforms the games into organized entertainment for viewing by a large segment of the population. Over the last twenty years, the public appetite for sports entertainment has provided the opportunity for skyrocketing franchise values, multi-million-dollar television contracts, average player salaries in excess of $1 million, flourishing markets for sports memorabilia, and hundreds of millions of public dollars directed toward stadium construction.

The growth in sports economics research, in my view, results from the unique opportunities the sports industry provides for both theoretical and empirical analysis. First, the sports industry generates a level of interest much greater than other industries. Issues in sports are prominent in daily reports in the press—including news, business, and sports sections—in discussions at the office water cooler or with neighbors or friends, and frequently are used as examples in books, speeches, and the classroom. Second, there are the peculiar aspects of the industry (Neale, 1964). The output of sports is a joint product where the firms in the industry must compete and cooperate for the league to thrive. In addition, the output of the industry is fixed so that the average winning percentage is always 0.5. Also, employment levels are fixed and complicated by several unique institutional rules about employee mobility, salary negotiations, and so on. Third, the basis of economic analysis is individual decision-making motivated by self-interest, which is a perfect fit with the sports industry. In sports, one can easily collect detailed measures of player and team productivity, identify individual decisions (e.g., player, manager/coach, or arbitrator decisions), and determine how judgments and performance change as incentive structures are altered. Finally, the economic analysis of sports employee productivity, labor relations, marketing, and profitability often parallel the analysis of business in general. The wealth of data about sports makes the industry a laboratory to observe economic and business behavior and theory not possible in other industries where there is a dearth of public information.

In the next chapter, Jewell addresses the quality of the research in sports economics. He finds that sports economics has moved from a diversionary and occasional academic exercise to a place of prominence and legitimacy within the economics discipline. Jewell reviews a number of articles that have been published in the best economic journals, highlighting the innovative methodologies, excellent data, and well-crafted arguments that are now common in sports economics research.

In short, sports economics is an influential and rigorous field of study that has experienced significant growth in a short time. The *Handbook of Sports Economics Research* is an opportunity to reflect on these changes and assess the state of the art.

The dynamic nature of the sports industry continually introduces new issues and uncovers new aspects of old issues. The chapters in this book examine what we know, what we do not know, what is stable, what is changing, what is certain, and what is controversial in sports economics. They present surveys of specific sports economics topics and suggest new and untapped avenues of research.

The *Handbook of Sports Economics Research* allows a reader to address issues in a particular sport or make comparisons along major topics of importance such as:

- Revenues and costs
- Labor markets (restrictions, discrimination)
- Market structure (league and association organizations)
- Market outcomes (competitive balance, the pursuit of winning versus profits)
- Public and league policy

Part II offers six chapters that review and analyze specific sports. Berri begins this part with an examination of the National Basketball Association

(NBA). He notes that NBA research is dominated by studies on discrimination, perhaps because of the historically high minority participation levels. He finds mixed results for salary, hiring, and customer discrimination research, but concludes that definitive analysis is elusive because replication across different data sets and methodologies is absent. Berri continues with a review of player productivity as related to salaries and team objectives. In this context, he provides a number of interesting and provocative insights. Much more is available in the chapter.

Leadley and Zygmont turn our attention to the National Hockey League (NHL). They find that much of the research about the NHL, like that on the NBA, addresses discrimination. In this case, the focus is on discrimination toward French Canadian players. No consensus is apparent. Leadley and Zygmont turn next to the effect of player violence on player salaries and team attendance. They find attendance increases with the level of violence. They also find that players designated as enforcers seem to receive compensation for violence, which is consistent with the value of violence reflected in higher attendance. A unique aspect of labor market studies addressed in Leadley and Zygmont's review is the joint production of teammates. Additional insights are offered about attendance and franchise location, each of which is particularly important in light of the positions held by players and owners that led to the cancellation of the 2004–5 NHL season.

Fizel and Hadley offer a synopsis of the research issues involving the unique, three-tiered labor market of Major League Baseball (MLB). Not surprisingly, they find that the reserve clause has been shown to consistently lower player salaries relative to salaries of free agents. However, the relationship of all players' salaries relative to marginal revenue product is an increasingly unsettled issue, as new models of measuring MRP appear in the literature. Some research even indicates that with the choice of free agency, players early in their careers may opt to select to operate under the reserve clause as part of an optimal contracting arrangement with owners. The applicability of the invariance principle is also unresolved. New models of arbitration negotiation have resulted in useful insights into player and owner decision-making, but aspects of discrimination, MLB structural changes, arbitration panels, and more offer significant future research opportunities.

Matheson continues the analysis of specific sports with his survey of European football (soccer). Among other topics, Matheson discusses three aspects of soccer that are distinctly different than North American sports. First, players in soccer are frequently traded for cash settlements, not for other players or draft choices. Second, soccer is played in leagues that do not have a fixed set of teams. Teams may move from one league to another as they are promoted to a better league for a good team performance or relegated to a lower league for a poor team performance. Third, the playing and regulatory aspects of soccer are quite unique.

Humphreys takes us to the world of women's collegiate athletics. The key issue is Title IX. Humphreys adds clarity to the discussion on definition, application, compliance, and effects of Title IX by removing the emotional rhetoric and applying an economic foundation for analysis. A number of additional issues are weaved into the presentation of the Title IX literature, with some intriguing and surprising conclusions. Humphreys also addresses gender regulation and compensation among coaches and players.

The last chapter of Part II focuses on individual sports and how individual sports fit into economic theory. As von Allmen points out, it is not how well one performs that matters in an individual sport, it is the rank order of one's finish that counts. As a result, von Allmen reviews the research on rank-order tournaments and their relevance to optimal contest design and optimal compensation systems. He also reviews applications within a number of individual sports including golf, track, motor racing, tennis, thoroughbred racing, and more. [1]

Part III offers two chapters that deal with issues relevant across various sports. Krautmann and Hadley offer an analysis of the literature on demand for sporting events. Although demand analysis may seem rudimentary and straightforward, it is not. Krautmann and Hadley explain the complications in measuring output and price, the foundation for any demand analysis. These complications, they find, cause some counterintuitive empirical results. Theoretically, one would expect a profit maximizing firm to price in the elastic portion of the team's demand curve, but empirical evidence for this behavior is lacking. Sometimes, the research even finds a positive relationship between price and ticket sales. Krautmann and Hadley do their own empirical analysis to highlight the issues surrounding price as well as address other important demand determinants.

Next, Fort examines the existing research on competitive balance in North American professional sports. A peculiar aspect of sports described earlier is that the output of sports is a joint product where the firms in the industry must compete and cooperate for the league to thrive. Teams compete to be successful, but if one team is "too successful" and competitive balance within the industry is compromised, fans lose interest and the league fails. Fort points out that competitive balance is multidimensional, and, as a result, he assesses the competitive balance in sports using three different measures of competitive balance. He also incorporates an assessment of cross-sectional and time-series analyses using these measures. This review paints an interesting picture of where competitive balance is and how it has changed over time. Fort also suggests that policy choices by North American sports leagues appear to have little effect on competitive balance and that the research on competitive balance has only just begun.

Part III, the concluding part of the *Handbook*, examines the econometric tools and theoretical framework that have been underutilized in sports economics research and that provide an opportunity for several new threads of research.

This part of the book starts with Lee's discussion of efficiency estimation. Efficiency is determined by how well a team or manager uses player talent to generate wins or team profits. Measuring and understanding efficiency is critically important in industries faced with salary caps, taxes on high payrolls, and the disparity in market size of teams, which almost mandates that small-market teams be efficient to survive. Lee begins with an overview of the existing literature, indicating the variety of estimation techniques used to assess production or cost efficiency. He also addresses the important role of using *ex ante* or *ex post* player talent data. He follows with a discussion of stochastic frontier models, how they can provide new insights into efficiency estimation, and how they can incorporate the peculiar aspects of sports economics.

Leeds and McCormick also explore the econometric possibilities in sports economics research. Their presentation addresses specification issues in cross-sectional and time-series analysis. More specifically, some of the topics include sample selection bias, quantile regressions, and causality issues. Many relationships in sports involve endogenous variables, but seldom are endogeneity issues explicitly addressed. Leeds and McCormick explain the implications of this oversight and provide guidance on how to treat the issue. Also, comparative analyses of players within a sport focus on a distribution around the average performance or compensation. Leeds and McCormick demonstrate how quantile analysis examines the entire population not just the average player. In addition to addressing the foundations of time-series analysis, Leeds and McCormick suggest that causality analysis is underutilized.

In the final chapter of the *Handbook*, Szymanski creates a framework for theoretically analyzing contests, whether they exist as individual sports competitions or games played within a sports league. This framework and the analysis it permits is clearly in its infancy. In my opinion, Szymanski provides a result that will cause all of us to explore more about modeling contests. Typically, economists expect talent to be allocated to its most valuable location. Doing so, the marginal revenue of a win will be equalized across the league. Szymanski's models find that this is not true. The implication of his result is that the total profits of the league are increased when talent is moved from weaker to stronger teams (is this the Yankee dream or what?).

In closing, I want to thank all of the contributors for a job well done. Their work would have been outstanding if they had only presented the results of the voluminous research in their topic areas. But, as you will read, they have also provided critical analysis of the results and have shown great insights into suggestions for future research streams. My comments about each chapter are limited, with many more topics to be discovered in each chapter. I believe that you will find the *Handbook of Sports Economics* useful, thought provoking and, hopefully, enjoyable.

Note

1. Men's collegiate athletics (NCAA) was consciously omitted from the *Handbook of Sports Economics Research* because extensive and current reviews of this topic already exist. For more on the NCAA, see Fleisher, Goff, and Tollison (1992), Zimbalist (1999), and Fizel and Fort (2004).

2

Sports Economics

The State of the Discipline

R. Todd Jewell

Sports economics is firmly established as a legitimate field of economics. Given the apparent acceptance of sports economics, one might expect this would translate to academic self-respect and respect among ones peers. However, this appears not to be the case for those who study the sports industry. For instance, at a recent national conference frequented by sports economists, I heard various comments that lamented a perceived lack of respect for sports research within economics as a whole. This chapter provides some evidence that sports economics is a thriving and respected field of economics and that it has potential for continued growth. Most importantly, it appears high-quality sports-related research can be, and increasingly is, published in the best economics journals. This research is characterized by the use of innovative methodologies and outstanding data. In addition, a clear statement of the importance of the research to economics as a whole increases the probability of publication and should increase the impact of the research on future scholarship. My comments are designed to continue a dialogue among researchers who wish to analyze the position of the sports economist in the context of the entire economic discipline.

I define a sports economist as one who does research on sports-related topics. There are two unique, but not mutually exclusive, strains of sports-related research. First, in order of appearance in the literature, there is research that applies microeconomic theory to the sports industry in an attempt to understand the markets of sports. This strain can be referred to as "sports-microeconomics" and contains papers that develop or adapt economic theory for use in describing the sports industry. The history of such studies spans some fifty years. In the past thirty years, another literature has developed that uses sports data to test or explain various components of microeconomic theory. Goff and Tollison (1990) call this type of research "sportometrics," comparing it to experimental economics that uses data from sporting contests instead of laboratory data. The intents of these two strains differ; sports-microeconomics has a narrowing focus, from the larger field of microeconomics to the smaller field of sports economics, while sportometrics has an expanding focus, from sports economics to microeconomics. Although there is clearly room for both in sports economics, the "sportometrician" is more concerned with acceptance outside the subdiscipline than is the "sports-microeconomist."

It is incumbent upon sports economists to explain why their research can be generalized beyond the sports industry, something at which they have become increasing adept. Most arguments for the validity and importance of sportometric research hinge on two major issues. First, sportometricians have the advantage of excellent and detailed data. Specifically, sports data are often better suited for testing and analyzing economic theory than data from other industries. Second, the sports industry generates a level of interest that is greater than that of most other industries, and this is especially true for college students.[1] The most-used argument against the importance of sportometric research appears to be the following: Although sports data are almost always of better quality than data from other industries, the results are not easily generalized and are, therefore, unimportant except to help understand the sports industry. Based on this argument, sports-microeconomics is a legitimate area of research, but sportometrics is not. In addition, some feel a bias exists among "real" economists—and other scholars as well—that sport is frivolous and doing research on such trivial matters is unworthy of academic interest. Among sports economists, the view is that sportometric research is important in understanding the sports industry and gives insights that can help us understand behavior in other industries and situations.

A Brief Discussion of the Literature

In an effort to analyze the impact and relevance of sports research, it may be instructive to review the sports literature in order to understand its development over time, including how its impact on the economics discipline has developed. Since an exhaustive survey is beyond the scope of this chapter, a selected literature review will have to suffice. With apologies to those researchers who have published in other economics journals, I only consider papers published in two of the most-respected journals, the *American Economic Review* (*AER*) and the *Journal of Political Economy* (*JPE*). A scholar who publishes in these journals has received a level of recognition for his or her work that spans all the fields of economics. Readers are directed to the other chapters in this volume for more-detailed literature reviews.[2] Much of the empirical research in these two journals has analyzed baseball or used data from U.S. Major League Baseball (MLB). As sports researchers have attempted to incorporate information from other sports, recent papers have included data from such diverse sports as sumo wrestling, track and field, and soccer.

Early Research

When discussing the impact of sports research on the discipline of economics as a whole, it seems appropriate to begin with Simon Rottenberg's (1956) article in *JPE*, "The Baseball Players' Labor Market." It can be argued that this article marks the true birth of sports economics. The author's purpose in writing the article is to explain the labor market of professional baseball using economic theory; he does not appear to care about generalizing his analysis to other labor markets. Although clearly important due to its seminal nature, Rottenberg's paper also serves as both a positive and a negative example to those who wish to produce scholarship that has an impact beyond the bounds of sports economics. First and foremost, the paper contains some extremely good economics, is well written, and is accessible to those without a deep knowledge of the institutions and other details of professional sports. Thus, it is an excellent example of sports-microeconomics research.

However, the author concentrates solely on professional baseball and loses an opportunity to show how his economic insights could be used to illuminate issues in other industries. Consider, for instance, Rottenberg's analysis of the reserve clause and the role of property rights in the distribution of labor resources, referred to as the invariance principle, which has been compared to Coase's (1960) influential ideas on property rights, transaction costs, and social costs. Although the publication of Rottenberg's analysis predates Coase's by several years, Rottenberg is rarely cited outside of sports economics, while Coase's has been called "the most widely cited article in the whole of the modern economic literature."[3] Although Coase's work is undoubtedly more important than Rottenberg's—a Nobel Prize is a fairly good indicator—one wonders whether "The Baseball Players' Labor Market" would be cited more often and would have had a larger impact on the discipline had the author generalized the results of his study to other labor markets.

After Rottenberg's paper, no further studies on the sports industry appeared in these two journals until El-Hodiri and Quirk (1971) and later Scully (1974). El-Hodiri and Quirk follows the general pattern of Rottenberg's study;

specifically, it is designed as a purely theoretical application of economics to the sports industry. In addition, the innovative aspect of this paper is based on the fact that economic theory had not been applied to sports in this way before, which is also similar to Rottenberg's paper. The first empirical sports study to appear in these two journals is Scully's, which is one of the best known and most cited sports research paper of all time.[4] The Scully study is the first to empirically measure the marginal revenue product of a MLB player. Although his analysis has been criticized by some (e.g., Krautmann, 1999) and improved by others (e.g., Zimbalist, 2001), Scully's methodology for measuring the value of an athlete is still in standard use. Note that this paper shares an important characteristic with Rottenberg and El-Hodiri and Quirk: All three papers are part of the sports-microeconomic literature since they add to the overall economics literature with novel applications of existing economic theory to an area that had not been previously analyzed, namely the sports industry.

El-Hodiri and Quirk and Scully were quickly followed by two other papers: Gwartney and Haworth (1974) and Hunt and Lewis (1976). The Hunt and Lewis study is similar to Scully's paper in that the authors use economic theory to empirically analyze MLB. However, among the papers surveyed here, the publication of Gwartney and Haworth's marks a turning point: Previous papers only attempted to apply accepted economic models to explain the sports industry, while Gwartney and Haworth illustrate how sports data can be used to empirically test economic hypotheses. Thus, this paper marks the birth of sportometrics in *JPE* and *AER*. Specifically, the authors use the racial integration of MLB to test Becker's (1957) theory as it applies to discriminating firms. As the authors state (p. 873), "this theoretical proposition is difficult to test in the real world." However, MLB during the 1940s and 1950s provides a "real world" test of the theory.

The 1980s saw the further development of sportometrics as researchers followed the lead of Gwartney and Haworth. Wittman (1982) illustrates how the institutions of the sports industry can inform economic theory concerning the existence of rules in markets, although his paper uses descriptive, rather than empirical, analysis. McCormick and Tollison's (1984) paper provides an excellent example of the advantages of sportometric research. The authors develop a theory of the market for crime, which considers both the supply and demand of crime simultaneously, concentrating on the impact of increasing the number of law enforcers on the number of arrests. To test their theoretical model, the authors use data on the Atlantic Coast Conference (ACC) college basketball tournament. Prior to 1979, the ACC tournament used two officials per game and then changed to three; thus, this exogenous change in the number of officials produces a natural experiment. McCormick and Tollison argue that their ACC data (p. 224) "provide an economic laboratory with a history of accurate reporting of events . . . unlike most criminal data, which are generally held to be subject to various types of reporting errors." Importantly, the authors discuss the implications of their empirical results in terms of a more general increase in the number of law enforcers on arrests.[5]

Recent Research

Since 1990, there has been a veritable explosion of sports-related research in *AER* and *JPE*, with about a dozen papers appearing in these journals. This is a clear indication of the level of acceptance that sports research has achieved. For the most part, these studies are empirical papers, both sports-microeconomic and sportometric in nature, which use excellent sports industry data. These studies cover a wide variety of sports topics, including baseball (Schmidt and Berri, 2004; Goff, McCormick, and Tollison, 2002; Chapman and Southwick, 1991), college sports (Anderson and Ceslock, 2004; Goff, McCormick, and Tollison, 2002), hockey (Carlton, Frankel, and Landes, 2004), sumo wrestling (Duggan and Levitt, 2002), soccer (Chiappori, Levitt, and Groseclose, 2002; Szymanski, 2000), tennis (Walker and Wooders, 2001), track and field (Munasinghe, O'Flaherty, and Danninger, 2001), basketball (Brown and Sauer, 1993), and golf (Ehrenberg and Bognanno, 1990a&b). These recent publications have much to teach scholars who have an interest in influencing the literature beyond the confines of sports economics. Continuing the concentration on sportometric research, I briefly discuss several of these papers below.[6]

The quality of sports data often provides opportunities for testing economic theories when data from other industries are not up to the task. This is of obvious importance when encountering new theoretical developments that have not been supported by empirical testing. Chapman and Southwick (1991) use sports data to test the validity of the job-matching model of Jovanovic (1979). Although the model is intuitively appealing, empirical testing of this model is difficult due to the need for data that are highly disaggregated and that contain detailed information on performance and productivity; given these constraints, previous studies had provided inconclusive results. Since no other data are as disaggregated or contain as much information on worker productivity as do sports data, the authors' solution is to use the detailed, individual-level data of MLB. Given the advantage of using sports data, the authors are able to directly test whether the match between the manager and the team is a determinant of productivity (in terms of winning percentage), finding that the job match is significant after controlling for other determinants. In addition, the authors are able to show that manager tenure and the probability of job separation are related in the way implied by the model. Thus, MLB data give empirical support to the job-matching model.

Munasinghe, O'Flaherty, and Danninger (2001) creatively use several sources of track and field data to test for the effects of globalization and technological change on the rate of change of records. More importantly, the authors persuasively argue the merits of using track and field records to measure technical progress. Using statistical and economic theory to establish a model of discrete changes in track and field records, the study's empirical results indicate that the impact of technological change dominates globalization. The paper also makes a clear statement concerning the value of the research to economics as a whole. The authors state (p. 1146) that the major contribution of the paper is "to bring the theory of records to the attention of the economics profession," and they discuss how records theory can be applied to other research questions. In addition, they point out that their methodology can be applied to other studies on technological change and globalization (p. 1134):

> Records are a natural way to look at discrete changes by optimizing agents. . . . Economists are interested in how globalization and technological change affect a host of discrete decisions: how often workers move or lose their jobs, how often firms start up or shut down, how often comparative advantage in different products shifts, and how often new versions of software are introduced. For these questions, records are more relevant than performances.

Note that the quote refers to the interests of economists and how available sports data (i.e., records) correspond to that interest, clearly stating the value of their work.

Szymanski (2000) continues a long history of testing for discrimination using sports data begun by Gwartney and Haworth. The sports industry has provided opportunities to test for the existence and the source of wage discrimination due to the availability of detailed data on performance, thus validating the basic arguments in favor of sportometrics. The author's innovation in this paper is in devising a test for employer discrimination that does not rest on the assumption that all information on productivity is known; instead, his test is based on an assumption of a competitive labor market. On the basis of this assumption, the results give evidence of employer-based discrimination against black soccer (football) players and imply that competitive forces may not drive out employer discrimination. However, the author is careful not to stress the last point too strongly, due to the possibility that noncompetitive forces are at work in the output market of English soccer. Like previous examples, he details why sports can be viewed as a laboratory that produces interesting data and shows how his results inform microeconomic theory on racial discrimination.

Kahn (2000: 91) contends that "while it would be unwise to extrapolate too strongly from the labor market experience of sports, evidence on a particular labor market should not be discounted just because the market has a high profile." Perhaps Szymanski is heeding Kahn's advice when not stressing the more general implications of his results, or it may just be that an editor or referee would not allow a broader interpretation. However, Szymanski could have made a stronger case for the fact that his evidence suggests that it may not be easy for competition to drive out employer discrimination and that employer discrimination may be more widespread than neoclassical economists think; that is, if there exists any market power, then there is room for employers to indulge discriminatory tastes if they have them. Szymanski's most valuable contribution is his methodology, which is likely the main reason this paper was published in *JPE*. Although not explicitly stated in the paper, Szymanski's methodology could be used to test for employer discrimination in other industries, as long as data are available on the racial characteristics of employees and total salaries.

Goff, McCormick, and Tollison (2002) use data from MLB and college basketball to analyze the impact of racial integration on firm behavior. The authors place their study in the context of the economics of innovation, treating racial integration in sports as a process of teams taking advantage of an increased pool of talent. The hypothesis tested is whether strong teams or weak teams were the first to integrate. Their results suggest that teams with better won/loss records tended to integrate first, an outcome that the authors state is due to managerial efficiency. An interesting aspect of this study is its empirical simplicity; the paper presents results from OLS estimations with few independent variables. Clearly, this paper was not published in *AER* due to its empirical complexity, proving that sports researchers need not perform statistical magic to publish in the top journals.[7] However, the paper could have been improved by the inclusion of a discussion generalizing these results. Similar to Szymanski, perhaps the authors chose not to make the stretch or the editor did not allow it.

Experimental economics applies laboratory methods of inquiry to the study of economics. In this rapidly growing field, researchers design experiments in which the behavior of individuals is observed under controlled conditions. Game theory is often tested in such controlled environments; in fact, empirical testing of game theoretic models is based almost solely on experiments. Unfortunately, these models have not always been consistent with empirical evidence from experiments using human subjects. However, the laboratory of the sports industry has provided opportunities for creative researchers to test these models in the real world using non-experimental data. In order to test whether agents behave as game theory predicts, Chiappori, Levitt, and Groseclose (2002) use data on penalty kicks from French and Italian first division soccer league games and Walker and Wooders (2001) use data on serves in professional tennis matches from the 1970s to the 1990s. In these two studies, sports data validate the propositions of the respective theoretical models. If the success of these recent attempts to use nonexperimental sports data is any indication, "experimental sports-economics" may well be a growth industry.

Conclusion

This brief review of sports-related literature in *AER* and *JPE* shows that research containing innovative methodologies and data has been published in top economics journals. While there is every reason to expect that this will continue to be true into the foreseeable future, expanding beyond these two journals gives a clearer picture of the status of sports economics as a field. The number of published studies on sports in all economic journals increased from less than five per year in the 1970s to an average of thirty per year in the 1990s (Kahane, Idson, and Staudohar, 2000). In addition, during the 1980s and 1990s, sports research appeared in top-tier journals such as *Quarterly Journal of Economics*, *Journal of Economic Literature*, *Journal of Economic Perspectives*, *Review of Economics and Statistics*, *Economic Inquiry*, *Economics Letters*, *Southern Economic Journal*, *Journal of Human Resources*, *Journal of Labor Economics*, and *Industrial and Labor Relations Review*. In 2000, sports researchers even got their own academic journal, the *Journal of Sports Economics* (*JSE*), which can be interpreted as a sign that the demand for and supply of research by sports economists is now large enough to necessitate a field journal.

It is not surprising that some sports economists find the level of respect for their work unacceptable. No doubt many academics wish their chosen field were afforded greater respect. This issue is more profound in areas that may seem trivial to other scholars. Some sports economists feel they face prejudices against the value of their work, which impacts their ability to influence the discipline. The brief literature review provided in this chapter shows that any prejudices do not compose a significant barrier to publishing sports-related research. On the contrary, sports research can be published in top-quality economics journals, whether it is a sports-microeconomic or a sportometric study. Characteristics of high-quality empirical research in any discipline include innovative methodologies, excellent data, and well-crafted arguments for the value of the scholarship. Sports researchers who aspire to any level of scholarship would be well advised to include all of these in their papers.

In summation, consider the advantages the sports economist has over other economists. First, there is the quality of the data and the relative ease with which it is obtained. For example, Kahn (2000: 75) considers the data available to a typical labor economist and to a sports economist—who happens to study labor issues—and concludes the sports economist has access to data that "are much more detailed and accurate than typical microdata samples such as the Census or the Current Population Survey." Clearly, the availability and quality of sports data have positively affected the productivity of sports researchers; in addition, this advantage will continue to generate opportunities for sports researchers in the future.[8] Second, many academics, including sports economists, have problems communicating with and influencing the decisions of industry practitioners. However, sports economists are in a better position than other economists, since sports economists are in some sense "closer" to the practitioner. This is a result of the existence of more and better data on the sports industry than on other industries. Third, there is the interest that sport engenders in the population at large and, more importantly, in our students. So, the next time you feel disrespected for your work, instead of getting angry, pity those economists who did not have the foresight to study the sports industry.

Notes

1. Although it is not the focus of this chapter, I would be remiss if I did not mention the impact that sports economics has had on the teaching of economics, especially at the undergraduate level. It could be argued that sports economics has had its largest and most important impact in the classroom. This can be seen in the proliferation of sports economics courses at universities throughout the world. In addition, examples from the sports industry are commonly used to explain and reinforce economic concepts in theory courses.

2. Papers published in *AER* and *JPE* on betting markets are not considered here, although the use of data from betting at racetracks and other sporting venues dates back at least as far as Weitzman (1965). See Jullien and Salanie (2000) for a review of this literature.

3. This quote can be found in Coase's biography on the Nobel Prize website (nobelprize.org). The online edition of the *Concise Dictionary of Economics* (www.econlib.org/library/CEE.html) reports that Coase (1960) was cited 661 times between 1966 and 1980. As of October 16, 2004, the Social Science Citation Index reports that Rottenberg (1956) has been cited 69 times.

4. As of October 16, 2004, the *Social Science Citation Index* reports that Scully (1974) has been cited 105 times.

5. It could be argued that the theoretical papers of Lazear and Rosen (1981),

Rosen (1986), and Dixit (1987) on tournament theory qualify as sports-related research, especially since these papers have spawned an extensive literature designed to test this theory with sports data. A similar argument can be made for Rosen's (1981) theoretical treatment of superstars. However, these papers are additions to microeconomic theory and make no attempt to analyze the sports industry or to show how sports data could be used to test this theory. See Szymanski (2003a) for a survey of tournament theory as applied to the sports industry.

6. Again, I apologize to those scholars whose papers are not discussed here; their exclusion in no way implies that they are inferior to the ones chosen.

7. It could be argued that reputation played a part in this paper being published in *AER*. For instance, Robert Tollison has an impressive curriculum vitae and has published more than a dozen articles in *AER* and *JPE*. Even if reputation has something to do with whether work is published in these top journals, it does not take away from the importance of the research.

8. Although not all sports data can be accessed easily, much is available on the Internet. For instance, if one is looking for some data, one might try Rodney Fort's website (users.pullman.com/rodfort/), which contains a wealth of information on several different sports.

Part II

Review and Analysis of Specific Sports

3

National Basketball Association

David J. Berri

The world of professional sports provides a unique environment to examine economic and business issues. As Kahn (2000: 75) notes, "There is no research setting other than sports where we know the name, face, and life history of every production worker and supervisor in the industry." This chapter will review the research utilizing the unique environment of the National Basketball Association (NBA). The chapter summarizes what has been learned and what remains unknown about the world of professional basketball.

Much of the research on the NBA has focused upon the issue of racial discrimination. Such a focus is inspired by the prominence of minority participation in the NBA. Of the major North American professional sports leagues, the NBA has by far the highest rate of African American participation. Still researchers wonder if racial discrimination is an issue in the sport that has been frequently labeled "the black man's game."

This review will also reveal a most surprising result—decision-makers in the NBA may not process information as efficiently as neoclassical theory suggests. This result emanates from a variety of published research on the NBA and is but the first hint that data from the NBA can tell stories beyond the subject of racial discrimination. A brief review of these "other" stories will suggest that research employing data from the NBA is closer to the beginning of the game than to the end.

The Evidence of Racial Discrimination

The story of racial discrimination dominates the study of basketball economics. Becker (1971), in his seminal work on discrimination, defines discrimination as "the unequal treatment of workers who offer equal levels of productivity." Given this definition, the challenge facing researchers is to adequately evaluate a worker's productivity. Although one can find ample evidence that pay can vary across workers according to both gender and race, one cannot establish a case for discrimination without an assessment of worker productivity that demonstrates equal level of output received unequal levels of compensation. As Kahn (1991) notes, such an objective is hampered in most industries where accurate measures of productivity are not available to the academic researcher.

Given such a problem, researchers have often turned to the study of professional sports. Professional team sports devoted considerable resources to track the productivity of individual workers. Additionally, as Kahn (1991) argues, data from professional sports allow us to examine various aspects of discrimination. One can discuss wage discrimination, via the extensive data on worker productivity, employment history, team revenue, and consumer demand, but data are also available to address both the issues of hiring and consumer discrimination.

Kahn (1991) reviewed over sixty discrimination studies, including more than twenty examinations of the NBA. Consequently this discussion begins with a review of several studies noted in Kahn (1991), but concludes with a review of more recent scholarship. The work of Kahn begins with the issue of salary discrimination before moving on to the issue of hiring and consumer demand. Like Kahn, we will follow this progression and review what these studies have to say about race relations in the NBA. Unlike Kahn, though, we will take the discussion one step further and review what these studies tell us about decision-making in the NBA. One should note that the post-1991 review is assisted by an additional Kahn review, offered in 2000.

Salary Discrimination

The standard approach to uncovering the existence of salary or wage discrimination is to estimate the following model:

$$S = \beta_0 + \beta_1 X + \beta_2 R + e_i, \tag{3.1}$$

where S is worker's salary, X is a vector of firm characteristics and worker productivity measures, R is a dummy variable or set of dummy variables of worker race and/or ethnicity, and e_i is an error term.

If one finds that β_2 is statistically significant, then the researcher concludes that evidence of discrimination has been uncovered. As noted, all other factors that may influence salary must be accounted for in X. If not, the estimation and interpretation of β_2 is compromised.

Table 3.1

Studies of Wage Discrimination in the NBA

Studies	Years	Sample	Results
Kahn and Sherer (1988)	1985–86	226	Significant (1%) positive coefficient for whites
Koch and Vander Hill (1988)	1984–85	278	Significant (10%) positive coefficient for whites
Wallace (1988)	1984–85	229	Significant (10%) positive coefficient for whites
Brown, Spiro, and Keenan (1991)	1984–85	227	Significant (5%) negative coefficient for blacks
Jenkins (1996)	1983–94	368	Insignificant race coefficient
Dey (1997)	1987–89, 1990–93	1,306	Insignificant race coefficient
Hamilton (1997)	1994–95	332	Quantile regression reveals evidence of a premium to white players at the upper end of the income distribution
Gius and Johnson (1998)	1996–97	328	Insignificant race coefficient
Bodvarsson and Brastow (1998)	1990–91	151	Insignificant race coefficient
Bodvarsson and Brastow (1999)	1985–86 and 1990–91	226 and 263	Significant race coefficient for 1985–86 season, insignificant race coefficient for 1990–91 campaign
Bodvarsson and Partridge (2001)	1985–86 and 1990–91	226 and 263	Evidence of coworker discrimination by white players and customer discrimination by black fans
Eschker, Perez, and Siegler (2004)	Regression per season 1996–97 to 2001–2	Sample ranges from 330 to 368	Significant race coefficient from 1998–99 season, insignificant in all other seasons.

Although a number of studies were offered in the 1970s and early 1980s, much of this work evaluated only samples of fewer than thirty players. Beginning in 1988 published papers began to examine samples in excess of 200 players. Table 3.1 lists twelve such studies.

These studies appear in two clusters. The first cluster consists of the first four papers listed in Table 3.1. These papers were originally reviewed by Kahn

(1991), examined the 1984–85 or 1985–86 season, and all found evidence that black players in the NBA were paid a lower wage than white players for equivalent productivity. Perhaps due to the consistency in findings offered by the first four papers, scholarship on this issue took an apparent break.

The work of Jenkins (1996) ended the hiatus. Jenkins argued that the inclusion of both free agents and non-free agents biased the previous study of wage discrimination. As noted, studies in this field attempt to link a worker's wages to productivity. Jenkins argued that as one moves further from the time the contract was signed, the link between productivity and wages becomes increasingly tenuous. Consequently, Jenkins restricted his study to the population of free agents in professional basketball from the 1983 to 1994 seasons. Using free agents, the only workers in the industry currently seeking to link wages and productivity, Jenkins found no evidence of racial discrimination. The nonexistence of a relation between race and salary was not only found in the entire sample, but also in a restricted sample focused only on the 1980s.

The Jenkins study had little impact on other writers on this subject. Of the remaining studies listed in Table 3.1, only Eschker, Perez, and Siegler (2004) cite Jenkins. Not surprisingly, none of the remaining studies restricts the sample of NBA players to free agents. Despite this failure, the insignificance of the coefficient on race is an increasingly common finding. Dey (1997), Gius and Johnson (1998), Bodvarsson and Brastow (1998), and Eschker, Perez, and Siegler (2004) all find an absence of racial discrimination. Summarizing these results, Bodvarsson and Brastow (1999) replicate the original Kahn and Sherer (1988) finding for the 1985–86 season but find evidence of discrimination no longer exists for the 1990–91 season. In essence, racial discrimination appears to have vanished by the 1990s. Of course, if we follow the work of Jenkins, it was not an issue in the 1980s either.

Before we embrace this conclusion, one should consider the work of Hamilton (1997). Like the other studies listed in Table 3.1, Hamilton regresses player salaries on worker productivity, firm characteristics, and a dummy variable for race. Like much of the work of the latter 1990s, evidence of racial discrimination was not found. Hamilton then turned to a censored quantile regression, which sought to uncover differences in pay at different points of the salary distribution. For those at the lower end of the distribution, primarily consisting of a team's non-starters, no evidence of discrimination was reported. In contrast, at the upper end of the distribution, Hamilton does report evidence that blacks were paid less for equivalent performances. Again, Hamilton does not restrict the sample to recent free agents. Nevertheless, the examination of discrimination at different points of the distribution is a promising methodology for future studies.

The final study we wish to note from Table 3.1 comes from Bodvarsson and Partridge (2001). These authors take perhaps the most ambitious approach to assessing discrimination by attempting to identify if the source of discrimination comes from customers, coworkers, or employers. By employing measures of the race of the player, his teammates, his managers, and his host city, these authors sought to uncover the specific cause of discrimination. The results suggest that coworker discrimination does occur in the NBA. Furthermore, some evidence of black fans engaging in customer discrimination was offered. The results, as these authors stress, should not be considered definitive but rather should inspire future research.

To summarize, the study of NBA salary discrimination has utilized a variety of methodologies and offered a mix of results. Although early studies consistently presented evidence of wage discrimination, more recent studies have often been unable to find evidence of discrimination. One should stress that most of these studies utilized data from the 1980s, with the latest year examined being the 1996–97 season. As noted, recent salary data are readily available on the Internet. Consequently, studies of racial discrimination with more recent data, utilizing the methodology of Jenkins (1996), Hamilton (1997), and Bodvarsson and Partridge (2001) will hopefully be forthcoming.

Hiring Discrimination

Professional sports, with the exception of baseball's Negro Leagues, were strictly the province of white males in the early twentieth century. When the Brooklyn Dodgers hired Jackie Robinson for the 1947 season, baseball's era of all-white players ended. Three years later the NBA followed baseball's lead when Earl Lloyd, Nat Clifton, and Chuck Cooper joined the league. The history of exclusion, though, leads one to ask if black athletes have exactly the same opportunities as whites to find employment in professional sports.

Unlike the issue of salary discrimination, the study of hiring in the NBA has been relatively sparse (studies summarized in Table 3.2). The work of Kahn and Sherer (1988) examined the NBA draft in an effort to see if race played a role in determining a player's draft position. This work found no evidence of racial discrimination. As these authors admit, though, the ideal study of the college draft would include players who were not drafted. These authors did not have access to such data, consequently the proposition that blacks are more likely to be passed over completely by the draft was not tested.

Hoang and Rascher (1999) sought to uncover the impact of race on the probability that a player would lose his job in the NBA. These authors do report evidence that blacks are more likely to lose their job in the NBA. They find that white players have a 36 percent lower risk of being cut.

Table 3.2

Studies of Hiring and Consumer Discrimination in the NBA

Studies	Dependent variable	Years	Sample	Results
Kahn and Sherer (1988)	Draft position	1985–86	226 players	Insignificant coefficient for race of player
Hoang and Rascher (1999)	Employment	1980–91	275 players	Significant (5%) negative coefficient for whites; whites less likely to be cut
McCormick and Tollison (2001)	Playing time	1981–88	2,481 players	Significant (1%) positive coefficient for black players; blacks receive more minutes than whites, ceteris paribus
Burdekin, Hossfeld, and Smith (2005)	% of team that is white	1990–91 to 1998–99	251 teams	Significant coefficient of percent white of SMSA. Coefficient is insignificant; sample is bench players
Kahane (2004)	Team wins	1990–91 to 1998–99	251 teams	Insignificant coefficient for percentage of white players employed by the team
Kahn and Sherer (1988)	Attendance	1980–86	138 teams	Significant (2%) positive coefficient for percentage of white team members
Brown, Spiro, and Keenan (1991)	Attendance	1983–84	23 teams	Insignificant coefficient for black playing time
Burdekin and Idson (1991)	Attendance	1980–86	131 teams	Significant (1%) positive coefficient for racial matching variable; increase attendance by hiring more white players
Hoang and Rascher (1999)	Attendance	1980–91	235 teams	Significant (1%) positive coefficient for racial matching variable; increase attendance by hiring more white players
McCormick and Tollison (2001)	Attendance	1981–87	156 teams	Insignificant coefficient for ratio of white players to black players on the team; negative coefficient in cities with relatively larger African American population
Kanazawa and Funk (2001)	Nielsen ratings for televised NBA games	1996–97	258 games	Significant (1% and 10%) positive coefficient for number of white players on local and visiting team
Berri, Schmidt, and Brook (2004)	Gate revenue	1992–93 to 1995–96	108 teams	Insignificant coefficient for racial matching variable
Burdekin, Hossfeld, and Smith (2005)	Gate revenue	1990–91 to 1998–99	251	Significant coefficient when racial composition of team is interacted with racial composition of city and time

White players will enjoy a longer career relative to similarly gifted and productive black players.

McCormick and Tollison (2001) offered a very different conclusion when they examined the relationship between race and the allocation of minutes played. They find that race matters in terms of the allocation of playing time. But their evidence points out that the bias is against white players, with black players receiving more playing time than comparable whites.

Bias in favor of whites was uncovered in the work of Burdekin, Hossfeld, and Smith (2005). These authors examined the relationship between the racial composition of a team and the composition of the team's host city. The evidence suggests that an effort is made to match the composition of the team to the city. When the sample was restricted to bench players, though, the relationship disappears. From this study we would conclude that racial discrimination in hiring only applies to the team's starters.

Kahane (2004) provides a study that examines the implication of hiring discrimination. If discrimination exists and less productive players of a favored race are overutilized, output or wins should be compromised. Kahane found that the number of white players employed by the team did not impact the number of wins the team achieved. In other words, Kahane found no evidence of discrimination in the NBA.

Kahane's work did offer an additional finding that will surely inspire additional research. In an examination of the relationship between wins and the race of both the coach and the general manager, Kahane found that black decision-makers were often employed by teams that achieved fewer wins than their payroll would suggest. In other words, black coaches and general managers tend to be employed by underperforming teams. Although Kahane found that race is not relevant to the hiring of players, race does matter when one considers the management of NBA teams.

The review of the few studies of hiring discrimination in the NBA offered in the literature finds ambiguous results depending on the specific hiring process addressed. The lack of consistent results offers opportunities for additional research on the topic.

Customer Discrimination

As Kahn (1991) notes, one can expect market forces to eventually eliminate employer and coworker discrimination. Competitive forces, though, will not eliminate customer discrimination. Certainly one would expect that the initial segregation of the NBA to be reflected, at least partially, in the preferences of the NBA's customers. In the fifty years since the integration of players, have the attitudes of the NBA's customers changed?

The study of customer discrimination is hampered by the attendance data the NBA provides (see studies in latter part of Table 3.2). As Berri, Schmidt, and Brook (2004) note, over 40 percent of NBA teams from the 1991–92 season to the 1995–96 campaign sold out each game during the regular season. Because a significant number of NBA teams play at capacity, attendance understates actual demand. Given the truncation of demand, the standard OLS methodology for demand estimation using attendance data is inappropriate. Consequently, the attendance studies offered by Kahn and Sherer (1988), Brown, Spiro, and Keenan (1991), Hoang and Rascher (1999), and McCormick and Tollison (2001), which did not account for the demand truncation in estimating their models, offer results that are difficult to interpret. Only the study of Burdekin and Idson (1991) addressed the upward bound of the data. The evidence from these studies, for what is worth, suggests that customer discrimination did exist in the NBA in the early 1980s but as indicated by Berri, Schmidt, and Brook (2004) was not an issue for NBA teams in the early 1990s. In a study of gate revenue, the racial match between the team and the host city was not found to be significant.

Does this mean customer discrimination has ended? Kanazawa and Funk (2001) suggest otherwise. In a departure from studies of attendance, these authors examined Nielsen ratings for the telecasts of NBA teams. Kanazawa and Funk present evidence that the number of white players, on both the home and visiting teams, positively impacts the ratings these games receive. This work suggests that customers of the NBA, who are often white, still have a preference for white players.

The work of Kanazawa and Funk is disputed by Burdekin, Hossfeld, and Smith (2005). Specifically, Burdekin et al. (2005) note that one of the whitest teams in the sample considered by Kanazawa and Funk also employed Michael Jordan, perhaps the most popular player in NBA history. The popularity of Jordan and, hence his relatively white team, may have driven the results found by Kanazawa and Funk.

Although Burdekin et al. (2005) dispute the study of television ratings, they present other evidence indicative of customer discrimination in the NBA. They begin by noting that NBA league revenues hit unprecedented highs in the 1990s. At the same time, participation by blacks increased while whites became increasingly scarce. Such results suggest that customer discrimination does not exist in the NBA today. However, before making this conclusion, the study continues by providing evidence white players are found to migrate to cities that are predominantly white. This result was uncovered when these authors examined gate revenue and also the movement of players from team to team in the NBA. Such work indicates that customer discrimination was still prevalent in the NBA in the last decade of the twentieth century.

Race and the NBA: A Summary

What has been learned from the study of racial discrimination in the NBA? The results are mixed. Recent work indicates little salary discrimination, ambiguous hiring discrimination, and probably some customer discrimination. Discrimination in all areas appears to be diminishing over time. One should be cautious, though, in comparing results. Because each new study examines new data and new methods (if it hopes to be published), comparisons are often between apples and oranges. More studies should consider taking the approach offered by Jenkins (1996) and compare data from both the 1980s and 1990s and now the 2000s with the same methodology. When such a practice becomes more common, our knowledge of how racial attitudes have changed over time will be improved.

Measuring Player Productivity

As noted in the preceding section, one cannot examine the role of race in decision-making without controlling for worker productivity. Consequently, the studies of race are also studies into the value decision-makers place on the actions players take upon the court. One may presume that players who contribute the most to wins or profits would be paid the most and be least likely to be cut from the team. To test this presumption, we will begin with an additional review of the studies examining both wage discrimination and employment discrimination in the NBA.

Player Salary Determinants

Table 3.3 presents the results of ten papers that studied the relationship between player productivity statistics and salary. Twelve different salary models were used. In all but one model a player's production of points was found to be a statistically significant determinant of the player's salary.[1] However, a player's accumulation of points is dependent on the number of shots taken. Lofty point totals can be achieved simply by taking an inordinate number of shots. Clearly, efficiency in utilizing shot attempts should also be an indicator of a player's worth to a basketball team.[2]

Only six of the salary models considered field goal percentage. Of these six, only the studies that examined the 1985–86 season found shooting efficiency to be both statistically significant and positively correlated with a player's sal-

Table 3.3

Player Productivity Variables in NBA Salary Studies

Author(s)	Kahn and Sherer (1988)	Koch and Vander Hill (1988)	Brown, Spiro, and Keenan (1991)	Dey (1997)	Hamilton (1997)	Gius and Johnson (1998)
Sample	1985–86	1984–85	1984–85	1987–89, 1990–93	1994–95	1996–97
Points scored (+)	+	+	+	+	+	+
Field goal percentage (+)	+	NA	NA	NA	NA	NA
Free throw percentage (+)	NS	NA	NA	NA	NA	NA
Offensive rebounds (+)	NS	NA	NA	NA	NS	NA
Defensive rebounds (+)	NS	NA	NA	NA	NS	NA
Total rebounds (+)	NA	+	+	+	NA	+
Assists (+)	NS	Mixed	NA	NS	NS	+
Steals (+)	NS	NA	NA	NA	NS	NA
Blocked shots (+)	NS	NA	NA	NA	NS	+
Personal fouls (−)	NS	NA	NA	NA	NA	NA
Turnovers (−)	NA	NA	NA	NA	NA	NA

Author(s)	Bodvarsson and Brastow (1998)	Bodvarsson and Brastow (1999)	Bodvarsson and Brastow (1999)	Bodvarsson and Partridge (2001)	Bodvarsson and Partridge (2001)	Eschker, Perez, and Siegler (2004)
Sample	1990–91	1985–86	1990–91	1985–86	1990–91	1996–97 to 2001–2
Points scored (+)	NS	+	+	+	+	+
Field goal percentage (+)	–	+	NS	+	NS	NA
Free throw percentage (+)	–	NS	NS	NS	NS	NA
Offensive rebounds (+)	NA	NS	NS	NS	NS	NA
Defensive rebounds (+)	NA	NS	NS	NS	NS	NA
Total rebounds (+)	NS	NA	NA	NA	NA	+
Assists (+)	NS	+	+	NS	+	+
Steals (+)	NA	NS	NS	NS	NS	NS
Blocked shots (+)	NA	+	+	NS	+	+
Personal fouls (–)	NA	NS	NS	NS	NS	NA
Turnovers (–)	NA	NA	NS	NA	NA	NA

Note: Expected sign in parentheses; NS = not significant; NA = not applicable.

ary. This point is highlighted in the work of Bodvarsson and Brastow (1999). These authors tested the same model with data from the 1985–86 and 1990–91 seasons. For the earlier years, field goal percentage is statistically significant; for the later years, field goal percentage is insignificant. In sum, a player who scores points can expect to receive a higher salary, but evidence that scoring needs to be achieved via efficient shooting is not as clear.

Scoring is not the only aspect of a player's performance one can consider. For example, in five of the salary models total rebounds were found to be both a positive and statistically significant determinant of a player's salary. Six models sought to break total rebounds into offensive and defensive rebounds. Interestingly, in these studies rebounds were not found to be a significant determinant of salary.

The only other factors in these studies to be significant determinants of player salaries were assists and blocked shots. With respect to assists, five studies failed to find a significant relationship, five models estimated a coefficient that was both positive and statistically significant, and one study, offered by Koch and Vander Hill (1988), produced a statistically significant coefficient for assists that was positive in one regression and negative in another. Blocked shots were tested in eight regressions, with five reporting a statistically significant relationship.

Taken together, one can argue that player salary in the NBA is a function of points scored, and perhaps total rebounds, shooting efficiency, assists, and blocked shots. All other factors do not appear to matter in ascertaining a player's salary. The list of factors is interesting because, with the exception of blocked shots, all of this data has been collected since the 1950–51 season. In fact, the only other data collected in the 1950s were free throw percentage and personal fouls. Not until the 1970s did the NBA tabulate both offensive and defensive rebounds and report for each player steals, blocked shots, or turnovers.[3] Still the results with respect to steals, offensive rebounds, and defensive rebounds suggest that much of the statistical innovations of the 1970s were not yet incorporated into the decision-making of people in the NBA by the 1980s or early 1990s. Before we reach any conclusions with respect to these studies, let us first consider the three studies that sought to model the non-salary aspects of a player's employment.

Determinants of Employment

The non-salary studies are summarized in Table 3.4.[4] Kahn and Sherer (1988) considered the relationship between a player's college production and the player's order of selection in the annual NBA draft. Of the player statistics considered, a negative correlation between points scored and draft position was reported. Given that one would expect that the more points a player

NATIONAL BASKETBALL ASSOCIATION 33

Table 3.4

Player Productivity in Other NBA Studies

Author(s)	Kahn and Sherer (1988)	Hoang and Rascher (1999)	McCormick and Tollison (2001)
Dependent variable	Draft position	Employment	Playing time
Sample	1985–86	1980–91	1981–88
Points scored (+)	–	–	+
Field goal percentage (+)	NS	NS	+
Free throw percentage (+)	NS	NS	–
Offensive rebounds (+)	NA	NA	NS
Defensive rebounds (+)	NA	NA	+
Total rebounds (+)	NS	NS	NA
Assists (+)	NA	NS	+
Steals (+)	NA	NS	NS
Blocked shots (+)	NA	NS	+
Personal fouls (–)	NA	NA	–
Turnovers (–)	NA	NA	NA

Note: Expected sign in parentheses; NS = not significant; NA = not applicable.

scores in college the higher the player would be taken in the summer draft, a negative relationship was expected. The other factors these authors considered were not found to be statistically significant. Such a result is similar to the work of Hoang and Rascher (1999), who found that scoring more points reduced the probability a player would be cut from a team. Again, all other aspects of a player's on-court performance were found to be insignificant.

McCormick and Tollison's (2001) study of playing time presents the only evidence that a number of facets of a player's performance enter into the decision-making process of NBA management. They found that increases in a player's per-minute production of points, defensive rebounds, assists, and blocked shots led to increases in playing time. Field goal efficiency also had a positive impact, while personal fouls led to a decline in minutes played. Only offensive rebounds and steals were found to be statistically insignificant determinants, while free throw percentage came in with a surprising negative coefficient. Interestingly, the data set these authors considered came from the 1980s. Such evidence suggests that NBA coaches incorporated some of the statistical innovations of the 1970s fairly quickly.

Explaining the Perceptions of Productivity

When one examines the manuscripts reviewed in Tables 3.3 and 3.4, one learns that a player's accumulation of points is the only factor that virtually all studies agree is important to coaches and general managers in the

Table 3.5

Summary of Player Productivity Studies

Player productivity variable	Significant coefficient	Insignificant coefficient or incorrect sign	Not tested
Points scored	14	1	0
Field goal percentage	4	5	5
Free throw percentage	0	9	5
Offensive rebounds	0	7	7
Defensive rebounds	1	6	7
Total rebounds	5	3	7
Assists	6	6	2
Steals	0	9	6
Blocked shots	6	4	5
Personal fouls	1	5	8
Turnovers	0	0	14

NBA. This finding is highlighted in Table 3.5, which reports the frequency each aspect of a player's performance was found to be statistically significant, insignificant or of the incorrect sign, or not tested. Beyond scoring, only total rebounds and blocked shots were found to be significant more often than they were found insignificant. In contrast, offensive rebounds and steals were never found to be significant.

How do we explain the dominance of points scored in the decision-making of NBA economic actors? More specifically, how do we explain the lack of a relationship between much of what a player does on the court and either a player's wage or prospects for employment? One possible explanation may be the design of the estimated models. For example, if multicollinearity is an issue, then a potential consequence is statistically insignificant coefficients. Certainly as a player's minutes increase, his per-game production of points, rebounds, steals, assists, and so will also increase. Hence the correlation between these statistics may have muddied the waters to such an extent that a statistical relationship could not be uncovered. Certainly this particular issue warrants further study. Beyond this simple econometric issue, two additional explanations deserve consideration: (1) the primacy of scoring in the NBA, and (2) the assumption of rationality inherent in most studies in economics.

The Primacy of Points Scored—Why?

An easy answer to the primacy of points scored is to simply say, "What puzzle? Scoring is necessary to wins games, therefore players are paid to score." The literature on team wins production, though, suggests that wins

Table 3.6

Estimated Coefficients for Equation (3.2)

Dependent Variable = Team Winning Percentage
(OLS with White Heteroskedasticity-Consistent Standard Errors & Covariance)

Variables	Coefficients		t-stats
Constant	(0.744)***		4.892
PTS	0.013***		8.247
Adjusted R^2		0.160	
Observations		315	
Sample		1993–94 to 2003–4 seasons	

*** Significant at 1% level.

are about more than points scored per game. An empirical examination of the question can add clarity. Consider the following model:

$$WINS = \alpha_0 + \alpha_1 PTS + e_{2i}, \qquad (3.2)$$

where *WINS* is team winning percentage and *PTS* is points scored per game. The estimation, reported in Table 3.6, reveals that only 16 percent of team winning percentage is explained by points scored. In other words, points scored per game did not explain 84 percent of the variation in team winning percentage.

Such a result is hardly surprising. A team wins when its points scored exceed those of its opponent. Knowing this basic truth, though, does not tell us much about player productivity. Let us expand the model to ascertain the value of such factors as rebounds, steals, and turnovers:[5]

$$WINS = \alpha_0 + \alpha_1 \times PTS/PE + \alpha_2 \times DPTS/PA + e_{2i}, \qquad (3.3)$$

where *PTS/PE* represents points per possession employed and *DPTS/PA* is points surrendered per possession acquired. Possession employed (*PE*) and possession acquired (*PA*) are derived accordingly:

$$PE = FGA - RBO + TO + 0.44 \times FTA \qquad (3.4)$$
$$PA = DTO + RBD + RBTM + DFGM + 0.44 \times DFTM,$$

where:

FGA = field goals attempted   *RBO* = offensive rebounds
FTA = free throw attempts   *DTO* = opponent's turnover
DFTM = opponent's free throw made   *RBTM* = team rebounds
DFGM = opponent's field goal made   *RBD* = defensive rebound

Table 3.7

Estimated Coefficients for Equation (3.3)

Dependent Variable = Team Winning Percentage
(OLS with White Heteroskedasticity-Consistent Standard Errors & Covariance)

Variables	Coefficients		t-stats
Constant	0.495***		5.288
PTS/PE	3.122***		50.945
DPTS/PA	−3.118***		48.330
Adjusted R^2		0.947	
Observations		286	
Sample		1993–94 to 2003–04 seasons–	

*** Significant at 1% level.

Equation (3.3) builds upon the work of Oliver (2004) and Hollinger (2003). These authors argue that wins in the NBA are determined by points scored and points surrendered per possession. Possessions were defined in terms of field goal attempts, offensive rebounds, turnovers, and a fraction of free throw attempts. Berri (2004b) introduced the concept of possessions acquired, which were defined in terms of the opponent's turnovers, defensive rebounds, team rebounds, opponent's field goals made, and a fraction of the opponent's made free throws. The estimation of equation (3.3), reported in Table 3.7, reveals that points scored and surrendered per possession explain 95 percent of wins. Additionally, if one takes the derivative of wins with respect to points scored, possessions employed, points surrendered, and possessions acquired, one can see that the value of a point, field goal attempt, rebound, steal, and turnover is virtually equal.[6] In other words, points scored are not the only factor that determines wins in the NBA.[7]

Team Wins Drive Team Revenue

Do teams focus on maximizing wins or maximizing profits? If it is the latter, perhaps high-scoring players are what a team needs to employ. Although these players may not produce many wins, such players do put fans in the seats. This view is contradicted by the aforementioned work of Berri, Schmidt, and Brook (2004), who examined the relationship between gate revenue and team wins, a team's aggregate star power, and a collection of additional demand factors. The results revealed the importance of winning to a team's revenue generation. Although star power, as measured by the all-star votes a team's players received for the mid-season All-Star Game, was found to be statistically significant, the economic impact was relatively small.

Berri, Schmidt, and Brook (2004) did not explicitly examine the link between gate revenue and points scored per game. The addition of this factor to the double-logged model these authors report reveals a surprising result. Points scored per game are statistically significant, but the sign is negative. Such results indicate that assembling a team of scorers who cannot win is not a strategy consistent with profit maximization.[8]

Team Payroll Is Not Highly Correlated with Team Wins

Thus we have learned the following:

1. Points scored per game primarily determine player salaries.
2. Wins are about much more than points scored.
3. Team revenue is driven primarily by team wins, not points scored.

Given these three statements, it is not surprising to learn about the lack of a strong relationship between team payroll and team wins. Both Berri and Jewell (2004) and Szymanski (2003a) examined the relationship between wins and team payroll. The former examined how changes in wins were impacted by changes in a team's payroll. The results revealed that increasing payroll via the addition of new players impacted team wins. Simply increasing the pay of existing players did not have a statistically significant impact. Interestingly, only 6 percent of the changes in team wins could be explained by the independent variables Berri and Jewell employed.

A similar result was revealed by Szymanski, who examined the link between a team's relative payroll and winning percentage. From the estimation of equation (3.2) we learned that only 16 percent of the variation in team wins was explained by the number of points a team scored per game. Similarly, Szymanski found that only 16 percent of team wins was explained by a team's relative wage bill. Such results suggest that the link between pay and productivity, like the link between team scoring and team wins, is quite weak.

NBA Decision-Makers Do Not Always Process Information Efficiently

Economists typically assume that economic actors are rational. Such an assumption has been criticized by a few notable economists, including

Nobel Laureates Herbert Simon and Douglass North. As the latter received the Nobel Prize in economics in 1993, he made the following observation (1994: 360):

> Players must not only have objectives, but know the correct way to achieve them. But how do the players know the correct way to achieve their objectives? The instrumental rationality answer is that, even though the actors may initially have diverse and erroneous models, the informational feedback process and arbitraging actors will correct initially incorrect models, punish deviant behavior, and lead surviving players to correct model. . . . Individuals typically act on incomplete information with subjectively derived models that are frequently erroneous; the information feedback is typically insufficient to correct these subjective models.

Given North's discussion of decision-making and our literature review to this point, one might wonder if economic actors in the NBA follow the dictates of instrumental rationality. For information on this topic, we next turn to the work of Staw and Hoang (1995), Camerer and Weber (1999), and Berri and Schmidt (2002).

The work of Staw and Hoang (1995) and Camerer and Weber (1999) examined escalation of commitment. This term is defined by Camerer and Weber (1999: 59–60) as follows: "When people or organizations who have committed resources to a project are inclined to 'throw good money after bad' and maintain or increase their commitment to a project, even when its marginal costs exceed marginal benefits."

This idea is basically the same as sunk cost fallacy. When this occurs it suggests the possibility, although not the certainty, that the decision-makers are irrational. With respect to the NBA, Staw and Hoang (1995) and Camerer and Weber (1999) investigated the impact a player's draft position has on playing time. Both of these studies offer evidence that the initial assessment of a player, embodied in the place he was selected in the draft, still impacts the amount of playing time the player receives after the first two seasons of a player's career. This result exists even when one controls for the quality of a player's on-court performance. Such a finding suggests that NBA decision-makers are slow to adopt new information, maintaining an assessment of a player when the available evidence suggests that the initial perspective is incorrect.

In a less sophisticated study, Berri and Schmidt (2002) investigated voting for the All-Rookie team. This award is one of the few post-season honors decided by NBA coaches. In essence, this award is a statement by coaches of who the most productive rookies have been in the past season. The evidence presented suggests that a simple, yet inaccurate, productivity model is quite consistent with the voting pattern. In contrast, a complex yet accurate productivity model is unable to explain the number of votes a rookie receives. In other words, given the complex nature of NBA productivity data, NBA coaches have developed a simplified model that is easy to implement, but unfortunately is not an accurate indicator of a player's contribution to team wins.

These studies suggest but do not definitively establish that decision-makers in the NBA are incapable of making correct decisions. Camerer and Weber (1999) stress the importance of seeking alternative explanations before one settles on the charge of irrationality. The results noted above merely indicate the possibility that people in the NBA make systematic errors. Certainly the potential existence of such behavior should be a subject of future investigations.

Seven Other Stories

The data generated by the NBA have often been employed in the study of racial discrimination. As noted above, the research on racial discrimination also tells a story about decision-making in the NBA. Although the subject of economic rationality is of interest, the data generated by the NBA have the potential to tell many more stories. The following list of seven statements illustrates the diversity of stories that have been told to date.

1. A superstar externality exists in the National Basketball Association.
2. NBA teams played to lose in the years before the institution of the NBA draft lottery. Furthermore, as the probability of earning the top pick in the draft changed, NBA teams adjusted the effort level offered.
3. Inconsistency in performance reduces the wages paid to NBA players.
4. The NBA experienced an increase in salary dispersion in the mid-1990s.
5. A winner's curse may have existed with respect to the signing of international players for the 1996–97 and 1997–98 seasons. In the years thereafter, the premium for foreign players disappeared.
6. The NBA moved to the 2-3-2 format for the NBA finals in an effort to increase the probability that the championship series would not end in five games, but rather proceed to a revenue-generating sixth contest.
7. The impact of wins on team revenue will vary from team to team, while the impact of player performance on wins is constant across all teams.

What follows is a brief discussion of each of these statements. Refer to the articles noted below for more information and evidence in support of these propositions.

1. A superstar externality exists in the National Basketball Association.

Perhaps more than any other North American sports league, the NBA promotes its individual players. This may be due to the lack of competitive balance in the league.[9] Although uncertainty of outcome may not be at the level enjoyed by other sports, consumers may still buy tickets for the chance to see the stars of the NBA.

One should note that the NBA does not share revenue between teams from games or local broadcasts. Consequently, a star player can generate uncompensated revenues for his opponent. Hausman and Leonard (1997) were the first to report evidence of a "superstar externality." Utilizing data from gate revenue, television revenue, and the sale of NBA properties, these authors found that Michael Jordan generated $53 million in revenue in the 1991–92 season for teams other than his own team, the Chicago Bulls. Given his salary of $3.125 million, Jordan was clearly exploited by the NBA.[10] In the later 1990s Jordan received a substantial pay raise. For the 1997–98 season, his last year with the Chicago Bulls, he was eventually paid $33,140,000. Still, even such a substantial pay raise fails to approach the revenues he generated for the league.

The superstar externality was also examined in the work of Berri and Schmidt (2005), who examine the link between the attendance a team draws on the road in the NBA and the team's star power, measured via All-Star votes received, and the number of wins a team accumulates. With respect to the Chicago Bulls' Michael Jordan, it was noted that the combination of his star appeal and on-court productivity generated $930,593 for the Bulls' opponents on the road. Evidence was also offered that Jordan's star appeal was actually worth more to Chicago's opponents than it was to the Bulls.

2. NBA teams played to lose in the years before the institution of the NBA draft lottery. Furthermore, as the probability of earning the top pick in the draft changed, NBA teams adjusted the effort level offered.

Like the other major North American professional sports associations, the NBA conducts a yearly amateur draft. In an effort to promote competitive balance, the NBA allows the teams with the worst records to pick first, while the better teams pick last. NBA observers in the 1980s suggested that the worst NBA teams were not playing to win in the latter portions of the NBA season.

The reasoning behind this behavior is quite clear. Often only one or two players are truly expected to immediately alter the fortunes of an NBA team. For example, consider the players for the 1985 NBA draft. The first player chosen was Patrick Ewing. Although the New York Knicks actually lost one more game with Ewing than it had without him the season before, Ewing eventually produced at a very high level for the Knicks. Ewing's career highlights included selection to 11 All-Star Games, appearances in 139 playoff games, and inclusion in the list of the 50 greatest players in the history of the NBA. The second and third choices in 1985 were Wayman Tisdale and Benoit Benjamin. Although each enjoyed fairly lengthy careers, neither player ever appeared in an All-Star Game and together these players only played in forty playoff contests.[11] Such anecdotal evidence is not unique to the 1985 draft. In essence, if a team has a poor season, yet is not truly the worst team in the NBA, a draft where selection follows a strict reverse order will result in several poor teams choosing among a collection of players who will not dramatically alter the team's fortunes. Hence there is an incentive to lose as many games as possible to secure the rights to that one talent that might turn a franchise into a contender.

Of course, the NBA has denied that teams would ever take such actions. Nevertheless, the NBA did institute a draft lottery in 1985. For the draft in 1985 the seven non-playoff teams were placed in a lottery, with each team having an equal chance to secure the top spot. In 1986 the lottery was limited to just the first three choices, so that the worst team could not choose any lower than fourth. After the very worst team consistently failed to secure the top spot, the NBA in 1990 introduced a weighted lottery where the very worst teams would have a greater chance to garner the first choice.[12]

Taylor and Trogdon (2002) examined how these changes in incentives altered the behavior of NBA teams. The evidence these authors present suggests that teams eliminated from the playoffs during the 1983–84 season were approximately 2.5 times more likely to lose than playoff teams, even when one controls for team quality. For the 1984–85 season, though, the first year of the NBA draft lottery, there is no significant difference between the behavior of playoff and non-playoff teams. When the weighted lottery was introduced in 1990, the behavior of NBA teams changed once more. The worst teams had an incentive to lose, and once again this is the behavior we observe. The size of the effect, though, fell from 2.5 to 1.7. Given that the incentive to lose was also reduced relative to the 1983–84 campaign, one is not surprised that the magnitude of the effect fell.

3. Inconsistency in performance reduces the wages paid to NBA players.

Bodvarsson and Brastow (1998) suggest that inconsistency lowers the salary a worker receives in the NBA. On the surface, such a result is not surprising. The implication of this work goes beyond this simple statement. As Bodvarsson and Brastow (1998) note, one would expect that increases in monitoring costs would lead to reductions in a worker's wage. Monitoring costs, though, are difficult to tabulate. In an effort to empirically examine the link between wages and the cost of watching workers, these authors turned to the NBA.

We do not have a wealth of data on coaches' salaries in the NBA, nor do we know the cost of monitoring workers in basketball. Undeterred, Bodvarsson and Brastow (1998) examined the link between the variation in a player's performance and the wage the player received. As the authors argued, greater variation in productivity implies increases in monitoring costs. Hence, when Bodvarsson and Brastow found that increases in the variability of a worker's output led to reductions in wages, they argued that they had "found strong support for this monitoring costs hypothesis" (Bodvarsson and Brastow, 1998: 156).

Esteller-Moré and Eres-García (2002) point out that the work of Bodvarsson and Brastow (1998) fails to distinguish between the hypotheses that monitoring costs or risk aversion on the part of employers is driving the observed results. If it is risk preference that drives the result, the findings suggest that risk aversion on the part of NBA decision-makers leads them to take consistency over flashes of potential.

4. The NBA experienced an increase in salary dispersion in the mid-1990s.

In 1999 the NBA experienced its first loss of regular season games due to a labor dispute. A primary issue in the dispute was the NBA's vanishing middle class. While a few athletes had garnered the attention of the media for contracts in excess of 100 million dollars, a larger number of veteran players were playing at the minimum wage, albeit NBA style.[13] The changes in salary equity were primarily a result of the 1995 collective bargaining agreement (CBA).[14] Not only did this agreement increase the team payroll cap by 45 percent, it also eliminated the institution of restricted free agency. Hence, all players without a contract at the conclusion of the 1995–96 season were free to negotiate and sign with any team in the NBA. As a result, several organizations began the summer of 1996 with relatively empty rosters and significant amounts of money to spend on the acquisition of talent. The path taken by many of these teams was to devote a substantial amount of team payroll to a few star players. The remainder of the roster was then filled with players offered only the minimum NBA wage.[15]

Both Banaian and Gallagher (1999) and Hill and Groothuis (2001) present evidence that the distribution of salaries in the NBA became increasingly unequal after the 1995 CBA. Banaian and Gallagher note the top ten players in the league during the 1997–98 season earned 15 percent of the league's payroll. As these athletes enjoyed increasing success, the population of players earning the minimum wage was expanding. For the 1993–94 campaign, only 9 percent of the league was playing at the NBA minimum wage, with only three teams employing as many as three players at the league's lowest wage. By 1997–98, the number of minimum wage employees had risen to 20 percent, with over half of the teams employing at least three minimum wage players. Via a variety of statistical measurements, Hill and Groothuis confirmed the earlier work of Banaian and Gallagher, demonstrating that the middle class in the NBA had become considerably less populated by the close of the 1997–98 season.[16]

The implications of this change in salary dispersion have been tentatively explored. Frick, Prinz, and Winkelmann (2003) find that increases in salary dispersion led to increases in a team's winning percentage. In contrast, Berri and Jewell (2004) fail to find a statistically significant relationship between wage disparity and team wins. Furthermore, Berri (2001) presents evidence that increases in pay inequality diminished the performance of individual players in the NBA. Hence, like the studies of hiring discrimination, all the possible relationships between inequality and performance in the NBA are now present in the literature. More research needs to be done.

5. A winner's curse may have existed with respect to the signing of international players for the 1996–97 and 1997–98 seasons. In the years thereafter the premium for foreign players disappeared.

Over the past decade there has been an influx of foreign players into the NBA. Of the fifty-eight players chosen in the 2003 NBA draft, twenty-one were not from the United States. In 2004, twenty international players were taken. In other words, over a two-year period 35 percent of the players chosen in the draft were from countries other than the United States. This trend is clearly worthy of some academic inspection.

Eschker, Perez, and Siegler (2004) were the first to address the internationalization of the NBA, focusing specifically on the link between a player's wage and his nationality. Following the methodology laid forth by the aforementioned racial discrimination studies, a player's wage was regressed upon measures of worker productivity and a dummy variable equal to 1 if the player was born in a foreign country and did not attend a U.S. college. In essence, these authors wished to know if foreign training affected the worker's wage.

Nationality was statistically significant in the 1996–97 and 1997–98 seasons, but insignificant for the 1998–99 season through the 2001–2 season. Surprisingly, the estimated impact was positive. A premium in these two seasons was paid for foreign-trained players. The authors also reestimated their equation with a dummy variable equal to 1 if the player was foreign born but trained in either the United States or in another country. For this second estimation the finding of a wage premium for foreign-born athletes disappeared. Given these findings, the authors argue that their initial findings were driven by a winner's curse, which was alleviated as more information became available.

6. The NBA moved to the 2-3-2 format for the NBA finals in an effort to increase the probability that the championship series would not end in five games, but rather proceed to a revenue-generating sixth contest.

The NBA decides its champion via a best-of-seven game playoff series. Before 1985 the NBA utilized a 2-2-1-1-1 format. After 1985 it introduced a 2-3-2 pattern.[17] Caudill and Mixon (1998) sought to understand the motivation behind this change.

The NBA claimed that this change was introduced to save travel time. With only two changes of venue, the 2-3-2 format would clearly impose less travel. However, Caudill and Mixon (1998) argue that the 2-3-2 format was actually introduced to increase the revenues earned by the NBA by increasing the probability that a sixth game (or more) would be played by the final participants. In other words, the odds of a series ending in five games were reduced. The sixth game tends to generate higher television ratings, and hence more revenue, than a fifth game. Thus, Caudill and Mixon suggest that the change in formats is not about travel time but rather about the desire of the NBA to maximize its profits.

7. The impact of wins on team revenue will vary from team to team, while the impact of player performance on wins is constant across all teams.

Rottenberg (1956) and El-Hodiri and Quirk (1971), in their seminal works in sports economics, both argue that the value of a win will vary by market size. A win to a team located in Minnesota will not have the same revenue potential as a win to a team located in New York City. Despite this contention, revenue functions in the sports economics literature have often utilized a linear functional form.[18] A linear specification forces the value of a win to be constant across all teams.

In examining the determinants of NBA gate revenue, Berri, Schmidt, and Brook (2004) compared the results of a log-log model, which would allow the value of a win to vary from team to team, with a linear model. The statistical evidence indicated that a double-logged model was the appropriate functional form.

Although researchers have often estimated revenue functions with a linear model, production functions in the NBA have often taken the log-log, or Cobb-Douglas, functional form. In other words, researchers have argued that the impact of a point, rebound, steal, and so on would vary across all teams in the NBA.[19] The work of Berri (1999) examined the appropriate choice of functional form. The results indicated that a linear functional form was the proper choice. This finding indicates that a point generates the same number of wins for each team in the NBA. Teams win, not because their statistics are worth more than other teams, but rather because they accumulate larger quantities of positive statistics and/or lower quantities of negative factors. Teams lose when they do the opposite.

Concluding Observations

At the end of this review we make an observation: we are closer to the beginning of research utilizing data from the NBA than we are to the end. At this point the numbers generated by the NBA have been most frequently employed in the examination of racial discrimination. Not only does such research improve our understanding of race relations in the NBA, but also sheds significant light upon how information is processed by decision-makers employed in professional basketball.

Beyond the issues of race and rationality, though, an abundance of additional stories can be told. We concluded our discussion with a list of seven stories that have been told. An astute observer would note that many of our additional stories came from research that also studied racial discrimination. In other words, the topic of race in the NBA is hard to avoid.

Although the subject of race and the NBA is important, the worker productivity data generated by the NBA have the potential to tell many stories, both unique to the literature and also found presently in the examinations of Major League Baseball. With respect to the former, additional studies on the college draft would be interesting. Productivity information on most Division I college players now exists on the Internet. Such data would allow one to see which factors cause a player to be selected or passed over in the annual NBA draft. Furthermore, one could also look at the relationship between college and pro performance. Can we predict the future stars of the NBA via the data generated by players in college? The data exist to answer such a question.

Such data also allow one to examine issues that have most often been viewed via the lens of Major League Baseball data. At the onset of this review we noted that baseball produces productivity data that are relatively easy to employ. For example, Scully (1974) simply employed slugging percentage to measure the output of a hitter in baseball. In contrast, the research on productivity in basketball has been much more complicated. From the Cobb-Douglass models of Zak, Huang, and Siegfried (1979) to the system of equations developed by Berri (1999), research on productivity has often been quite complex and nonintuitive.

At the risk of being thought a self-promoter, I would note that a simple, yet accurate model of productivity is offered in Berri (2004b). Such a model should lower the cost of NBA research and allow the consideration of a wider range of questions. For example, are NBA player's exploited? Other than the work of Scott, Long, and Sompii (1985), no one has sought to answer this question for basketball in the fashion laid forth in Scully's seminal 1974 article. The issue of managerial input could also be better examined if player productivity was first accurately measured. In fact, an assortment of factors that influence a worker's level of output can now be easily investigated.

These are but a few of the untold stories one can tell with NBA data. With the abundance of data the NBA generates and the ease that such data can be evaluated, one hopes the research on the NBA continues to shed further light on the economics of sports specifically and the subject of economics in general.

Notes

1. The term "statistical significance" is open to interpretation. A common rule of thumb is that the t-statistic should be greater than 2. The discussion offered will focus upon the insignificance of much of what a player does on the court. Given that the conclusions reached depend upon the conclusion of insignificance, one should seek to error in the opposite direction. Consequently, a coefficient will only be considered insignificant in this discussion if its t-statistic falls below 1.5. One should also note that a number of studies considered more than one salary model variation. If one of these models found a statistically significant relationship, then it is reported herein as statistically significant. The one exception to this rule was the review of Eschker, Perez, and Siegler (2004). The authors estimated the same model thirty-six times. In one of these regressions, steals were statistically significant with the incorrect sign. In the other thirty-five regressions, steals were found to be statistically insignificant. This latter result is reported in Table 3.3.

2. The majority of studies considered used either a player's total accumulation of the statistic or his per-game average. Of the salary studies examined, only Brown, Spiro, and Keenan (1991) considered a player's per-minute performance. Per-minute performance

would be considered a better measure of a player's ability, since a player could accumulate higher per-game averages or totals simply by playing more minutes. Of course, with respect to scoring, shooting efficiency is the preferred measure since a player could achieve a higher per-minute scoring mark by taking a large number of shots per minute.

3. Although data on turnovers were available to each of the studies noted in Table 3.3, this factor was ignored in each and every study. An unpublished study by Berri, Brook, and Schmidt (2004) did look at turnovers with free agent data from 2001 to 2003. This study found turnovers to be insignificant. In fact, only points scored, blocked shots, and personal fouls were found to be statistically significant.

4. Of the employment studies examined, only Kahn and Sherer (1988) considered a player's total accumulation of the statistics employed. Both Hoang and Rascher (1999) and McCormick and Tollison (2001) employed a player's per-minute production.

5. This model was developed in Berri (2004b), and employed by Berri and Krautmann (2004), Lee and Berri (2004), Berri and Eschker (2004), Berri, Brook, Fenn, Frick, and Vicente-Mayoral (2005), Berri, Brook, and Schmidt (2004), and Berri and Fenn (2004).

6. Berri (2004b) made this point explicitly. The estimation of equation (3.3) reveals that much of what a player does on the court has an equivalent impact on wins. Consequently, the following equation can be used to measure player productivity:

$$Player\ Productivity = PTS - FGA - 0.44 \times FTA + RBO - TO + STL + RBD$$

7. The work of Berri (1999) also demonstrated the importance of factors beyond points scored to determining team wins.

8. This result is available from the author upon request.

9. Schmidt and Berri (2003), Berri (2004a), and Berri, Brook, Fenn, Frick, and Vicente-Mayoral (2005) each examined competitive balance across a variety of professional team sports leagues. The results indicated that the NBA, relative to leagues playing soccer, American football, hockey, and baseball, had the lowest level of competitive balance. Such a result was also noted by Quirk and Fort (1992).

10. The NBA salary data used in this chapter can be found at the website of Patricia Bender: www.dfw.net/~patricia. The term "exploited" is being used according to the definition first offered by Joan Robinson in 1933 and restated (1972: 281–82). "It is usually said that a factor of production is exploited if it is employed at a price which is less than its marginal net productivity."

11. Data on the career performances of Ewing, Tisdale, and Benjamin were taken from various issues of the *Sporting News NBA Register*.

12. In 1985, the two worst teams were Golden State and Indiana. Indiana picked second, while Golden State picked seventh. In 1986, the worst team was the New York Knicks, which picked fifth. For the 1987 draft, the worst team was the L.A. Clippers, which selected fourth. The Clippers repeated as the worst team in 1988 and were rewarded with the first overall selection. Finally, in 1989, the last year without lottery weights, the worst team was the Miami Heat, which selected fourth.

13. According to Hill and Groothuis (2001), the minimum salary in the NBA for the 1994–95 season was $150,000. By the end of the decade, this wage had doubled to a value in excess of $300,000.

14. For details of this agreement, see Banaian and Gallagher (1999) and Hill and Groothuis (2001).

15. The best example of this was the 1996–97 Houston Rockets, who paid $19.85

million to three players, while giving significant minutes to five players who were paid the NBA minimum. This list of five players included the starting point guard.

16. The list of measurements includes the basic descriptive statistics—standard deviation, skewness, and kurtosis—as well as the calculation of the Gini coefficient. As noted by Hill and Groothuis (2001), all of these measures indicate an increasingly less equal salary distribution before the 1999–2000 season.

17. These numbers refer to the location of each game in the series. A format of 2-2-1-1-1 means that the first two games are played at the home arena of the team with the best regular season record. The next two are played at the other team's home arena. The final three games are then rotated between the two teams, with the team with the best regular season record hosting games five and seven. A format of 2-3-2 results in the team with the best record hosting the first two and last two games of the series. The middle three games are played at the arena of the other team.

18. A representative sample of this literature would include Scully (1974), Medoff (1976), Scott, Long, and Sompii (1985), Zimbalist (1992b), Blass (1992), and Berri and Brook (1999). Not all researchers followed the lead of these authors. Sommers and Quinton (1982) present evidence that the marginal revenue generated by a win varies from small- to large-market teams in Major League Baseball. More recently, Burger and Walters (2003b) also provide evidence that market size significantly affects the valuation of player productivity.

19. The double-logged functional form has been employed in the work of Zak, Huang, and Siegfried (1979), Scott, Long, and Sompii (1985), McCormick and Clement (1992), and Hofler and Payne (1997).

4

National Hockey League

John C. Leadley and Zenon X. Zygmont

This chapter examines thirty-three articles about the National Hockey League published in academic journals and scholarly publications between 1969 and 2004. Articles written in languages other than English and publications on amateur, collegiate, or minor league hockey are not included in this survey. The hockey literature is dominated by two research topics, discrimination and violence; of the literature surveyed, eighteen (42 percent) of the papers are primarily concerned with discrimination and ten (23 percent) focus on violence. Other research topics include the market structure of the NHL, player compensation, franchise location, attendance demand, antitrust issues, contingent valuation of a franchise, and the impact of a rules change on team incentives. Two articles concern competitive balance (Jones and Davies, 1978; and Richardson, 2000). Since that subject is discussed in Chapter 10 of this volume, we include only that portion of Richardson covering topics other than competitive balance.

The next section discusses articles by topic (mostly in the sequence in which they were published). This is followed by a section that offers possible directions for future research. Table 4.1, at the end of the chapter, summarizes the empirical results.

Labor and Product Market Studies: The Structure of the NHL

Jones (1969) described the NHL as a collusive oligopoly where both cooperation and competition among firms are present. First pointed out by Neale (1964) and now well recognized in the sports literature, the dilemma inherent in operating a professional sports league is to strike a balance between the collective interests of the league and the interests of individual teams. What is optimal for the league as a whole is high uncertainty of outcome, while the incentive of each profit-maximizing franchise is to stockpile talent to increase winning percentage.

Jones indicated the interests of NHL franchises are protected through league rules that allow each team to reserve its rights to players as well as protect specific players from being acquired by another club. The combination of the amateur draft and the possibility of claiming unprotected players should more equally distribute talent and promote the objectives of the league. Yet, as Jones averred, this is often not enough. The persistent dominance by teams like Montreal and Detroit at the expense of perennial underdogs Chicago and New York necessitated institutional changes to the amateur draft system and an increase in the number of teams eligible for post-season play. These changes were designed to promote greater financial stability and allow the NHL to claim it was acting in the public's best interests (even though there was no overall reduction in the league's monopolistic or monopsonistic powers). The existence of the reserve clause, the "protected list," and the relationship between the NHL and the Canadian Amateur Hockey Association reinforced each franchise's leverage over its players.[1]

In 1972 the NHL faced a competitive threat from a rival league, the World Hockey Association (WHA). In light of this development, Jones (1976) re-examined the impact on the product and labor markets. The entry of the WHA promoted competition in the product market to the extent that cities previously without a professional hockey franchise got one (e.g., Houston, Indianapolis), and some cities now had competing franchises (e.g., Chicago, Los Angeles). In addition, the entry of the WHA effectively changed monopsony into duopsony as the WHA, in an effort to produce a quality product, bid talent away from the NHL, causing average salaries to rise and a restructuring of labor contracts in favor of the players.[2] Jones recognized the challenges any rival league faces and envisioned—accurately—the demise of the WHA (which ceased operations in 1979), the acquisition of selected WHA franchises by the NHL (Edmonton, New England, Quebec, and Winnipeg joined the NHL), and the renaissance of monopoly and monopsony (but with an increased likelihood of labor unrest). To counter the reemergence of the monopoly/monopsony outcome, Jones advocated government regulation and/or application of the Combines Act (the Canadian equivalent of the Sherman Act) as remedies.

Salaries, Player Performance, and Discrimination

The most vigorously debated issue in the hockey literature concerns discriminatory practices against Canadian Francophone players, particularly the Québécois. The discussion can be traced back to an article by Marple (1975) in French, and it first appeared in English with Lavoie, Grenier, and Coulombe (1987). At issue is the extent to which French Canadian players are subject to entry and salary discrimination in comparison to their English Canadian counterparts, especially in the case of French Canadians playing for franchises located outside Quebec. Entry discrimination is said to occur at two points: at the time of the draft, and subsequently during training camp and finalization of the roster. Those French Canadians who successfully hurdle those barriers may then find themselves victims of salary discrimination.[3]

Player Performance and Entry Discrimination

Lavoie, Grenier, and Coulombe (1987) alleged that French Canadian players outperform players from other ethnic/linguistic groups yet, except in the case of goalies, are underrepresented in the overall population of NHL players, especially at defense. Uncertainty and subjectivity are the factors responsible for this discrimination. Because it is more difficult to determine the likelihood of future success of a young defenseman than that of a forward or a goalie, NHL coaches, general managers, and scouts (who are typically English Canadians) are biased against nonnative English speakers.[4] As a result, "only the very best members of the minority group gain entry and therefore performance differentials in their favor are substantial" (Lavoie, 1989: 27).

As evidence of superior performance, Lavoie, Grenier, and Coulombe found that French Canadians outperform English Canadians and Americans (especially in offensive categories), that Francophone players performed better than Anglophones drafted in the same round, and that Francophones performed at least as well as Anglophones even when the former were chosen later in the draft. Other notable results involved the plus/minus statistic and player size, both potential proxies of defensive skill.[5] The plus/minus statistic is significantly greater for Francophone forwards and defensemen, indicating that French Canadian players are not only better offensively but also superior defensively. Player size is believed to be irrelevant, but even if it is not, since there is no statistically significant size differential by ethnicity, it cannot explain entry discrimination against Francophones.[6]

However, when Lavoie and Grenier (1992) used player performance data from the late 1980s to replicate the 1987 study, it appeared that entry discrimination against French Canadians had lessened over time.[7] They attributed this to the increase in French-speaking coaches and general managers in the NHL. McLean and Veall (1992) also replicated the Lavoie, Grenier, and Coulombe study but detected no offensive advantage for French Canadian defensemen. Since defensemen—not forwards—are alleged to be the victims of discrimination, these results are problematic and suggest that the normative prescriptions to combat discriminatory practices (as advocated by Lavoie, Coulombe, and Grenier, 1989) may be unnecessary.

Krashinsky (1989) argued that competitive pressures to win should erase most discrimination against Francophones. Coaches and general managers who systematically discriminate against these players jeopardize their job security if team winning percentage is compromised.[8] A better explanation for any apparent entry discrimination is communication difficulties among teammates and between players and the coaching staff. If a team has more Anglophone players and coaches than Francophones, and the costs of communication are higher between these groups, a team may opt for a marginally less talented Anglophone rather than a marginally more talented Francophone. This pattern of hiring may be especially pronounced for defensemen if more communication and coaching are required to develop the skills of a defender than of a forward or goalie. If a reduction in entry barriers is desirable, the appropriate solution is to promote bilingualism.

In a reply article, Lavoie, Grenier, and Coulombe (1989) disagreed with this interpretation. Poor communication between a Francophone player and his teammates and coaches should hinder that player's productivity, yet how can this explanation be reconciled with evidence indicating that French Canadians are better players and are often drafted before Anglophones?[9] In response to the assertion that it is harder to learn to play defense than any other position, Lavoie, Grenier, and Coulombe showed that French Canadian players are on average younger when they are drafted by the NHL than their English Canadian, American, and European colleagues. If Krashinsky is correct, the opposite result would be expected.[10]

Entry discrimination and language issues aside, there are other possible interpretations of the empirical evidence. For example, Lavoie (1989) considered style of play and reservation wage explanations. The former has considerable support from anecdotal evidence and suggests that since French Canadian players are interested in scoring and not in the hardscrabble and unglamorous work of playing defense, it makes sense for them to be underrepresented among defensemen. Lavoie tested and rejected this premise.[11] The reservation wage thesis assumes that Francophones incur considerable social costs in adjusting to life in NHL cities outside Quebec. As a result, only the most talented Francophones—the players most confident they will have a successful NHL career—will be willing to leave the "comforts of home." If this is true, it explains the performance advantage demonstrated by French Canadian players *and* the reason for their underrepresentation. This is tested by comparing the percentage of French Canadians on an NHL team's training camp roster to the percentage on the final roster.[12] If discrimination is not present, then a decline in these percentages may be attributable to homesick players returning to Quebec. Based on data collected for the 1984–85 season, Lavoie rejected the reservation wage hypothesis.[13]

To Walsh (1992), the fact that Francophone players are more proficient scorers than Anglophones is inconclusive in determining a player's total productivity because it ignores defensive skills, which previous studies failed to measure adequately. The use of the plus/minus statistic as a signal of defensive skill is spurious because defensive ability is not always positively correlated with a higher plus/minus ranking.[14] Walsh illustrated this by examining the plus/minus statistic of the winners of the Selke Trophy (an award presented to the NHL player considered to be the best defensive forward) from 1978 to 1991 and concluded that the plus/minus statistic does "not provide a reliable measure of defensive proficiency" (Walsh, 1992: 445).

Walsh also disagreed with the assertion that player size is irrelevant. He claimed that durability, checking, and the ability to intimidate opposing players are directly related to player size and contribute to a team's success; hence, size is a valuable asset for an NHL team. Observing similarly sized players across ethnic groups *in the NHL* does not mean that no size differential occurs *in the minor leagues*. Forwards and defensemen in the Anglophone-dominated Ontario Hockey League (OHL) and Western Hockey League (WHL) are significantly taller and heavier than their peers in the Quebec Junior Major Hockey League (QJMHL).[15] These inter-league differentials suggest that when an NHL team drafts a defender, more often than not he comes from the OHL or WHL rather than the QJMHL because there is a smaller pool of big players to choose from in the QJMHL. *If* NHL teams believe that size matters *and* players are larger in the Anglophone-dominated OHL and WHL than in the QJMHL, then "the *indirect* effect . . . is the underrepresentation of Francophones in the NHL" (Walsh, 1992: 452). This means that although a kind of systemic discrimination against French Canadian players exists, it is unintended not deliberate.[16] And if this *indirect* discrimination Francophone players face is undesirable, then the QJMHL should develop bigger players or the NHL should consider changing the rules of the game to make size less important (e.g., expanding the size of the rink).

Lavoie, Grenier, and Coulombe (1992) acknowledged the imperfections of the plus/minus statistic and proposed an alternative, the number of power play goals scored against a player. When a team is shorthanded, the coach will have his best defenders on the ice. Over time, since these players are likely to have more goals scored against them than their less defensively talented teammates, power play goals are a reasonable proxy for defensive ability.[17] They compared how often Anglophone and Francophone players were on the ice when their team was shorthanded and scored upon, and concluded that "there is no evidence that the defensive performance of Francophone skaters in the NHL is deficient" (1992: 463).[18]

Longley (2000) contended that the aforementioned studies overlooked a crucial element, team location. Discrimination not observable when looking at the NHL as a whole, nevertheless may be present in specific cities. He compared the total number of games Francophones played for franchises in the "rest of Canada" (hereafter ROC) and U.S.-based franchises versus the number of games they played for ROC teams. Absent discrimination, "the distribution of French Canadian players between English Canadian . . . and U.S.-based franchises should be consistent with the proportion of English Canadian teams in the league relative to U.S.-based teams" (2000: 239). The data suggested otherwise, and Longley considered possible theories consistent with the evidence.[19] The language cost argument does not fit the facts; if linguistic skill is the criterion, a French speaker should be penalized whether he plays in Toronto or St. Louis. He dismissed the Francophones "have poorer defensive skills" and "are too small" criticisms for exactly the same reason.[20]

Longley believed either fan-based or employer-based discrimination is the root cause. Fans in ROC cities harbor prejudices against Francophones because of longstanding "tensions between English . . . and French Canadians" (2000: 250), which are exacerbated by periodic threats of secession from the federal government in Ottawa by Québécois political groups.[21] Because underrepresentation is significantly greater (and statistically significant) during these episodes of political tension, Longley contended discrimination "could be viewed as [English Canadians] retaliating against French Canadians for French Canadians wanting to separate from Canada" (2000: 252).[22]

But an employer-based explanation is also appealing because of the relative scarcity of French Canadian coaches and general managers in the NHL compared to their Anglophone peers.[23] Longley (2003) found that French Canadians play more games if they are on a U.S.-based franchise rather than an ROC team. Longley also recognized that the pressure to win games can swamp any inherent biases on the part of a general manager (GM) regardless of location, so a fan-based explanation may be more plausible. To test this conjecture, Longley regressed a different dependent variable, the number of French Canadians drafted by a team in a given season, against location (ROC or the United States), the ethnicity of the GM (French Canadian or American) and a time trend.[24] Neither GM dummy is significant, which indicates there is no discernable difference between the drafting tendencies of French Canadian, American, or English Canadian GMs. The location variable remained positive and significant, supporting a fan-based rather than employer-based explanation for the underrepresentation of French Canadian players.

Lavoie (2003) reestimated the specification used in Lavoie and Grenier (1992) with a broader set of dummy variables that interact ethnicity with team location. This allowed him to determine if Quebec-based franchises engage in entry discrimination against non-Francophone players, if ROC franchises discriminate against non-Anglophones, and if U.S. teams discriminate against players who were not born in the United States. The interaction variables produce interesting but problematic results. No entry discrimination by Quebec teams is apparent, but Europeans appear to suffer from entry discrimination when they play in the ROC. Strangely, French Canadians are not discriminated against in the ROC but they are in the United States. These results differ significantly from Longley and are inconsistent with a simple theory of fan-based discrimination. As Lavoie (2003: 398) mentions, "if customer discrimination were present, one would have expected the teams from a given location to discriminate systematically against players of all foreign origins."

Despite considerable research effort thus far, no consensus has emerged from the entry discrimination studies. The superiority of French Canadians in terms of their offensive and defensive performance is still disputed and the issue of defensive skill is compounded by the lack of an agreed upon metric.[25] The introduction of ethnicity/location interaction terms is a promising approach, but to date has produced inconsistent results, which may be due to a combination of methodological improvements and lack of sufficient data.[26] But certainly those who believe that entry discrimination continues to occur may find their suspicions supported not only by anecdotal evidence but by the contributions of researchers like Lavoie.[27]

Player Performance and Salary Discrimination

Irrespective of any entry discrimination, once French Canadian players join an NHL team, are they then subject to salary discrimination? Lavoie and Grenier (1992) analyzed the 1977–78 and 1989–90 seasons and concluded that any salary discrimination against defensemen that occurred in the 1970s appeared to have diminished (Francophone forwards were not victims of salary discrimination).[28] Similar results were generated by McLean and Veall (1992), who argued that competitive pressures reduced discrimination over time and that the number of French-speaking coaches and general managers may have increased. Jones and Walsh (1988) offered only qualified support for the discrimination hypothesis.[29] They found that salaries are roughly 10 percent less, ceteris paribus, for Francophone defensemen but that Francophone forwards and goalies are not subject to salary discrimination.[30] When Longley (1995) introduced ethnicity/location interaction terms into the salary specifications, a different picture emerged. French Canadians playing for ROC teams are paid an estimated 37 percent less than English Canadians playing for those same teams. A French Canadian playing in the ROC is paid 33 percent less than he would be if he played in Quebec, and English Canadians are paid 14 percent less when playing for teams in Quebec than in the ROC. Longley said the language cost thesis does not explain why salary discrimination applies to Francophone forwards because this discrimination occurs only in Canada and not in the United States. Longley dismissed player-based discrimination for similar reasons; Anglophone Canadian players comprise roughly 70 percent of the roster in the United States and the ROC, yet discrimination is only observed in the latter. The more likely explanation is the bias and prejudice of coaches and general managers or fan-based discrimination.[31]

Lavoie (2000) used a model similar to Longley (1995) yet produced different results. American forwards playing in the ROC suffer an estimated 23 percent reduction in salary compared to English Canadians, and European forwards get 34.5 percent lower salaries than French Canadians. For defensemen, the only evidence of salary discrimination is for French Canadians playing in the United States, while European defensemen playing in Quebec appear to be significantly overpaid (75 percent more) compared to Francophones.

Jones, Nadeau, and Walsh (1999) tested several propositions concerning ethnicity. The hypothesis that salary discrimination exists against Francophone players regardless of location was rejected. Salary discrimination by location (because of customer biases) was rejected for Canadian franchises and only weakly supported for U.S. cities (and then in favor of non-veteran American players only).

The most recent contribution to this debate is Curme and Daugherty (2004), who claimed that wage discrimination should be observed only prior to free agency. Once a player becomes a free agent, any attempt by his club to continue to engage in wage discrimination should be unsuccessful, as the player can exercise his exit option.

Using player salary as the dependent variable, the authors created two regressions. The first tests Longley's (1995) model using data from the 1998–99 season to estimate player salaries for 1999–2000, while the second adds several player productivity characteristics commonly found in previous empirical work. The specifications were estimated for forwards separately, and for forwards and defensemen combined. Points per game, team revenue, and several productivity measures (penalty minutes, plus-minus, all star status, and years of experience for defensemen), were positive and significant. Experience squared, and the round in which the player was drafted, were negative and significant. None of these results was unexpected.

Of the dummy variables used to capture the myriad permutations of ethnicity and franchise location (French Canadian in the ROC, European in the United States, English Canadian in Quebec, and so forth), only the coefficient for French Canadian players in the ROC was consistently negative and significant, indicating these players were subject to a substantial wage penalty (in the range of 31–41 percent). To test the hypothesis that this penalty diminishes as players age and qualify for free agency, Curme and Daugherty (2004) split the sample by age (creating dummies for "young" and "old" players). In the subsequent regression, not only is no support for this premise found but the wage penalty increases as players become eligible for free agency. Using an alternative specification—with years of experience rather than age—also produces poor results. The authors indicate that (p. 199) "the results provide little conclusive evidence that competitive pressures erode the FC earnings penalty as players spend more time in the league."

As with research on entry discrimination, a similar lack of consensus exists among the salary discrimination studies. In part, this may be due to an increased number of regressors being tested against smaller subsamples of data. But it may also be a result of insufficient data. Prior to 1990, salary data were only available for two seasons, 1977–78 and 1989–90. Salary information post-1990 is now obtainable, but its current availability cannot answer whether discrimination by pay occurred in the 1970s and 1980s or whether discrimination diminished over time (a trend that would be consistent with other sports).[32]

Salaries and Player Performance

Following the pioneering work of Scully (1974), several researchers investigated the relationship between player performance and pay. Eastman (1981) presented the first attempt at a salary determination model by constructing a system of simultaneous equations jointly determining salaries and productivity (points per season) and testing it using unpublished data for forty-four players during the 1976–77 season. In the salary function, player age (positive sign on the coefficient), experience (positive), and education (negative) are significant. The result on the latter variable conforms to a reservation wage explanation (his estimate is that an additional year of education decreases salary by $16,000).[33]

A more sophisticated examination of player salaries is Jones and Walsh (1988), who investigated the impact on player salaries due to the presence of a rival league. Over the course of seven seasons (1972–78) the WHA competed with the NHL for talent; this caused player pay to increase significantly and moved compensation closer to marginal revenue product (MRP). Based on a sample of players and teams from the mid-1970s, Jones and Walsh estimated player MRP and salary.[34] Regardless of the level of player productivity, salaries exceeded MRP, which indicated that monopsonistic exploitation was not widespread as of the 1977–78 season.[35] Examination of a subsample of fourteen NHL players showed several instances in which a player received a substantial salary "overpayment" and, in those cases where some exploitation remained, the margin between player salary and MRP was small.

Based on the estimated MRP for 520 players in the 1993–94 NHL season, Richardson (2000) raised a variety of issues related to player pay, performance, and monopsony power. Equations for team revenue and team production (winning percentage) determine each player's marginal contribution to team revenue and performance (player per-game performance is measured by goals, assists, points, penalty minutes, and, for goalies, saves). The player's "marginal salary" is then subtracted from MRP to determine the player's "surplus." Marginal salary is determined by calculating "the difference between a roster player's salary and the average salary of the reserve players at that position" (Richardson, 2002: 400). Richardson then determines whether, ceteris paribus, free agency has an inverse relationship with surplus; that is, do free agents capture more of their MRP than non-free agents? A regression of surplus on free agency and other explanatory variables (primarily player performance and experience) indicates that surplus is reduced by free agency but not significantly.

Richardson considered whether players tend to be paid less than their MRP early in their careers and more than MRP later (a human capital/life cycle explanation) or if teams systematically overpay better players to induce other players to improve their performance (a rank-order-tournament explanation). The data suggested that these explanations apply to forwards but not defensemen or goalies. Richardson also considered whether an ultimatum game (see Telser, 1995) is going on between players and owners. The hypothesis is that players with higher MRPs should receive salaries closer to their MRP than players with lower MRPs (as MRP increases, the ratio of a player's salary to his MRP should decrease) because these players are more likely to succeed in negotiating with owners. The ultimatum game explanation is supported for players at all three positions.

In the aforementioned research, player MRP was estimated strictly on the basis of the player's own performance and not that of his teammates. Idson and Kahane (2000) addressed the issue of the impact of coworker productivity on NHL player salaries.[36] Their hypothesis is that a player's salary is determined both directly (through individual and team performance) and indirectly (depending on the extent to which that player is considered a complement or substitute for his teammates). For example, if Player A is better at killing penalties than his teammate Player B, the former will earn a higher salary, all else equal. If Players A and B have the same skill at killing penalties but play on different teams, the player on the more successful team should earn a higher salary, all else equal. But if Player A is on a team with many other good penalty killers, his salary may increase or decrease depending on whether the coach and GM believe the player's skill is complementary or substitutable in relation to his teammates. If the latter, the team may derive little value from having another penalty killer on the roster and will not reward this skill as much as teams without other penalty killers. Interacted variables suggest that taller players and players who commit more penalties are likely to have lower salaries when they play on a team with several other tall and penalty prone players. These attributes are considered substitutes. Interestingly, the weight of a player appears to be a complementary input. Although an individual's weight has a negative effect on salary, this effect is diminished by the positive interaction coefficient with average team weight. Estimation of models without the team and interaction effects suggests that the estimates of coefficients on individual performance are generally biased upward in studies that omit such effects.[37]

Kahane (2001) recognized that a player's salary can also be influenced by team-level characteristics; he noted "players with the same level of skill may in fact have different salaries if they play on different teams, due to team-specific effects" (p. 629).[38] Teams with greater revenues pay higher mean salaries, as well as provide larger increases in salary based on productivity, than clubs with lower revenues. He found considerable variation in player salaries "both in terms of mean salary as well as rewards to greater performance" (p. 631).

Salaries and Player Violence

Violence is a complex and unique phenomenon that separates hockey from other professional team sports and other industries. If two economists came to blows during a seminar, either one, or both of them, could be subject to prosecution and sanctions such as fines or jail. Yet a similar act of aggression on the ice rarely results in more than a short stint in the penalty box or clubhouse. Many fans, players, and coaches and GMs consider fighting to be just another form of physical play that is inherent to the game of hockey, even though displays of fisticuffs violate NHL rules. Moreover, even if a fight is said to be an act of violence, it is may be justified if it deters worse forms of violence (e.g., using the stick as a weapon) or serves as a way to protect smaller offensively talented teammates from goons on the opposing team. Many researchers have explored various aspects of hockey violence.[39] Among economists the primary focus has been the relationship between violence and player compensation, and between violence and attendance.

If fighting attracts spectators to the arena, players with a reputation for brawling should be rewarded for this talent, just like their teammates who get paid to generate assists and goals. Using a sample of 388 players from the 1989–90 season, Jones, Nadeau, and Walsh (1997) tested for the impact of violence on the salary determination of NHL players. They divided the sample into two categories: "grunts" (goons and enforcers) and "non-grunts" (scorers and playmakers) to determine the similarity, or lack thereof, in the salary determination between these two groups. The hypothesis is that the estimated coefficients of the salary determination model for the two groups are significantly different; players are rewarded on the basis of significantly different performance characteristics.[40] For forwards, the rewards from a high first-round draft choice, years of experience if taken in the second or third round, and team rank two years previous are larger for grunts than non-grunts, while the effect of veteran status is smaller. For defensemen, the coefficients for grunts are larger for career games played and games squared, first round draft choice, free agency, arena capacity, and previous team rank. The intercept and coefficients for veteran status, career points per game, and draft number if taken in the first round are smaller for grunts. Finally, despite clear differences in the salary structure that applies to grunts and non-grunts, a Wald test to determine whether these differences translate into a total salary differential for a grunt player when evaluated at the means of the independent variables is rejected.[41]

Attendance Demand Studies

The Influence of Violence

Stewart, Ferguson, and Jones (1992) hypothesized that violence increases the demand for tickets in two ways. First, it may have a direct impact on attendance by appealing to fans' tastes and preferences, making it more likely they will attend a hockey match if they expect to see some on-the-ice melees. Second, it may impact demand indirectly via winning percentage. A common assumption in the sports economics literature is that winning percentage contributes positively and significantly to attendance demand in all professional sports. If violence leads to more games won, then another causal link between violence and demand is established. In terms of the estimated impact of violence on attendance, the "direct influence" is positive but the "indirect influence" (via winning percentage) is negative. The authors interpreted these results to mean that teams have reached a saturation point and additional violence "would significantly compromise winnings" (Stewart, Ferguson, and Jones, 1992: 62).

The relationship between the role of violence and profit maximization by NHL teams is further explored in Jones, Ferguson, and Stewart (1993). They tested the "taste for violence" hypothesis using data from the 1983–84 NHL season to estimate two nonsimultaneous reduced-form equations with attendance and price as the dependent variables. They also tested a secondary hypothesis that U.S. spectators have a stronger preference for "blood" than Canadians.

Regarding the appropriate measurement of violence, the authors indicate that while penalty minutes is the obvious aggregate measure, this measurement does not allow a distinction to be made between penalties for nonviolent and violent actions (e.g., cursing the referee versus fighting). In addition, penalties for physical contact differ by level of severity (minors, majors, misconducts), and these are subject to the discretion and interpretation of the referees. Because no a priori ideal measurement of violence exists, Jones, Ferguson, and Stewart ran separate regressions using each measure: total penalty minutes, misconducts, majors, and minors.

The results for the attendance equation are as follows.[42] For both Canadian and U.S. teams, the effect of total penalties is positive and significant, which supports the proposition that violence attracts spectators regardless of city location. But other results are mixed. Home team misconducts are significant in both sets of cities but with different signs; this implies this form of violence attracts U.S. fans but reduces Canadian spectators' interest. Visiting team misconducts are not significant. Home team majors and visiting team minors are significant only for the United States, while home minors are important in Canada but not the United States. The authors argue that these results indicate that "in the U.S., attendance increases with the more extreme degrees of home team violence . . . but in Canada attendance falls" (Jones, Ferguson, and Stewart, 1993: 73).

An important normative conclusion of this paper is that the level of violence exhibited in NHL games is excessive and should be reduced, either by internal (league sanctions) or external (judicial) means. Given the positive relationship between attendance and violence, the authors conclude that the league itself has no incentive to reduce violence and government intervention may be necessary.

Jones, Stewart, and Sunderman (1996) generated similar results using game-by-game data from the 1989–90 season. They added two new explanatory variables—the average number of fighting majors and style of play—to the model used in Jones, Ferguson, and Stewart (1993).[43] For the independent variables designed to capture the degree of violence, the coefficient for total penalty minutes is significant and positive in the United States only. The variable for misconduct penalties for home and visiting teams is significant, but the signs for home team misconducts differs (negative in Canada, positive in the United States). The coefficients indicate these types of penalties by the home team have a larger impact on attendance than those of the visitors. The results are similar for majors. Home minors, however, are positive and significant for both the home and visiting team. For the new violence proxies discussed above, the results for the average number of fighting majors prior to the game mimic those for misconducts and majors. Overall, a fairly consistent pattern emerges: Canadian audiences do not mind watching rough visiting teams but dislike violence by the home team.

For the variables designed to capture a team's style of play (fighting or skating), the results for the United States are positive and strongly significant if at least one team is a "fighter." The coefficient is even larger if both have a reputation as fighting teams. Canadians appear indifferent to a match between pure fighting teams but dislike games featuring one fighting team or two skating teams. These results buttress earlier findings; fans in Canada and the United States each enjoy some scuffles during the game but it is the latter group that derives more utility from it.

The authors are more explicit about possible countermeasures to violence in the NHL than were Jones, Ferguson, and Stewart (1993). Of the three remedies considered, two—self-regulation by the league itself and direct control via the establishment of a regulatory agency—are dismissed. The latter's impact is deemed to be minimal while the former is unlikely so long as brawls and brouhahas put paying customers in seats. The remaining option—the use of the judiciary—is problematic given legal differences in U.S. and Canadian jurisdictions and the fact that individual players, not teams, are the subject of prosecution.

Paul (2003) evaluated recent changes by the NHL to increase scoring, decrease fighting, and increase the number of times each team plays division rivals.[44] Although many of these results conform to earlier studies, the evidence indicates hockey spectators prefer a more rugged and grinding style of play than a free-flowing, up-and-down-the-ice game. This is at odds with policy changes by the NHL to increase scoring (e.g., changing the dimensions of the rink) and decrease fighting. Only the decision to schedule more games among division rivals (and between Canadian teams) makes sense in the light of the evidence.

The Influence of Other Factors

Noll (1974) provides one of the first estimations of attendance demand in professional sports, including hockey. Based on data from the 1972–73 NHL and WHA seasons he concluded that arena capacity, membership in the NHL, and locations in colder climates are important determinants of demand. Weaker influences on attendance include winning percentage, number of competing professional sports franchises, and playoff contention.[45] Not surprisingly, larger cities are better able to support a hockey team; Noll estimates that a franchise locating in a city in the United States requires a population of at least 900,000 to survive. In Canada the population threshold is lower, about 520,000. Four Canadian cities (Edmonton, Ottawa, Quebec, and Winnipeg) fell below this number, leading Noll to question their long-run potential. Only one U.S. franchise, Atlanta, was problematic.

The determinants of attendance demand are explored in greater detail in Jones (1984). He found lagged winning percentage, playoff contention, local population, arena capacity, and Canadian cities to be significant determinants of attendance in the pre-expansionary period (1946–67). In the 1977–78 season (post-expansion and competition with the WHA), population, Canadian cities, the number of superstar players, style of play, weekend games, and the number of other sports teams led to higher attendance. Teams ranked lower in the standings drew fewer spectators. Team success, regardless of whether it is defined as winning percentage or playoff contention, is clearly important in both the short- and long-run. As the NHL expanded, increasing the number of teams eligible for the playoffs was clearly in the best interests of the league and individual franchises.

Ferguson, Stewart, Jones, and Le Dressay (1991) tested the hypothesis that ticket prices are set to maximize profits. Assuming that the cost of accommodating an additional fan is zero, this corresponds to revenue maximization. They used a system of two equations, with the first equation the inverse demand function. Because a team may be constrained by the size of its arena, profits are maximized at the point where marginal revenue is zero *or* attendance is at capacity (so capacity minus attendance equals zero). The second equation is the product of these conditions. The intercept and slope coefficients of the inverse demand function are assumed to be linear functions of six home cities and team attributes. The slope coefficient also appears in the first order condition equation. The system of equations was estimated using full information maximum likelihood for all NHL teams and three seasons.

The first and second derivatives for the estimated revenue function are calculated for all twenty-one teams. If firms maximize profits, then the first derivative should be equal to zero and the second derivative negative, unless the team is constrained by the capacity of its arena, in which case the first derivative should be positive. The results for the first order conditions are mixed, with marginal revenue not statistically different from zero in sixteen of thirty-nine cases of non-sellout teams. The estimated second derivatives are more supportive of profit maximization, with statistically significant negative values for all cases where teams did not have sellouts.

Franchise Location Studies

The recent financial difficulties of the Ottawa Senators, a team that advanced to the 2003 Eastern Conference finals before losing, illustrates the importance of location. Jones and Ferguson (1988) and Seredynski, Jones, and Ferguson (1994) tested an attendance demand model in which team revenues and profits are a function of both the quality of the team and the attributes of the location.[46] At the time of their study, Canadian cities, even those without a franchise, appeared to be better locations than most U.S. locations. This result supports the NHL's decision to allow former WHA franchises in Edmonton, Quebec City, and Winnipeg to join the NHL in 1979, and it also explains the relocation of the Atlanta Flames to Calgary in 1980.[47]

In addition, Seredynski, Jones, and Ferguson (1994) estimated attendance revenues and operating costs to determine the short- and long-run profitability of existing franchises and other potential locations.[48] Although several Canadian cities—Hamilton, Ottawa, and Saskatoon—appeared to be more viable locations in the early 1980s than franchises located in Minnesota, St. Louis, and Washington, several other U.S. cities—Denver, Houston, Tampa Bay— may be even better locations.[49] Also, moving weak U.S franchises across the border is questionable because television revenue among Canadian teams is shared unequally and Canada's tax laws are not as favorable as those of the United States.[50] Thus, the profitability of a relocated or expansion team north of the border without widespread revenue sharing is questionable.[51]

The vulnerability of financially handicapped small-market franchises is highlighted by Cocco and Jones (1997), who showed that franchises in Calgary, Edmonton, Quebec, and Winnipeg are at a distinct financial disadvantage vis-à-vis Montreal, Toronto, and Vancouver. Much of this is attributable to a poor location (attendance and media revenues differ widely between the large- and small-market franchises) and the fact that small-market teams tend to have a higher ratio of salary to non-salary costs than their larger-market brethren.[52] In addition, since three of the four small-market teams also had the smallest profits, the NHL's concerns were well founded. Accordingly, four potential options must be considered: revenue sharing, a salary cap, government subsidization, or relocation.

The problems with the first three are familiar to sports economists. Although owners of professional sport franchises may publicly express concern about the plight of small-market teams, they are privately loathe to do anything about it.[53] Even if revenue sharing were imposed by some deus ex machina, we would expect team owners to engage in even more "creative accounting" practices to shield revenues and profits from redistribution.[54] Team owners tend to support option two, but the Players Association typically opposes a cap on player salaries unless it is tied to option one.[55] The subsidy approach is difficult to defend on purely economic criteria (such as net economic growth).[56] That leaves only relocation within Canada or to the United States as an alternative. A simulation showed that an intra-national shift in franchises is not attractive because location quality and potential profitability of cities such as Ottawa and Saskatoon are worse than the extant small-market franchises. Relocation to the United States is, as history demonstrated for Quebec and Winnipeg, more appealing and, for Calgary, Edmonton, and Ottawa, a distinct possibility.[57]

In 1983 the owners of the St. Louis Blues franchise proposed to relocate the club to Saskatoon, Saskatchewan. Because the NHL, like all professional sports leagues, grants each franchise an exclusive territory, franchise shifts require prior league approval. In the case of the Blues, their request was denied by the league's Board of Governors. Carlton, Frankel, and Landes (2004) examine the extent to which a negative externality—in the form of a decline in attendance at away games—explains the league's decision.

Clearly, the owners of the Blues believed the present value of the flow of profits from operating the franchise in Canada was greater than in St. Louis, otherwise why propose the move? However, such a franchise shift, while good for the Blues, could adversely impact other franchises if, after relocation, the franchise drew fewer spectators to away games than before the move. The authors mention the rivalry between St. Louis and the Chicago Blackhawks; would Saskatoon attract as many fans as St. Louis to games played in Chicago? Because 100 percent of the gate revenues are collected by the home team, a franchise such as Chicago has no interest in allowing a team to relocate if it anticipates that revenues from ticket sales and ancillary revenue streams such as concessions would fall.

Using data for sixteen NHL seasons (1967–83), Carlton et al. estimate a reduced-form equation using away attendance as the dependent variable. Explanatory variables include population and dummies for season, division, team quality, new team, and relocated team (arena capacity was included in one estimate and excluded in the other). The coefficients for the variables of interest—new team and relocated team—are negative and significant. Given that new teams are frequently of low quality, a negative sign is to be expected. However, a relocated team also results in lower away attendance, on the order of 3.5–6.7 percent during the first three years (for the time period under consideration, the relocation effect appeared to be stronger in the United States than in Canada). The authors argue that a 3–4 percent reduction in attendance can result in a "substantial decrease in profits," so it is not surprising that NHL owners are risk averse when it comes to approving franchise relocation requests.[58]

Additional Studies on Player Violence

Hockey violence is also discussed in the legal literature. Jones and Stewart (2002) maintained that violence creates pronounced negative externalities in the form of fan misbehavior (fighting among spectators or between spectators and players) and through increased societal violence (particularly in the "trickle down" from professional to amateur leagues). Although they do not discount the fact that some fans enjoy watching fights and violence may serve some therapeutic function, they nevertheless believe the benefits are outweighed by the costs. Given this assumption, and the fact that teams have no economic incentive to curb violence, the question is what remedies should be used reduce violence.

In recounting two recent legal cases, they concluded that criminal and civil law in Canada and the United States is ineffectual in reducing hockey violence.[59] The application of criminal law is weakened because it is directed at the player rather than the team even though it is the latter that encourages and rewards violent behavior. Civil law—particularly the doctrine of vicarious liability (which allows an employer to be liable for an employee's actions)—is a more promising avenue of deterrence, but no significant precedent involving the NHL has yet been established. An alternative to a judicial remedy is self-regulation on the part of the NHL. But this is unlikely given the structure of economic incentives and the impotence and inability of the commissioner's office to discipline teams. Consequently, Jones and Stewart do not reject the possibility of a third remedy: direct regulation by a third party, presumably a government bureau.

An example of a self-regulation occurred in the 1998–99 season when the NHL conducted an experiment in which roughly 35 percent of the games played were officiated by two referees rather than the usual one. The use of two referees should result in a greater rate of apprehension with more penalties being observed and called. However, the addition of a referee can also lead to deterrence, with fewer penalties being committed and fewer therefore observed. Allen (2002), Levitt (2002), and Heckelman and Yates (2003) considered these possibilities.

Allen (2002) tested a time-allocation model for legal and illegal activities to determine if the increased presence of "policemen" on the ice results in fewer penalties. He used three sets of independent variables, the first set measuring the legal and illegal gains from on-ice performance. The second set measures the costs of illegal activities and the presence of police (referees). The last set consists of control variables, such as player experience, overtime games, and player position. For the first group, points scored in the game and career points per game have negative effects on penalties, although the effect is only significant for nonviolent penalties. Allen argued that this result is consistent with the time-allocation model; the rewards from legal activity (scoring goals and generating assists) outweigh those from illegal ones.[60] The number of fights in a game contributes significantly to the number of penalties, both violent and nonviolent. For the second set, a team's penalty-killing percentage has a significant positive effect on violent penalties. Penalties should be of less concern to a team that has confidence in its ability to kill penalties. Interestingly, the presence of an additional referee also has a positive and significant effect on violent penalties. Allen interpreted this to mean that the apprehension (or monitoring) effect dominates the deterrence effect. In terms of non-violent penalties, only the scoring ability of a player's teammates is positive and significant. This indicates that players are unconcerned if they are sent to the penalty box for a few minutes because their team is not greatly inconvenienced.[61]

Levitt (2002) compared games in the 1998–99 season in which one referee was present to those in which two were used. He found that the rate of apprehension rose when two referees were used, as the additional referee resulted in a statistically significant increase in minor penalties whistled. The number of majors did not change, but this is not surprising given that these penalties are more easily observed than minors (e.g., fighting versus tripping) even with a single referee. Levitt also attempted to ascertain the impact of deterrence. He argued that an appropriate test of deterrence is to determine whether the use of an additional referee leads to increased scoring. Since penalties are usually committed to prevent the opposing team from scoring, an increase in the number of goals scored when two referees are present suggests deterrence is occurring. Unfortunately, the signs for goals scored are inconsistent across specifications and are not significant.

Overall, Levitt attributes the inconclusive results to the small change in the probability of detecting infractions, not the lack of a deterrence effect in hockey per se. He was unable to reject the hypothesis that adding a second referee had no effect on the probability of detection. If there was no significant change in the probability, it is not surprising that the estimated deterrence effect was "small and imprecisely measured."[62] Given the results found by Allen and Levitt, it remains an open question why the NHL made the two-referee system permanent beginning with the 1999–2000 season.

Heckelman and Yates (2003) explored similar terrain as Allen and Levitt. In the 1999–2000 season, the NHL continued its experiment with two referees but significantly increased the number of games in which they were used. Using a difference-in-means test, the authors established that significantly more total penalties, penalty minutes, and minors were called during the two-referee contests. They interpreted this as a pronounced monitoring effect.

To test for the presence of a deterrent effect, an instrumental variables approach was used in which team offensive and defensive skills, the frequency in which a team is penalized, player and coach characteristics, and the percentage of previous games played with only one referee are regressed on the total number of infractions committed per game. The instrumental variable for referees appeared to have no influence on infractions committed. This led the authors to dismiss the deterrence effect and conclude (p. 710) "that an additional referee catches infractions that otherwise might be missed, but the players themselves do not take this into consideration."

Given the empirical results of the previous three papers, a question remains why an NHL franchise or the league would implement a rules change adding a second referee. If the argument made by Jones, Ferguson, and Stewart (1993) about the positive relationship between violence and attendance is correct, and since gate receipts are retained by the home team, it is not profit-maximizing for a team to use two referees.

Depken and Wilson (2004b) explore the public goods aspects of the use of a second referee. Their conjecture is that although the addition of a second referee will not increase a team's revenue via increased attendance, its future share from national television broadcasting rights will rise with the rules change. If this hypothesis is true, no single franchise has the incentive to hire a second referee, preferring instead to free ride. This leads to the classic public goods/prisoner's dilemma problem and suggests why the league itself has an incentive to intervene.

Based on a sample of 2,222 games played during the 1998–99 and 1999–2000 seasons, their empirical results show that the addition of a second referee leads to increased scoring, and fewer fights and penalty minutes (which, in contrast to Heckelman and Yates, indicates a deterrence effect), but no change in the closeness of competition (this uncertainty of outcome variable is measured by the absolute difference in the competing team's points per game prior to their match). To establish the impact of the second referee on revenue, they estimate the impact of these game outcome variables on attendance and national television viewership. Interestingly, they find, contra Jones et al., that the *decrease* in fighting due to the presence of a second referee neither reduces attendance nor adversely impacts television viewership. The increase in goals scored does have a positive impact on the television audience and therefore the revenue available to the NHL. Based on the television contracts in place during their sample period, the increase in potential revenue for the NHL was only $37,700 per referee, far less than the approximate cost for each additional referee of $100,000 per season.

Beginning with the 2000–2001 season, a new television broadcasting contract went into effect. ABC and ESPN paid the NHL $120 million per year for rights through the 2004–5 season. This represented an increase of 178 percent over the prior $45 million per year deal with ESPN and Fox. Using parameter estimates from the period of the previous contract, Depken and Wilson determine that the value per televised game of adding a second referee rose from $4,597 to $14,051. Using the assumption that roughly 10 percent of all NHL games are televised nationally, the value of a second referee per game played increased from $460 to $1,142. For an entire season of eight-two games, each additional referee would add $93,673 to television revenue for the NHL. Although this is still less than their working estimate of $100,000 as the cost per referee, it suggests that a surplus may exist for the NHL (the upper bound for a 95 percent confidence interval for the revenue impact is $417,745). A free-rider problem exists because the second referee does not have a significant impact on attendance, the revenue source directly controlled by the teams. Hence the mutually beneficial decision by the league itself to mandate the use of two referees.

Other Studies

Subsidization of sports facilities is an important public policy issue that has drawn considerable attention from economists. In contrast to the oft-repeated claims by team owners and allied interest groups that sports franchises spur local economic growth, numerous studies have presented convincing evidence that no such net growth takes place.[63] Proponents of stadium subsidies also rely on arguments concerning intangible benefits. They assert that a sports team generates a positive externality (in the form of local public goods like civic pride) that is so substantial as to merit public investment.

Johnson, Groothuis, and Whitehead (2001) used a contingent valuation method (CVM) to estimate the public goods contribution made by the Pittsburgh Penguins, an NHL franchise that continues to lobby for a new, publicly funded, facility to replace Mellon Arena, its current home. Distributing 1,100 CVM surveys to randomly selected households in the Pittsburgh metropolitan area generated 226 completed surveys (a response rate of 20.5 percent) from which a willingness to pay (WTP) model was estimated. Determination of the use value and non-use value components of WTP allowed the authors to estimate both the annual and the net present value of these components aggregated for the entire population of Pittsburgh. Three conclusions are notable: First, non-use value is about 2.7 times greater than use value, which indicates that intangible benefits are an important contributor to WTP. Second, aggregated WTP is estimated to fall in the range of $1.9 to $5.3 million per year and $23.5 to $66 million in perpetuity. Third, even if the largest estimate is believed to be the most accurate, a future flow of $66 million in benefits does not justify the construction of a facility that will cost at least three times that amount.

Beginning with the 1999–2000 season, the NHL implemented two rules changes designed to reduce the number of overtime games ending in a tie. The first rules change awarded one point to a team that loses in overtime. Before the change a team would earn one point for a tie but no points for a loss; this created an incentive for teams to act in a risk-averse manner by playing a more defensive style of play in overtime to avoid losing. The NHL's intent was that the change in the points system (in conjunction with each team skating with one fewer player during overtime) would encourage teams to play more aggressively. The rules change was a success as the percentage of overtime games ending in a tie fell from 71.1 percent in the period 1995–96 to 1998–99 to 55.5 percent during 1999–2000 to 2001–2. But the change was accompanied by an unintended, yet arguably foreseeable consequence, the percentage of games that went into overtime rose (from 19.8 percent to 22.2 percent).

Abrevaya (2004) used OLS and probit models to explain how the incentive structure changed when the NHL essentially guaranteed teams one point if they went into overtime. Both models included dummy variables for the rules change, inter-divisional and intra-divisional games, the day of the season, as well as proxies for home and visiting team quality (goals scored, goals yielded, and a team differential). Each model was run against three samples: all games played from 1995–96 to 2001–2, games that were tied at the start of the third period, and games tied with ten minutes remaining.

The OLS regression, using third-period shots on goal as the dependent variable, produced results that showed that more shots were taken in the third period prior to the rules change (supporting the hypothesis that teams are playing for overtime), and that shots taken rises when high-scoring and high-goal-yielding teams play. Two versions of the probit model were estimated; one featured the probability of overtime as the dependent variable and the other used the probability of no goals being scored in the third period. Although not consistently significant across samples, the coefficient for the rules change variable on the probability of overtime has the expected negative sign. Games played between division rivals are more likely to go into overtime (even if one team loses, that extra point is valuable in the division standings). The rules-change effect on "no goals in the third period" was ambiguous and insignificant; however, games played between division rivals increased the likelihood of "no goals" (again because both teams prefer to lose in overtime rather than the third period). Given the NHL's current concern with low-scoring games, future rules changes designed to increase offense might also include strategies to reduce the number of overtime games played.

Conclusions and Suggestions for Future Research

Hockey research is clearly plagued by a lack of data, especially consistent time-series data for team revenues, player salaries, ticket prices, and attendance. Given these gaps in data, historical and archival efforts may yield more information to allow replication and extension of the extant literature (especially in the murky waters of discrimination).

Despite the lack of data, many interesting avenues of inquiry remain open. For example, many of the studies discussed in this chapter use specific performance statistics (e.g., penalty minutes, goals) to address issues related to the labor market in the NHL. Future research could employ a broader theoretical perspective by investigating production and revenue functions from which estimates of marginal product and marginal revenue could be produced. This would yield more accurate empirical research concerning the NHL labor market, including the issue of discrimination.

There are numerous unanswered questions related to violence. For example, what is the relationship between ethnicity and propensity for violence? Did acts of violence fall with the increased supply of European players in the 1980s and 1990s? Is the intervention of a regulatory authority necessary to curb violence? If it is, how should a regulatory bureau be structured to avoid capture by the NHL? Is it possible that a criminal- or civil-law precedent will be established that sets boundaries on acceptable forms of hockey violence, thus obviating the need for direct regulation? Given that the average salary in the NHL is currently $1.64 million and these salaries include considerable economic rents, it seems reasonable to anticipate future lawsuits (at the time this was written Vancouver's Todd Bertuzzi was awaiting sentencing for his assault with intent to commit bodily harm on Colorado player Steve Moore).

In terms of other labor topics, McCormick and Tollison's (2001) NBA paper suggested future research on discrimination should also consider a reservation wage scenario in which players with different ethnic and racial characteristics have differing supply elasticities. This suggestion applies equally to the NHL, especially in light of the large influx of players from Europe and the former Soviet Union.[64] A related question concerns the impact players from these regions have had on attendance and revenue, especially among the Canadian franchises.[65] Given hockey's reputation as an important contributor to Canadian culture and identity, is there any possibility that the league might impose quotas on the number of foreign (European) players in an effort to boost attendance? Also, there is little existing research on the productivity and efficiency of NHL coaches and GMs in comparison to other professional (and collegiate) sports.[66] Finally, *if* more extensive salary information becomes available, changes in the NHL's monopsony power over time can be estimated.

In February 2004, the National Hockey League published the *Independent Review of the Combined Financial Results of the National Hockey League 2002–2003 Season*, more commonly referred to as the Levitt Report (it was coauthored by Arthur Levitt, the former chairman of the Securities and Exchange Commission). The Levitt Report estimated losses of $273 for the 2002–3 season (roughly $9 million per team) and supported warnings by team owners that contraction is inevitable without significant concessions by the Players Association (NHLPA) in the next collective bargaining agreement (CBA). The Players Association views the report with suspicion, given the proximity of the publication of the report to the expiration of the CBA in September 2004, and common knowledge of the accounting chicanery teams use to inflate their losses. However, the NHLPA did not reject the report outright, and it reportedly offered to reduce player salaries 5 percent across the board. Whether a restructured CBA will solve all the alleged financial misery of the NHL remains to be seen as there are issues other than labor costs that may explain why the average NHL franchise is at a financial disadvantage relative to other professional sports franchises.

How the NHL addresses its myriad problems, like a negligible television broadcasting contract and franchises teetering on the brink of bankruptcy, is certain to both renew interest in existing research questions and expand into new areas. For example, twenty-four of the thirty NHL teams (80 percent) are skating in arenas built since 1991. The presence of so many new arenas in a league that claims to be experiencing such severe losses raises questions about the relationship between a new arena and team operating income and whether any novelty or honeymoon was correctly estimated or understood to begin with. Given the league's financial problems, perhaps this is an opportune time for more attendance and location studies. Some earlier studies suggested hockey is an inferior good. Once any novelty effect wears off, is expansion into growing sun-belt cities, where household incomes are high

Table 4.1 Summary of NHL Research

Sample	Dependent variables	Independent variables	Results
		Labor Market Studies: Player Performance and Entry Discrimination	
Lavoie, Grenier, and Coulombe (1987)			
Canadian players for 1983–84 & 1984–85 seasons $n = 362$	CPoints Method: OLS	Draft# & Draft#^{2}, Defenseman, Origin (FC, EC = base)	**+ and sig:** FC, Draft#^{2} **– and sig:** Defenseman, Draft#
All players for 1983–84 & 1984–85 seasons $n = 515$	CPoints	Height, Age, Age^2, CPenalties, Defenseman, Origin (FC, AM, EU, EC = base)	**+ and sig:** Age, FR, EU **– and sig:** CPenalties, Defenseman
McLean and Veall (1992)			
	CPoints Method: OLS	CPenalties, Age, Age^2, Height, Defenseman, Origin (FC, AM, EU, EC = base)	**– and sig:** CPenalties, Defenseman, Height Coefficient for FC is positive but not significant
Lavoie and Grenier (1992)			
Players for 1989–90 season $n = 436$	CPoints	Draft#, Draft#^{2}, Defenseman, Origin (FC, all other = base)	**+ and sig:** Draft#^{2} **– and sig:** Draft#, Defenseman Positive coefficient for FC is significant at 12.5%, weak support for entry discrimination
Teams outside CUE for 1989–90 to 1999–2000 seasons $n = 248$	# of games played per season by French Canadians Method: Fixed-effects OLS	US, FC coach, FC GM, AM coach, AM GM, linear trend, 1994–95 season dummy	**+ and sig:** US **– and sig:** GM – FC, 1994–95 season This indicates FCs are less likely to play for teams in English-speaking Canada = customer discrimination
Teams outside QUE for 1989–99 to 1997–98 seasons $n = 203$	# of FC players drafted per season (draft# 100 or less) Method: Fixed-effects OLS	US, FC GM, AM GM, linear trend, team effects	**+ and sig:** US This indicates FCs are less likely to be drafted by teams in English-speaking Canada = customer discrimination

(continued)

Table 4.1 (continued)

Sample	Dependent variables	Independent variables	Results
Players for 1993–94 season $n = 436$	CPoints Method: OLS	Draft#, Draft#^{2}, Age, Defenseman, Defensive skill (used in powerplays), Weight, Height, CPenalties, Origin (FC, EU, AM, EC), Draft location (QUE, ROC, US) Results are for equation with draft location × player origin	<u>Base case</u> = FC forwards drafted in QUE **+ and sig:** Draft#^{2}, Age **– and sig:** Draft#, Defenseman, CPenalties <u>Base case</u> = EC forwards drafted in ROC **+ and sig:** Draft#^{2}, Age, EU × ROC **– and sig:** Draft#, Defenseman, CPenalties <u>Base case</u> = AM forwards drafted in US **+ and sig:** Draft#^{2}, Age **– and sig:** Draft#, Defenseman, Height, CPenalties, FC × US

Labor Market Studies: Player Performance and Salary Discrimination

---

Sample	Dependent variables	Independent variables	Results
Jones and Walsh (1988) Players for 1977–78 season $n = 306$	Salary (ln) Method: OLS	<u>Player</u>: CGoals, CPoints, CPenalties, 1st Round draft, Late draft, Height, Height^2, Weight, Weight^2, Trophies, All-Star picks, QUE born <u>City</u>: Canada location, Population, Income per capita, ArenaSize, OtherProSports (Comp)	<u>Forwards</u> **+ and sig:** CPoints, CGames, CPenalties, Height, Trophies, No1Draft, Population **– and sig:** CGames^2, Height^2, Weight, Weight^2 <u>Defensemen</u> **+ and sig:** CPoints, CGames, Weight, Trophies, No1Draft **– and sig:** Games^2, Weight^2, QUE, Comp <u>Goaltenders</u> **+ and sig:** CGames, Trophies **– and sig:** CGames^2

McLean and Veall (1992)
Players for 1989–90 season
$n = 460$

Salary (ln)
Method: OLS

CPoints, CPoints², CPenalties, Age, Height, CPlusMinus, Origin (FC, AM, EU, EC = base)

Forwards
+ **and sig:** CPoints, CPoints², Age
– **and sig:** Age², AM, EU
Defensemen
+ **and sig:** CPoints², Age, Height, CPenalties, CPlusMinus
– **and sig:** Age²
Goalies
+ **and sig:** Games played per season

Lavoie and Grenier (1992)
Players for 1989–90 season
$n = 436$

Salary (ln)
Method: OLS

Player: DeferredComp, NotDrafted, Draft#, Draft#², CSeasons, CSeasons², CPenalties, CPoints, CPoints², Weight, CPlusMinus, Defensive (powerplay), GoalAvg (Goalies), CGamesSeason (Goalies), All-star, Origin (FC, EU, AM)
Team: ArenaSize & utilization, City population, Canada location

Forwards
+ **and sig:** CSeasons, CPenalties, CPoints, CPoints², Population
– **and sig:** CSeasons²
Defensemen
+ **and sig:** CSeasons, CPenalties, CPoints, Defensive, All-star
– **and sig:** CSeasons²
Goaltenders
+ **and sig:** CSeasons, CGamesSeason, ArenaSize
– **and sig:** DeferredComp, CSeasons², Canada location

Longley (1995)
Forwards for 1989–90 season
$n = 250$

Salary (ln)
Method: OLS

Player: CGames, CPoints,
Team: Revenue
Player Origin (FC, EU, AM, EC)
x Location of team (QUE, CAN, US)

Base case = EC x CAN
+ **and sig:** CPoints, CGames, Revenue
– **and sig:** FC x CAN, EC x QUE
Base case = FC x QUE
+ **and sig:** CPoints, CGames, Revenue
– **and sig:** FC x CAN

(continued)

Table 4.1 *(continued)*

Sample	Dependent variables	Independent variables	Results
Jones, Nadeau, and Walsh (1999) Players for 1989–90 season Forwards *n* = 250, defensemen *n* = 138	Salary (ln) Restrictions on coefficients of interaction terms are used to test for (1) reservation wage effects, (2) player-borne bilingualism costs for Francophones, & (3) consumer ethnicity preferences	Player: Veteran (3+ years), CGoals, CAssists, CPenalties, CGames, CGames[2], Height, Height[2], Weight, Weight[2], Trophies + All-star, Years since draft, Goon (high CPenalties/low CPoints), Draft1, Draft2–3, Draft4+, NotDrafted, FreeAgent, Origin (FC, EC, AM, EU), NHL entry: University league (UNIV), European league (EURO), Major junior league (MAJR) Team: Rank in 1987–88 & 1988–89, Population, Income per capita, ArenaSize, OtherProSports, Location (QUE, ROC, US) Base = Draft2–3 & EC × MAJOR × ROC	Forwards **+ and sig:** Veteran, CGoals, CAssists, CGames, CPenalties, Goon, Weight, Weight[2], Trophies, Draft1, #Sports, Draft1 × Draft#Years, EC × UNIV × ROC, AM × UNIV × US **– and sig:** CPenalties × Goon, Height × Weight, Draft1 × Draft#, Draft1 × Years, Income, Rank88–89, VET × EC × UNIV × ROC, VET × EC × MAJR × US, VET × AM × UNIV × US, VET × EU × EURO × ROC Defensemen **+ and sig:** Veteran, CAssists, CGames, CPenalties, Trophies, #Sports, Rank87–88, EC × UNIV × US, EC × MAJR × QUE, EC MAJOR × US, AM × MAJR × US, VET × EC × UNIV × ROC, VET × AM × UNIV × QUE, VET × EU × EURO × ROC, VET × EURO × EU × US **– and sig:** CGames[2], Rank88–89, VET × EC × MAJR × QUE, VET × EC × MAJR × US Evidence of a weak consumer ethnicity effect

Lavoie (2000)
Players for 1993–94 season
Forwards $n = 308$, defensemen $n = 178$

Salary (ln)

Method: OLS

Team revenue, Draft#, NotDrafted, All-star selections, CGames, CGames², CPoints, CPoints², CPenalties, CPlusMinus, Weight, Defensive (used in powerplays), Origin (FC, EU, AM, EC, OTH), Team location (QUE, ROC, US)

Team revenue, Draft#, NotDrafted, All-star selections, CGames, $CGames^2$, CPoints, $CPoints^2$, CPenalties, CPlusMinus, Weight, Defensive (used in powerplays), Origin (FC, EU, AM, EC, OTH), Team location (QUE, ROC, US)

Forwards

For origin × ROC, base case = EC × ROC:
+ **and sig:** CGames, Weight, CPenalties, CPoints, $CPoints^2$, OTH × ROC
– **and sig:** $CGames^2$
For origin × US, base case = AM × US:
+ **and sig:** CGames, Weight, CPenalties, CPoints
– **and sig:** NotDrafted, $CGames^2$, OTH × US
For origin × QUE, base case = FC × QUE:
+ **and sig:** CGames, Weight, Defensive, CPenalties, CPoints
– **and sig:** $CGames^2$, EU × QUE

Defensemen

For origin × ROC, base case = EC × ROC:
+ **and sig:** All-star, CGames, Weight, Defensive, CPoints, OTH × ROC
– **and sig:** $CGames^2$
For origin × US, base case = AM × US:
+ **and sig:** All-star, CGames, Weight, Defensive, CPoints
– **and sig:** Draft#, $CGames^2$, FC × US, OTH × US
For origin × QUE, base case = FC × QUE:
+ **and sig:** All-star, CGames, Weight, Defensive, CPoints, EU × ROC, OTH × EU
– **and sig:** $CGames^2$

(continued)

Table 4.1 *(continued)*

Sample	Dependent variables	Independent variables	Results
Curme and Daugherty (2004) Players for 1999–2000 season Forwards $n = 366$, all non-goalies $n = 563$	Salary (ln) Method: OLS	Player: Draft round, All-star, CGames, Cpoints, CPenalties, CplusMinus, Weight, Weight², Height, Height², Years in NHL, Years², Defenseman, Origin (FC, US, EC, ER), Team location (QUE, ROC, US)	<u>Forwards</u> (Base case = EC × ROC) **+ and sig:** CGames; Weight, CPoints, CPenalties, Team revenue, All-star, **− and sig:** Years², Draft round, FC × ROC, US × US <u>All non-goalies</u> (Base case = EC × ROC) **+ and sig:** CGames, CPoints, CPenalties, CPlusMinus, Weight, Team revenue, All-star, Defenseman, Years **− and sig:** Years², Draft round, FC × ROC

Labor Market Studies: Salaries and Player Performance

Sample	Dependent variables	Independent variables	Results
Eastman (1980) Players for 1976–77 season $n = 44$	Salary, Points Method: Two-stage least squares	Age, Experience, Education, Draft#, Height, Weight, Penalties, MaritalStatus	<u>Salary</u> **+ and sig:** Age, Experience **− and sig:** Education <u>Points</u> **+ and sig:** Salary, Experience
Jones and Walsh (1987) Teams for 1975–76 to 1977–78 seasons $n = 36$ (12 teams for 3 years)	Winning% = % of maximum possible points Method: OLS	GoalsFor, GoalsAgainst Average Winning % prior 3 years	**+ and sig:** GoalsFor, AverageWinning% **− and sig:** GoalsAgainst
	Team Revenue	Winning%, ArenaSize, Income per capita, Population, Canada location, OtherProSports	**+ and sig:** Winning%, ArenaSize, Income, Canada

Players for 1977–78 season $n = 276$	Salary Method: OLS	Player: CPoints, CGames, CGames², CPenalties, Height × Weight, Star, Draft1, Draft6+, DefensiveAttributes City: Canada location City (lagged): ArenaSize, Income per capita, Population, OtherProSports	+ and sig: CPoints, CGames, CPenalties, Star, Draft1, DefensiveAttributes, LagPopulation − and sig: CGames²
Richardson (2000) Teams for 1988–90 to 1995–96 seasons $n = 161$	Revenue Method: OLS with fixed-effects by team	Winning%, Lagged Win%, #PlayoffGames Linear trend, 1994–95 lockout	+ and sig: Winning%, LagWinning%, #PlayoffGames, Trend − and sig: Lockout
$n = 166$	#PlayoffGames	Winning%, Winning%²	+ and sig: Winning% − and sig: Winning%²
	Method: Tobit regression model	Forwards: Goals, Assists Defensemen: Points, Penalties Goaltenders: Save%	+ and sig: Goals, Assists, Points, Save% − and sig: Penalties
	Winning%		
Players for 1993–94 season Forwards $n = 312$, defensemen $n = 156$	Surplus = Salary − MRP using MRP derived from above equation	Years (of experience), Years²	Forwards + and sig: Years − and sig: Years² Defensemen and Goaltenders: no significant variables
		SalaryRank (Player's salary rank on team—low is better), SalaryRank²	Forwards − and sig: SalaryRank² Defensemen: no significant variables
Defensemen $n = 520$		FreeAgent, MRP, MRP² All-Star, Years, Team effects	+ and sig: MRP − and sig: All-Star, Years

(continued)

Table 4.1 (continued)

Sample	Dependent variables	Independent variables	Results
League for 1979–80 to 1998–99 seasons $n = 17$	Ratio: std dev of win% divided by expected std dev under equal playing strength (= degree of competitive balance)	Linear time trend, #Teams	**– and sig:** Trend
Teams for 1979–80 to 1998–99 seasons $n = 298$	Winning%	Average draft pick order for years t–4 to t–6, Win% for years t–1 to t–2	**+ and sig:** Winning%(t–1), Winning%(t–2) **– and sig:** AvgDraftPick Implies early draft picks increase subsequent winning percentage, increasing competitive balance
Idson and Kahane (2000) Players for 1990–91 & 1991–92 seasons $n = 930$	Salary (ln) Method: White's robust variance-covariance matrix method with clustering on individual (due to panel data nature of dataset)	Player characteristics: CGames, CGames^2, CPoints, CPenalties, CPlusMinus, Height, Weight, HighDraft, Star, Forward, FreeAgent Team: Average of player characteristics Franchise: Revenue, CoachYears, CoachWin% Interaction terms: Player × Team performance	Individual characteristics **+ and sig:** CGames, CPenalties, CPlusMinus, Star, HighDraft, FreeAgent, **– and sig:** CGames^2, Weight, Forward Team average **+ and sig:** CPenalties, CPlusMinus, Height **– and sig:** Weight Franchise **+ and sig:** Revenue, CoachYears **– and sig:** CoachWin% Interaction (jointly significant at 5% level) **+ and sig:** Weight **– and sig:** CPenalties and Height

Kahane (2001)
Players for 1991–92 season
$n = 428$

Salary

Method: Hierarchical linear model using team-level effects for 22 teams

Player: Lagged CPoints
Team: Average lagged CPoints, Revenue

Intercept only, with random team-level effects:
Fixed effect on intercept statistically significant, random effect on intercept significant
Intercept & CPoints variable, with random team-level effects for intercept and slope:
Fixed effect on intercept & slope statistically significant, random effects on intercept & slope significant
Intercept and CPoints variable, with random team-level effects for intercept & slope plus fixed team-level effects on intercept & slope depending on team revenue: Fixed effect on intercept significant, random effects on intercept & slope significant, fixed effect of revenue on intercept & slope positive & significant

---

Labor Market Studies: Salaries and Player Violence

Jones, Nadeau, and Walsh (1997)
Players for 1989–90 season
$n = 388$

Salary

Method: Switching regression model with endogenous switching

Probit regression to determine Grunt status using penalty minutes & points per game in junior & minor professional leagues

Player: Veteran, FreeAgent, CPenalties, CGames, CGames^2, CPoints, Weight, Draft position (Draft1, Draft1 × Draft#, Draft1 × Draft# × Years, Draft2–3 × Years, NotDrafted × Years), Grunt status (affecting intercept & all slopes)

Team: City population, Income per capita, ArenaSize, OtherProSports, Rank in 1987–88 season, Rank in 1988–89

Grunt coefficient differentials
Forwards
+ and sig: TeamRank87–88, Draft1 × Draft#, Draft2–3 × Years
– and sig: Veteran
Defensemen
+ and sig: CGames, CGames^2 Draft1, FreeAgent, ArenaSize, TeamRank87–88
– and sig: Intercept, Veteran, CPoints, Draft1 × Draft#

Effect of Grunt status on salary when evaluated at means of independent variables is not significant

(continued)

Table 4.1 (continued)

Sample	Dependent variables	Independent variables	Results
		Attendance Demand Studies: The Influence of Violence	
Stewart, Ferguson, and Jones (1992) Teams for 1981–82, 1982–83, & 1983–84 seasons *n* = 63	Attendance Win% Price Violence (# penalties & misconducts for the season) Method: Full information maximum likelihood Model assumes price is set where elasticity = 1	City: Population, Income per capita, Canada location Team: Powerplay %, Penalty killing %, # AllStars, Points per season in last 3 seasons, # Defensemen with 20 points, # 20+ scorers, Negative of goals against for team's best goaltender	Attendance equation: + and sig: Population, Canada location − and sig: Income, Price Direct effect of violence on attendance is positive but small & not significant Indirect effect of violence on attendance via winning percentage is negative and larger but not quite significant
Jones, Ferguson, and Stewart (1993) Games for 1983–84 season *n* = 840	Attendance Price Method: Zellner's seemingly unrelated regressions	City: Population, Income per capita, Canada location Teams: Home Rank, Visitor Rank, Both teams top 3 rank, One team top 3 other bottom 3, Day game Violence (penalty minutes): Total for both teams or Misconduct each team or Major each team or Minor each team	Attendance (separate regressions for each violence measure) *All* + and sig: TotalPenalties *Canada:* + and sig: TotalPenalties, HomeMinors − and sig: HomeMisconducts *US:* + and sig: TotalPenalties, HomeMisconducts, HomeMajors, VisitorMinors Price (city variables only) + and sig: Population & Canada location − and sig: Income per capita

(continued)

Jones, Stewart, and Sunderman (1996)

Games for 1989–90 season

n = 552

Attendance
Price

Method: Zellner's seemingly unrelated regressions

City & Team: See Jones, Ferguson, and Stewart (1993)
Violence: Penalty minutes See JFS (1993)
# fighting majors each team, Styles of play (FF, SS, FS)
[Fighting = high previous season penalty minutes, Skating = low]

Attendance (separate regressions for each measure of penalty minutes)
Canada:
+ **and sig:** Home minor, Visitor total, Visitor misconduct, Visitor fighting
− **and sig:** Home total, Home misconduct, Home fighting, Visitor minor, FS, SS
US:
+ **and sig:** Total penalties, Home misconducts, Home majors, Home minors, Home fighting, Visitor misconduct, Visitor major, Visitor minor, Visitor fighting, FF, FS
Price (city variables only)
+ **and sig:** Population & Canada location
− **and sig:** Income per capita

Paul (2003)

Games for 1999–2000 season (teams excluded if all sellouts)

n = 984

Attendance
Price
Method: Zellner's seemingly unrelated regressions

Lagged Attendance
City: Population, Income per capita, NBA, MLB, NFL teams
Time of game: Opening night, weekend, first month, end of season
Previous season: Playoffs, 2nd round playoffs, points, goals scored
Current season to date: Points & goals per game
Rivalry: Division rivals, non-conference game, both Canadian teams
Violence: # fights per game each team for current season to date

Attendance
All:
+ **and sig:** Home fights per game
Canada:
+ **and sig:** Home fights per game
US:
+ **and sig:** Home fights per game
Price: results not reported

Table 4.1 *(continued)*

Attendance Demand Studies: The Influence of Other Factors

Sample	Dependent variables	Independent variables	Results
Noll (1974) Teams for 1972–73 season n = 27	Attendance Method: OLS	ArenaSize, Winning% × Population, CanadaLocation × Population, NHL × Population (0 for WHA), DecTemperature × Population, OtherProSports × Population, ClosePlayoffRace × Population	**+ and sig:** Winning%, NHL, ClosePlayoffRace **− and sig:** Temperature
Jones (1984) Teams for 1946–47 to 1966–67 seasons n =????	Attendance (ln) Method: OLS & ridge regressions, both corrected for serial correlation with Hildreth-Lu procedure	<u>City:</u> Population, Black%, Income per capita, OtherProSports, Canada location, ArenaSize <u>Team:</u> Winning%, #Stars, PlayoffPreviousYear, PlayoffCurrentYear	<u>OLS</u> **+ and sig:** Winning%, ArenaSize, <u>Ridge regression</u> **+ and sig:** Winning%, PlayoffCurrent, Population, ArenaSize, Canada
Games for 1977–78 season n = 720	Attendance Method: OLS & ridge regressions	<u>Teams:</u> HomeRank (League or Div.), VisitorRank (League or Div.), Both teams top 3 rank, One team top 3 other bottom 3, PlayoffDrive, FF, SS, or FS styles of play (Fighting = high previous year penalties, Skating = low), Weekend game <u>City:</u> Population, Black%, Income per capita, OtherProSports, Canada location, ArenaSize	<u>OLS</u> (League rank) **+ and sig:** PlayoffDrive, #Stars, FF, SF, Weekend, Population, Black%, Canada **− and sig:** HomeRank, VisitorRank, BothTop3, OtherProSports, ArenaSize, Income <u>OLS</u> (Division rank) **+ and sig:** #Stars, FF, SF, Weekend, Population, Black%, Canada **− and sig:** VisitorRank, OtherProSports, ArenaSize, Income

Franchise Location Studies

Study	Data / Method	Variables	Results
Jones and Ferguson (1988) Games for 1977–78 season	Attendance (n = 632 games) Price (n = 16 teams) Method: Zellner's seemingly unrelated regressions	Host city: Population, Income per capita, Canada location Teams: Home & visitor rank, Playoff drive, Both teams top 3 rank, One team top 3 other bottom 3, Weekend game, #Star Players, FF, SS, or FS styles of play (Fighting = high previous season penalty minutes, Skating = low)	<u>Ridge regression (League rank)</u> **+ and sig:** PlayoffDrive, #Stars, FF, SF, Weekend, Population, OtherProSports, Canada **– and sig:** HomeRank, VisitorRank, Income <u>Attendance</u> **+ and sig:** Canada, Population, Playoff, FF, #Stars, Weekend **– and sig:** Income, HomeRank, VisitorRank, BothTop3, SS <u>Price</u> (host city variables only) **+ and sig:** Canada, Population
Seredynski, Jones, and Ferguson (1994) Games for 1981–82 through 1983–84 seasons n = 1,674 games, n = 42 teams	Attendance Price Method: Zellner's seemingly unrelated regressions. Separate regressions for American & Canadian host cities	Host city: Population, Income per capita, New franchise honeymoon (franchise < 6 years old) Opposing teams: Home & visitor rank, Playoff drive, Both teams top 3 rank, One team top 3 other bottom 3, Weekend game, FF, SS, or FS styles of play (Fighting = high previous season penalty minutes, Skating = low)	<u>Attendance</u> *American host cities:* **+ and sig:** Population, Playoff, Weekend **– and sig:** Income, HomeRank, VisitorRank, FS *Canadian host cities:* **+ and sig:** Honeymoon, Population, Income, Playoff, Weekend **– and sig:** HomeRank, VisitorRank, BothTop3, FS, SS <u>Price</u> (host city variables only) *American host cities:* No significant variables *Canadian host cities:* **+ and sig:** Income **– and sig:** Population

(continued)

Table 4.1 *(continued)*

Sample	Dependent variables	Independent variables	Results
Cocco and Jones (1997) Games for Canadian teams for 1989–90 season n = 280 games, n = (not reported)	Attendance (ln) Price (ln) Method: Zellner's seemingly unrelated regressions	Host city: Population, Income per capita Teams: Home & visitor rank, Playoff drive, Both teams top 3 rank, One team top 3 other bottom 3, FF, SS, or FS styles of play (Fighting = high previous season penalty minutes, Skating = low), Weekend game	Attendance + **and sig:** Income, Weekend – **and sig:** Population, BothTop3, FS, SS, HomeRank, VisitorRank Price (host city variables only) + **and sig:** Population – **and sig:** Income
Ferguson, Stewart, Jones, and Le Dressay (1991) Teams for 1981–82 & 1983–84 seasons n = 63 (21 teams for 3 years)	Attendance Price System of nonlinear equations consisting of inverse demand & first order condition for constrained maximization (attendance ≤ capacity) Method: Full information maximum likelihood	Population, Income per capita, Canada location, #Stars, Rank in league (Average for current season, End of previous season) These variables affect both intercept (α) & slope (β) of inverse demand function. Only slope interaction effect is used in first order condition	Unrestricted model (uses δ's in first order condition equation rather than restrict coefficients to equal βs from inverse demand function) α: + **and sig:** Canada – **and sig:** #Stars, CurrentRank, PriorRank β: no significant coefficients δ: no significant coefficients Restricted regression (cross-equation restrictions based on model: δs = βs) α: + **and sig:** Income – **and sig:** Population β: no significant coefficients

Study / Sample	Dependent variables / Method	Independent variables	Results
Carlton, Frankel, and Landes (2004) Teams for 1989–90 season $n = 280$ games	Season attendance for away games (ln) Method: OLS	<u>City/arena characteristics</u>: Population, ArenaSize <u>Team</u>: Division leader, Top four in division, New team (first 3 years), Moved team (first 3 years) Fixed effect dummies for season & division	**+ and sig:** Capacity, Population, division leader, top 4 team **– and sig:** New team years 1 & 2, moved team years 1–3

Additional Studies on Player Violence

Study / Sample	Dependent variables / Method	Independent variables	Results
Allen (2002) Players by game during 1998–99 season $n = 27,722$ 587 players (minimum 11 games per player to maximum of 60)	Nonviolent penalties Violent penalties Method: Random-effects negative binomial model	2Refs <u>Player</u>: CPoints, CPlusMinus, CPenalties, CSuspensions, Defenseman, Rookie, Experience, Experience^2, AvgIceTime, European Player in game: GPoints, GShots, GPlusMinus, TeammateGPoints <u>Team</u>: TeamStandingPoints, PenaltyKill%, OpponentPowerplay% <u>Game</u>: TotalFights, Overtime, InCanada, DivisionOpponent	<u>Nonviolent penalties</u> **+ and sig:** GPlusMinus, CPenalties, TotalFights, Defenseman, TeammateGamePoints AvgIceTime, Experience **– and sig:** GPoints, CPoints, TeamStandingPoints, Rookie, Experience^2 <u>Violent penalties</u> **+ and sig:** CPenalties, CSuspensions, TotalFights, PenaltyKill%, 2Refs, AvgIceTime **– and sig:** Rookie
Levitt (2002) Games for 1998–99 season $n = 780$	Minor penalties Major penalties Goals per even-strength minute Goals per power-play minute Method: OLS with fixed effects	2Refs (in 270 of 780 games), Linear trend, Team fixed effects, Team-pair fixed effects	Results for 2Refs variable; other regression results not reported Minor penalties: **+ and sig** Major penalties: **– and not sig** Even-strength goals: **+ and not sig** Power-play goals: **– and not sig**

(continued)

Table 4.1 *(continued)*

Sample	Dependent variables	Independent variables	Results
Heckelman and Yates (2003) Games for 1999–2000 season $n = 770$	Home team penalty minutes Home team total penalties Home team minor penalties Home team major penalties Method: IV with instrument for number of referees	# of referees, Own team goon dummy, Opposing team goon Team differences: Age, Height, Weight, Coach Experience Own team (previous 15 games): Powerplay defense, Save percentage, Shorthanded frequency Opposing team (previous 15 games): Powerplay offense, Shooting percentage, Powerplay frequency	Penalty minutes + and sig: Own shorthanded freq., opposing powerplay freq., own goon, opposing goon, age difference − and sig: Own save percentage Total penalties + and sig: Own shorthanded freq., opposing powerplay freq., own goon, opposing goon, age difference − and sig: Own save percentage Minor penalties + and sig: Own shorthanded freq., opposing powerplay freq., own goon − and sig: Own save percentage, weight difference Major penalties + and sig: Opposing shooting percentage, own shorthanded freq., own team goon, opposing goon, age difference − and sig: Own powerplay defense

Study / Sample	Dependent variable	Independent variables	Results
Depken and Wilson (2004b) Games for 1998–99 & 1999–2000 seasons *n* = 2,222	Total goals scored	Number of referees, Month, Team fixed effects	**Total goals scored** **+ and sig:** # of refs, Mar., Nov., total shots on goal **– and sig:** Visitor PPG
	Total fights	Season-to-day team performance: Home points per game (PPG), Visitor PPG, Difference in PPG	**Total fights** **+ and sig:** Total powerplays, goal difference **– and sig:** Number of refs, visitor PPG
	Total penalty minutes	Game characteristics: Number of powerplays, Total shots on goal, Goal difference	**Total penalty minutes** **+ and sig:** Goal difference **– and sig:** Number of refs, visitor PPG
	Closeness of game (goal differential)		**Closeness of game** **+ and sig:** Difference in PPG **– and sig:** none
	Method: OLS with fixed effects		
Games for 1998–99 & 1999–2000 seasons *n* = 2,222	Attendance	Canada location, Network (ESPN, ESPN2), Month (base = April), Time of day (primetime vs. nonprimetime), Day of week (base = Friday), Host city fixed-effects, Season to date team performance: Home points per game (PPG), Visiting PPG, Difference in PPG	**+ and sig:** Higher of home/visiting PPG *or* home PPG and visiting PPG, Monday **– and sig:** Difference in PPG, Canada, all months (compared to April), all days except Sat. (compared to Fri.)
	Method: Fixed-effects Tobit censored at arena capacity		
Televised games for 1998–99 & 1999–2000 seasons *n* = 227	Television viewers	Home points per game(PPG), Visiting PPG, Difference inPPG, Home + visiting goals per game, H + V fights per game, H + V penalty minutes per game, Higher of home & visiting PPG	**+ and sig:** Home + visiting goals per game, higher of home/visiting PPG, Oct., Dec., Feb., Mar., primetime, ESPN, all days except Sat. (compared to Fri.) **– and sig:** none
	Method: Fixed-effects OLS		

Other Studies

Study / Sample	Dependent variable	Independent variables	Results
Johnson, Groothuis, and Whitehead (2001) Survey respondents *n* = 226	Willingness to pay (WTP) per year for a new arena for Pittsburgh Penguins	ProposedTaxIncrease,income per household, AttendedGame(s), #GamesAttended, #TVGamesWatched,	**+ and sig:** AttendedGame(s), #GamesAttended, #PublicGoods, WatchedStanleyCup

(continued)

Table 4.1 *(continued)*

Sample	Dependent variables	Independent variables	Results
	Model: Tobit model	#PublicGoodsConsumed (0–4), WatchedStanleyCup, SurveyedAtGame, Gender, Age, WhiteRace, Years education, #inHousehold	Evaluated at the mean of independent variables, use value & nonuse value both statistically significant. Estimated nonuse value 2.7 times use value, & the difference is statistically significant
Abrevaya (2004) Games for 1995–96 to 2001–2 seasons *n* = 7,821	Total third period shots on goal	Old rule dummy (NHL change in awarding of points for ties & overtime losses), Division rivals dummy, Number of days into season, Season performance (Home team goals per game, Visiting team goals per game, Home team goals allowed, Visiting team goals allowed, Home/visitor difference)	Third period shots on goal + **and sig:** old rule, home goals per game, visitor goals per game, home goals allowed, visitor goals allowed − **and sig:** home/visitor difference
	Overtime (Probit)		Overtime + **and sig:** division rivals − **and sig:** old rule, visitor goals allowed, home/visitor difference
	No goals last 20 mins. (Probit)		No goals last 20 mins. + **and sig:** division rivals − **and sig:** home goals per game, home goals allowed, visitor goals allowed
			[Results also reported for games tied with 20 mins. left to play & games tied with 10 mins. left]

Note: sig = statistical significance. *Players:* AM = American origin; Cassists = Career assists; CGames = Games played during career; CGamesSeason = Average games per season during career; CPenalties = Penalty minutes per game during career; CPoints = Points per game during career; CPlusMinus = Plus/minus statistic during career; CSeasons = Seasons played during career; DeferredComp = Deferred compensation; Draft# = Draft number if selected (lower is better); Draft1: Dummy equal to 1 if drafted in first round; Draft2–3 = Dummy equal to 1 if drafted in second or third rounds; EC = English Canadian origin; EU = European origin; FC = French Canadian origin; FreeAgent = Dummy equal to 1 if ever signed a contract as a free agent; GoalAvg = average goals per game; NotDrafted = Dummy equal to 1 if not selected in regular draft. *Teams:* Attendance = Average attendance per game during season; OtherProSports = Number of other professional sports in the same city; QUE = Quebec location; Rank = Rank in division or league (lower is better); ROC = Rest of Canada (outside Quebec)location; US = United States location; Winning% = Win Percent.

and substantial alternative forms of recreation exist, a wise choice? Is the presence of a minor league hockey club a reliable leading indicator for the viability of an NHL franchise? Is it possible that the rise of the so-called alternative sports associated with events like the X Games is finally killing off its first major professional sport?

Finally, as we finish this chapter, the fact that the NHL season remains in limbo points to a lack of empirical research on the economic impact of lockouts and labor stoppages. Evidence from Major League Baseball, and the strike in 1994, suggests that it may take at least a decade for the NHL to recover. And given that the NHL is in a much weaker financial position than baseball was at the time the season was suspended, recovery may not be guaranteed for all NHL franchises.

Notes

An earlier version of this paper was prepared for the Sports Economics: Past and Future session at the Western Economics Association meetings in Denver, July 2003. The authors greatly appreciate the comments made by Stacey Brook at that time and during subsequent discussions. We also wish to thank Hamid Bahari-Kashani, John Fizel, Dianna Hewett, Colin Jones, Marc Lavoie, and the staff of Hamersly Library at Western Oregon University. The usual caveat applies.

1. For a discussion on the evolution of the NHL's monopoly power, see Gruneau and Whitson (1993: 79–106).

2. The first NHL star to sign with a WHA team was Bobby Hull, who left the Chicago Blackhawks to join the Winnipeg Jets. The NHL's reserve clause was overturned in 1972 by the legal case Philadelphia World Hockey Club, Inc. v. Philadelphia Hockey Club, Inc.

3. These players may also be subjected to positional discrimination or stacking. The latter appears to be the case for French Canadians at the position of goalie.

4. They also mention that the NHL's use of a central scouting bureau means that scouts may be immune from competitive pressures that constrain their tastes and preferences.

5. When a player is on the ice, and his team is at full strength or shorthanded, he gets a "plus" each time his team scores. If his team is at full strength or on a power play, he gets a "minus" each time his team is scored upon.

6. Absent any precise way to assess defensive skill, teams will instead rely on "subjective or less relevant factors such as . . . the size of a player" and the biases of the front office (Lavoie, Grenier, and Coulombe, 1989: 99). See also Lavoie, Coulombe, and Grenier (1987: table 3, 412).

7. They use an "adjusted" plus/minus statistic designed to capture the fact that "teams that have good records have good players [and] average players playing for good teams will have better than average statistics" (Lavoie and Grenier, 1992: 171).

8. Krashinsky also disagreed with the claim that it is harder to evaluate the talents of defensemen: "While there may not be complete information about the future performance of young defensemen and forwards, there is surely some evidence that can be used in generating a probability distribution concerning ability" (1989: 96).

9. The apparent conflict between entry discrimination and the selection of Francophones *earlier not later* in the NHL draft can be described as follows:

> Final team rosters depend on decisions made from imperfect and unsure information. Training camps are usually too short to allow coaches and managers to make enlightened decisions. Cuts are often made depending on the previous reputation of the player, acquired through scouting reports and draft numbers. Poorly considered athletes are cut off unless they can quickly demonstrate their prowess. Francophone players, at least those who do not belong to Quebec teams, are not given the opportunity to show their talent, *unless* [italics added] they were drafted very early. Discrimination thus occurs twice: at the draft and when team rosters are finalized. (Lavoie, Grenier, and Coulombe, 1989: 28–29)

Lavoie, Grenier, and Coulombe provide an example of the role of uncertainty by examining the distribution pattern of the "stars of the game" award for the Montreal Canadiens in the 1987–88 season. They interpret the fact that forwards were almost seven times more likely to receive a "star" than defensemen as evidence of the difficulty in interpreting the latter's contribution to team success.

10. The drawbacks of the linguistic fluency idea, according to Lavoie (1989), are that it relies on an assumption that communication skills are somehow more important for defensemen than for forwards or goalies; that French Canadians have a perpetual language handicap that other nonnative English language players do not; and that the costs of investing in a linguistic form of human capital are completely internalized by the player. Also, existing labor market conditions make it unlikely that a player will be granted free agency until he is thirty-two years old, so it makes sense for an NHL franchise to help him improve his language skills if the franchise values his services.

11. Lavoie compared goals scored in the three junior hockey leagues NHL players are primarily drafted from: the Quebec Junior Major Hockey League (QJMHL), the Ontario Hockey League (OHL), and the Western Hockey League (WHL). Francophone players tend to be concentrated in the QJMHL, while Anglophones constitute a greater population in the OHL and WHL. Using data from the 1980s he determined that although the OHL is the most defensively minded league (lowest goals per game), the other two leagues had a similar goals-per-game average. Given the significant presence of former WHL players in the NHL, Lavoie asked why these English Canadian players are not subject to the same "too much offense, not enough defense" criticism as players coming from the QJMHL.

12. Marple and Pirie (1977) used a similar approach.

13. He also questions how this thesis can be reconciled with the overrepresentation of Francophones at goalie. Should not young Francophone goalkeepers also be daunted at the prospect of leaving Quebec to play for an NHL squad?

14. As Williams and Williams (1998: 148) indicated, "interpretations of this statistic can also be ambiguous, because some players who are very good at defensive play are consistently used by coaches against the other teams' most offensively-skilled players. The result is that these players get few goals but do collect minuses." On the interpretation of the plus/minus statistic, see Williams and Williams (1997).

15. Because more points per season are generated in the QJMHL, Walsh concluded that the QJMHL emphasizes offensive skills more than the other two leagues. This offensive emphasis comes at a cost however. During inter-league competition,

OHL and WHL teams dominate their QJMHL rivals, suggesting that it takes both offensive and defensive skills to win championships. Contrast Walsh's position with that of Lavoie (in Note 11). Also Lavoie, in correspondence with the authors, suggested Walsh's conclusion that OHL and WHL players are significantly bigger than those in QJMHL is overstated, as the size differential is minimal.

16. If size is an important determinant in assessing defense skill, then the uncertainty-based argument by Lavoie et al. may be exactly backward: there is *less* rather than more uncertainty in evaluating the talents of a potential NHL defenseman than a forward or goalie.

17. Other studies avoid measuring defensive skill. For example, Longley did not include defensemen in his sample because of the difficulty in identifying an unambiguous measurement of their performance (1995: 415). Berry, Reese, and Larkey (1999) presented a statistical comparison of player performance across time, but used data for forwards only.

18. Using a larger sample than Walsh, they found that during the period 1979–92 the average number of goals scored per team was roughly equal in the QJMHL and WHL and greater than the OHL. If Walsh's contention is true that the greater number of goals scored indicates more emphasis on offense and less on defense, then any criticism of the defensive abilities of players in the Francophone populated QJMHL applies equally to players in the Anglophone-dominated WHL. They also argue that Selke winners are smaller than most NHL forwards; this challenges Walsh's belief that size and defensive ability are positively correlated.

19. During the sample period (1948–98) Francophone forwards and defensemen played 8,640 games for English Canadian teams and 65,216 for all non-Quebec teams (13.25 percent). Yet in the same period, English Canadian teams comprised 18.66 percent of all non-Quebec teams. The actual participation rate is lower than would be expected were there no discrimination, and the difference in proportions is statistically significant.

20. He also argued that since Europeans are overrepresented on ROC teams compared to U.S. teams, there is little evidence that fans in Canadian provinces other than Quebec favor Anglophones at the expense of other ethnic groups.

21. This idea is tested by splitting the sample into two periods, the first covering the 1976–81 and 1993–98 seasons, and the second the 1967–76 and 1981–93 seasons. The first period encompasses those years that Longley believes represented greater political demands by the Québécois for sovereignty.

22. This possibility was raised in a paper by Curtis and Loy (1978: 299), who mentioned that "if discrimination against Francophones were operating and the cultural context had any influence, we might expect more evidence of such discrimination in English Canada . . . but not in French Canada or the United States."

23. During the period 1989–2000, Francophones and Americans represented, respectively, only 4 percent and 4.8 percent of the total population of head coaches, and 6.5 percent and 21.3 percent of the total population of general managers.

24. There is an important caveat concerning the dependent-variable-only picks after the 100th selection are included. Longley (2000) presented evidence that imbalances in the representation rate of French Canadians rose after the 100th pick. Since players chosen in these middle to late rounds are likely to be only marginally talented, and à la Lavoie et al. harder to evaluate, those players of Francophone origins may become victims of the tastes and preferences of English Canadian GMs.

25. Williams and Williams (1998: 145) mention that the "evaluation of hockey

players has been dominated by subjective professional judgment, perhaps influenced by a small number of selected statistics." Williams (1994) and Williams and Williams (1998) provide some alternative player performance measures based on principal components analysis.

26. As Lavoie (2003: 384) indicated, "as more sophisticated questions are being put to the test, more disaggregated data with fewer observations must be used, leading to more fragile results."

27. According to the 2002–03 edition of the *National Hockey League Official Guide and Record Book*, 47 percent of the players listed on the 2002–3 roster for the Montreal Canadiens were born in Quebec and 22 percent were born in the rest of Canada. Fifty-five percent of the Toronto Maple Leafs players were born in the rest of Canada and only one player, a goalie, was born in Quebec. In personal correspondence with the authors, Lavoie argues that the results in his 2003 paper (especially tables 1 and 2) should be interpreted as strongly indicative of entry discrimination.

28. In an earlier paper, Kahn (1991: 403) suggested these kinds of results are consistent with the statistical discrimination model in Aigner and Cain (1977).

29. Another issue is whether there are monopoly and monopsony influences on player salaries, a question originally raised in Jones (1969) and (1976). Jones and Walsh (1988) pointed out that the 1977–78 season coincided with one of the last seasons of a competing league, the World Hockey Association, which indicates a more pronounced monopoly labor market influence. The monopsony hypothesis is rejected and a monopoly influence on salary is only supported for forwards. In terms of lower salaries paid to defensemen, they discussed the plausibility that the relative anonymity of this position (from the fan's perspective) vis-à-vis forwards and goalies may result in lower bargaining strength during salary negotiations.

30. Jones and Walsh also explored whether playing in Montreal conveys any advantage to a player in terms of salary. They found that no such advantage occurs but an apparent salary penalty exists for Francophone defensemen playing outside Quebec.

31. Krashinsky and Krashinsky (1997) disagreed with the conclusions drawn by Longley. Their primary complaint concerns the lack of robustness in Longley's model resulting from a small sample size and omitted variable bias. Longley's salary discrimination argument is based on the number of French Canadians playing in the ROC, yet during the 1989–90 season there were only five such players. It is also possible that something other than discrimination may be explaining the salary results; for example, of the five French Canadian players in the ROC, four played for the Toronto Maple Leafs, a franchise run by an owner (Harold Ballard) considered tight-fisted regardless of the ethnic origins of his players. To answer the omitted variable bias criticism, Longley added dummy variables for the ethnicity of Maple Leaf players. The results for the coefficients on games played, points per game, and team revenue are the same as in the earlier paper (positive and significant). Only the French Canadian dummy is statistically significant (indicating French Canadians are paid 36 percent less, an estimate similar to the earlier finding).

32. For example, in professional basketball see Kahn (2000: 85).

33. Age and experience have the anticipated signs but, unlike later studies, Eastman does not investigate any nonlinear relationships between these variables and income or productivity.

34. The production function used goals scored, goals allowed, and team quality as the explanatory variables. The revenue function used player productivity, arena capacity, local income and population, the number of competing professional sports

franchises, and a Canadian dummy as the independent variables. Since a reliable metric for defensive skill was not available, the authors calculated MRP by weighing goals scored more for forwards, and goals allowed more for defensemen. Salaries were estimated using performance measures such as lifetime points, penalties, player size, and games played.

35. The fact that exploitation is negative (many players are overpaid relative to MRP) is suggestive of a widespread "winner's curse" phenomenon during this period.

36. Berry, Reese, and Larkey (1999: 668) also argue that interaction among players is very important in assessing a player's productivity.

37. Idson and Kahane began by regressing salary on the player performance variables and then added team measurements, a vector of variables to capture the productivity of teammates, and a series of interaction terms representing player attributes that are considered complements or substitutes. They argued that "if the coefficients on own productivity . . . fall when team measures are added, then we interpret this result as indicating that part of the measured effect of player characteristics on their salary is due to teammate contributions to their productivity" (2000: 352). An interacted term represents a complement if the sign of the coefficient is positive and a substitute if it is negative. Variables that are consistently statistically significant at the 10 percent level or better across all specifications of the model, and contribute positively to player salary, include: the number of games for the player; player and team penalties; player and team plus/minus statistic; player height; whether the player is an all star, a high draft pick or a free agent; the experience of the coach; and franchise revenues. None of these results is unusual. Variables that contribute negatively to player salary are the square of the number of games played (diminishing returns to experience), the total weight of all the team's players, a dummy if the player is a forward, and the coach's lifetime winning percentage. The last two results are not consistent with earlier studies. Other attributes that appear to be complements are points and the plus/minus statistic. Both variables have a positive coefficient but are not statistically significant. All-star status appears to be a substitute albeit not significantly.

38. To test this possibility, Kahane used a hierarchical linear model with lagged career points per game (as the player attribute variable) and team revenue (as the team-level variable) to explain the variation in 428 player salaries for the 1991–92 season. He recognized one of the limitations of the hierarchical linear model is that the number of player variables used is constrained by the number of observations for the team-specific variable. Since there were only twenty-two teams in the sample, player performance was limited to career points rather than additional observations (e.g., penalty minutes or power play goals).

39. There is considerable interest on the part of psychologists; see, for example, papers by Smith (1979), Widmeyer and Birch (1984), and Colburn (1985). Allen (2002) explores the history of violence in the NHL, and Gruneau and Whitson (1993, 175–96) interpret social aspects of hockey violence.

40. The classification of a player as a grunt or non-grunt is determined by applying a clustering procedure based on penalty minutes and points per game, with grunts identified as the players who accumulate more of the former and less of the latter. A further technical difficulty, mismeasurement of who the grunts are, is addressed using a probit model in which player weight, penalty minutes, and points scored while playing for junior and minor league hockey teams are regressed on the probability of being a grunt. The probit results suggest players classified as grunts are classified

correctly. To determine if the salary determination process differs between the two classifications of players, Jones, Nadeau, and Walsh (1997) used their OLS results to compare, via a Wald test, the coefficients for the two groups. They rejected the hypothesis that the salary determination process is identical.

41. The assertion that "NHL teams appear to use monopsony power to reduce the salaries of non-grunt forwards and defensemen" (Jones, Nadeau, and Walsh, 1997: 202) seemed intuitively plausible (non-grunts have greater outside sources of income, e.g., endorsements) but is only weakly supported by the regression results.

42. Violence "is measured as the total number of minor and major penalties, plus misconducts and game misconducts, incurred by the home team in its arena over the season" (Stewart, Ferguson, and Jones, 1992: 59). The important influences on attendance are the location variables: population, income, and a Canadian dummy are all positive and significant. "If the location is right, even a perennially mediocre team can draw large crowds" (Stewart, Ferguson, and Jones: 1992, 62). The coefficient on ticket price is strongly significant and implies the anticipated inverse relationship between price and attendance holds. In the price regressions, the population variable is consistently positive and significant and the income variable is positive and significant in Canadian cities but weaker for U.S. cities.

43. The style variable was determined by comparing the total number of penalty minutes a team accumulated in the 1988–89 season to the league mean. Teams one-half a standard deviation above or below the mean were classified as fighting and skating teams, respectively. Three style variables were used: both teams are fighters, one team is a fighter, or both teams are skaters.

44. Paul does not indicate the source of ticket price information or the kind of price variable used.

45. Noll normalized the data by multiplying all independent variables by population. He also indicated (1974: 153) that per capita income was never a significant variable and that price data was mostly unobtainable.

46. The sample is based on the 1977–78 NHL season. The price variable is average ticket price per team. When attendance is regressed against a set of team and location variables, the empirical results show income, population, and Canadian to be significant but only income negative. Attendance is higher when one or both of the teams have a "fighting" style of play, weekend game, in playoff contention. Increased uncertainty of outcome (Seredynski, Jones, and Ferguson, 1994) does not appear important and attendance is lower the lower the team is in the standings and if both teams have a "skating" style. In terms of price and market power, prices are higher in more heavily populated lower-income Canadian cities.

47. Of all major Canadian cities without a franchise, Saskatoon is the least favorable location but nevertheless is superior to Buffalo or Minnesota. Jones and Ferguson (1988) recognized that a poor location may be counteracted by the presence of a good team and a simple regression of team quality against location suggested the latter is an important influence on the former.

48. One factor influencing their (Seredynski, Jones and Ferguson (1994) revenue estimates is the honeymoon effect. They found the honeymoon to be much longer in Canadian cities than in the United States

49. Geddert and Semple (1987) defended Saskatoon as a viable franchise location.

50. Even U.S. cities like Tampa Bay appear unable to maintain a team in the long-run unless other significant sources of revenue (notably broadcast rights) besides ticket sales are developed.

51. Ottawa was granted a franchise in 1992. Minnesota moved to Dallas in 1993, Quebec moved to Denver in 1995, and Winnipeg went to Phoenix in 1996. Atlanta and Minnesota were expansion teams in the 1999 and 2000 season, respectively. Other commonly mentioned reasons for Canadian clubs' financial woes are the weakness of the Canadian dollar vs. the United States dollar (teams are required to pay salaries in U.S. dollars) and greater subsidization of arena construction in the United States. A broad perspective on the financial situation of pro sports franchises, including the NHL, is provided by Howard (1999).

52. Cocco and Jones (1997: 1543) noted that "no Canadian franchise covers its costs from regular season attendance revenue." Low media revenues are also important. Compared to the NFL, NBA, and MLB, the NHL had the lowest ratio of media revenues to player payroll in 1996 (see Fort, 2003: 77–80).

53. Cocco and Jones (1997) included the following quote by John McMullen, owner of the New Jersey Devils: "To hell with small market teams." The lack of cooperation among NHL teams in addressing financial difficulties is exemplified by the 1999 roundtable discussion convened to explore "shared solutions" to ensure the financial viability of Canadian franchises. Participants at the roundtable included representatives from the Canadian NHL teams, the NHLPA, and the provincial governments. No mutually agreeable solutions were established at this conference (see Public Policy Forum, 1999).

54. In the mid-1990s the NHL implemented two relatively low impact revenue sharing schemes, the Group 2 Equalization Plan (1995) and the Canadian Assistance Plan (1996). The first program appears to have ended in 1998. Edmonton, Calgary, and Ottawa continue to rely to some extent on the latter program.

55. In 1995 the players agreed to a salary cap for rookies.

56. Requests by Quebec and Winnipeg for new subsidized arena were denied. Calgary and Edmonton are being subsidized by local and provincial government.

57. According to Cocco and Jones's estimates, twenty-three U.S. cities, including Denver and Phoenix, had more viable locations than the weakest small-market franchises, Quebec and Winnipeg.

58. The authors also estimated the predicted impact of the relocation effect for five franchise relocations. Of the four that were approved, only one (Colorado to New Jersey) had an anticipated minimal relocation effect. For the remaining three (California to Cleveland, Kansas City to Colorado, and Atlanta to Calgary), only the move to Calgary appears, in retrospect, to have been a good idea. The largest relocation effect is for St. Louis, the move the league rejected.

59. The cases were *Regina v. McSorley* (tried in Canada) and *McKichan v. St. Louis Hockey Club* (the decisive case was tried in the Missouri Court of Appeals). Both cases were based on events that involved seemingly flagrant acts of violence directed at an opposing player. The McSorley case involved a Boston Bruins player who was charged by the attorney general of British Columbia with assault with a weapon. McSorley received an eighteen-month conditional discharge by the court and a one-year suspension by the NHL. The Bruins' franchise was not punished. The defendant in the McKichan case, a minor league player named Tony Twist, had charges against him dropped, but the parent club of his team, the St. Louis Blues, was found liable and the plaintiff was awarded damages.

60. Two specifications are estimated, one uses nonviolent penalties (e.g., delay of game) as the dependent variable and the other, violent offenses (e.g., spearing). Three subsets of explanatory variables are incorporated: measures of the gain from legal and

illegal activities; the costs of illegal activities and the presence of policemen; and several control variables. Misconducts and bench minors are not included as penalties.

61. Allen (2002: 50) refined this argument; he interacted players' performance variables with a dichotomous variable indicating whether a player is a forward or a defender. Unlike forwards, for defensemen points and penalties are positively related. Team ranking (measured by standings points) and the number of career suspensions a player has also are inversely related to nonviolent penalties. However, violent penalties are positively influenced by career suspensions. A direct and significant relationship exists between nonviolent and violent penalties and the total number of fights that occur during a game and a player's career penalty minutes per game. A player's plus/minus ratio contributes positively only to nonviolent penalties.

62. Former NHL referee Bruce Hood observed a match in which two referees were used. He commented, "The two worked well together. Generally what one saw, the other did too, and they obviously agreed not to make some calls. I wondered about some of their non-calls though. Maybe if there had been only one referee more would have been called. I also wondered with this system whether the intensity was the same as when a ref is out there alone, having the sole responsibility for making the calls" (Hood and Townsend, 1999: 87).

63. See, for example, Siegfried, Eisenberg, and Zimbalist (2000) and Noll and Zimbalist (1997).

64. Williams and Williams (1997) believe the reservation wage hypothesis explains why Scandinavians are paid more than comparably skilled Americans and Canadians, and significantly more than Russians, Czechs, and Slovaks.

65. Gruneau and Whitson (1993: 266) claim the decreased number of Canadians playing in the NHL has reduced the interest of Canadian fans.

66. For examples of similar research, see Koning (2003); Fizel and D'itri (1996); Scully (1995); Clement and McCormick (1990), and related papers in Goff and Tollison (1990) and Porter and Scully (1982).

5

Major League Baseball

John Fizel and Lawrence Hadley

Studies of Major League Baseball (MLB) represent the cornerstone of research in sports economics. As Todd Jewel states in Chapter 2, "Simon Rottenberg's (1956) article . . . marks the true birth of sports economics" with his *theoretical* analysis of "The Baseball Players' Labor Market." One may also argue that Gerald Scully's (1974) article, "Pay and Performance in Major League Baseball," marks the birth of *empirical* sports economics with his modeling and estimation of marginal revenue product for baseball players. For years after the publication of these seminal articles, MLB was the focus of research in sports economics due to vast amounts of publicly available industry data, easily interpreted individual and team performance measures, and a number of unique institutional arrangements. Even today, MLB continues to receive considerable research attention. The voluminous literature that has resulted from the attention to MLB is more than can be addressed in a single chapter, so we concentrate on the research that focuses on the distinctive features of the MLB labor market.[1]

MLB has a three-tiered labor market. Players with three or fewer years of experience operate exclusively under the "reserve clause," which perpetually ties a player to a specific team unless the owner of that team trades the player or sells the player's contract to another team. A monopsony is granted to team owners. The team owner becomes the one and only buyer of the player's services. Players with between three and six years of experience are also subject to the reserve clause, but are allowed to settle salary disputes through arbitration. Because the "outside arbitrator" can evaluate the market value and salary of a player relative to players with comparable performance and experience, team owners can no longer unilaterally decide what to pay players. Players with more than six years' experience, and not currently under contract with a team, can opt for free agency. Under free agency all teams have the option to competitively bid for a player's services. Players with more than six years experience may also invoke arbitration, but only with the consensus of the team.

This chapter will examine the components of this unique labor market, examining how each impacts player salaries and the performance of industry. The chapter will also highlight unresolved issues that provide opportunities for future MLB research.

The Reserve Clause

MLB has imposed a number of institutional rules that distort a free labor market outcome for players' services, the most noteworthy of which is the reserve clause, a permanent fixture for MLB since 1987. Until 1976 the reserve clause was mandated in all MLB player contracts. Since 1976, the clause ties a player to his team but only for the first six years of his MLB career. The obvious economic impact of this reserve clause is the creation of a monopsony in the MLB labor market.

The most important prediction of the standard monopsony model is that the wage paid to the worker (player) will be less than the wage that would be paid in a competitive labor market. Theory predicts that workers are paid a wage equal to their marginal revenue product (MRP) in a competitive market, and theory further predicts that with monopsony, workers will be paid a wage that is less than their MRP. Exploitation is defined as the difference between a player's MRP and his annual wage. Since the reserve clause eliminates competition on the owners' side of the labor market, it will reduce the wage below a player's MRP. Therefore, the reserve clause is a mechanism by which the owners engage in monopsonistic exploitation of the players.

Two other important predictions are that firms (teams) will employ fewer workers and will produce less output. In MLB, the realization of this last prediction involves a restriction on the number of MLB teams. If there are fewer teams than would exist in competitive markets, then there are also fewer roster spots. Therefore, fewer workers (players) are employed.

An important underlying economic reality that impacts the players' labor market is the unique athletic skills possessed by the players. For star players, the labor supply function is best represented as perfectly inelastic (vertical with respect to the wage rate) because *ex ante* the number of star players is approximately fixed for any particular season. A player's opportunity cost is his wage rate in his next best alternative employment outside of MLB, and any player-generated revenues greater than the player's opportunity cost are defined as monopoly rents. The demand for the labor services of a star player (equal to the star's MRP) is likely to be greater than the star's opportunity cost because the athletic skills are unique. Indeed, for most players, their MRP is much greater than their opportunity cost. Therefore, the MLB labor market will exhibit large monopoly rents. The central issue in this labor market is whether the owners or the players will capture these rents. With a reserve clause, it is expected that the owners will capture the bulk of these rents via monopsonistic exploitation.

MRP Estimations: Models and Results

Gerald Scully (1974) was the first economist to use a formal model to estimate the magnitude of marginal revenue product (MRP) and the monopsonistic exploitation of MLB players due to the reserve clause. Scully uses a two-equation recursive model that includes a team production function and a team revenue function. In short, team revenue depends upon team output measured as win percent, which depends upon hitting and pitching inputs. The contributions of individual players are weighted by a hitter's percent of team at bats or a pitcher's percent of innings pitched. Thus, each hitter's (pitcher's) MRP can be estimated as his marginal product, or the additional wins attributable to his contribution to team hitting (team pitching), times marginal revenue, or the extra revenue associated with the value of one more win percent.

Scully's results, estimated prior to the advent of free agency in 1976, indicate that players were typically paid only 10 to 20 percent of their MRP. Clearly, with no alternative owner to bid away the services of their players, team owners drove down the players' salaries to levels that just kept them employed, thereby confiscating most of the available monopoly rents.

Medoff (1976) argued that Scully's model is likely simultaneous rather than recursive. Using two-stage least squares to estimate the revenue function, Medoff estimates that players were paid 40–50 percent of their MRP, still substantial exploitation but rates much lower than estimated by Scully.

Andy Messersmith and Dave McNally soon challenged the reserve clause, and on December 23, 1975, Peter Seitz ruled on their case, declaring that the reserve clause applied for only one year. A player, therefore, could become a free agent if he played for one season without a contract. This led to a compromise between players and owners in the 1976 collective bargaining agreement and the development of the current structure of the MLB labor market. Players with less than six years of MLB would continue to work under the reserve clause, but players with six or more years of service could play out their contracts and declare as free agents.

This decision led to a plethora of studies using the Scully model, or the Scully model with minor modifications, to examine the impact of this structural change on player compensation.

The monopoly rents began to quickly shift to the players. Sommers and Quinton (1982) and Raimondo (1983) find that most of the "first family of free agents" received salaries commensurate with their MRP and, in aggregate, averaged between 95–98 percent of their MRP.

Subsequent studies continued to find exploitation of reserve clause players in ranges suggested by Scully and Medoff and minimal exploitation, if, any, of free agent players as suggested by Sommers, Quinton, and Raimondo (see Hill and Spellman, 1983; Hill, 1985; Cymrot, 1983; Zimbalist, 1992b; Marburger, 1994; and Gustafson and Hadley, 1995).

There are two notable exceptions to this summary. First, Bruggink and Rose (1990) find that the MRP-salary gap widened during the years 1986–87 when MLB owners were convicted of colluding in the free agent market. Their results suggest that the conviction may have been warranted. Second, Oorlog (1995) presents a variation of the Scully model by including broadcast revenues in his model. Theoretically, a player's MRP is independent of broadcasting revenue because such revenues are fixed in the short run. Although theory predicts that owners will not compensate players for their marginal broadcast revenue, the empirical evidence indicates that they do! Perhaps this is an indication that owners act more like sportsmen trying to maximize wins and team championships than business decision-makers who explore the relationships between benefits and cost of player inputs. Both of these papers suggest future research opportunities that examine the impact of interesting and unique institutional factors on MLB salaries.

Krautmann (1999) proposed an entirely different model for estimating players' MRPs. He begins by estimating a salary equation using only a sample of free agent players who earned a market-determined salary for the current year. The estimated salaries are assumed to approximate the free agent players' MRPs, and the regression coefficients in the salary equation calibrate the competitive market-determined rewards for player performance. Thus, the salary equation can be used to generate a predicted value of salary for any player using that player's MLB performance statistics. The predicted salary should approximate the player's MRP assuming that his performance is rewarded at the same rates as a free agent in the competitive market for free agents. By definition, there is no exploitation of free agents and much smaller estimates of exploitation of non-free agents using the Krautmann model relative to versions of the Scully model.

There are strengths and weaknesses with the Krautmann model. Most important, the model is firmly based in the microeconomic theory that labor inputs are employed by profit-maximizing firms up to the point that the MRP of the input equals the wage rate. The model is also consistent with the relatively low levels of exploitation of free agents found in earlier versions of the Scully model. Because of this foundation in neoclassical microeconomics and empirical support, it may be preferred to the Scully model. However, the potential weakness of the Krautmann model is that players' inputs may not be paid a wage equal to their MRP for reasons relating to market structure and other factors. This may cause the model to over- or understate player MRP.

Mullin and Dunn (2002) introduce "star quality" in the estimation of MRP. Star quality can relate to player charisma, community and charitable activities, on-the-field demeanor, and other factors that cause fans to place special value on a given individual. Mullin and Dunn use the value of each player's baseball card as a proxy for star quality emanating from customer perceptions. They find a significant level of underpayment of stars using the Scully model. Burger and Walters (2003b) also use the Scully model and find underpayment of free agent stars playing in large cities. Omitting star quality and market size from the Krautmann model is likely to result in biased MRP estimates.

Players may sign long-term contracts before they gain eligibility for free agency. Maintaining player skills until one is eligible for free agency is uncertain, and a long-term contract is a mechanism for a player to shift that uncertainty to an owner. A long-term contract that pays a player less than his current MRP may be a utility-maximizing decision for the player as part of a risk-return tradeoff. One could provide a similar analysis for owners who try to avert the risk of losing a star player to free agency by signing a long-term contract with the player at a salary that is greater than the player's short-term MRP. It is an empirical question to determine whether owners or players benefit more from long-term contracts, but Kahn (1993) has found that long-term contracts have increased during free agency.

Finally, one of the most cited examples that cause MRP and wages to differ is the winner's curse (Cassing and Douglas, 1980). The winner's curse occurs when the highest bidder for the talents of a free agent player bids or pays more than that player's MRP. The reason for this result is uncertainty surrounding the player's actual MRP. This uncertainty will generate a distribution of MRP estimates for the player that, in turn, will generate a distribution of bids around the actual MRP. Since the player is apt to select the highest bidder, with the most optimistic estimate of player MRP, the player will likely receive a salary greater than his actual MRP.

Future research into salary estimations and player exploitation will have to look carefully at current and evolving institutional relationships within baseball. The standard factors in salary estimation have been frequently used and provided similar results with regard to exploitation of reserve clause players, albeit over different time periods. New research should also examine estimation models that, like Krautmann's, allow us to examine the issues from a new but theoretically sound perspective. For example, work in search theory may identify rational decisions by players, not owners, that prompt player compensation to be below MRP.

Invariance Principle

Why does the reserve clause persist given the overwhelming evidence of exploitation due to its implementation? The mobility restrictions of the reserve clause have long been justified as necessary for competitive balance across MLB teams, which, in turn, is necessary to maintain the fan interest required for an economically viable product.

Owners argue that if the reserve clause is removed and all players have the freedom to move to the team of their choice, players will flock to the teams with the most financial resources, usually the large-market teams. The large-market teams would then dominate play, winning significantly more than the small-market teams. If the league became sufficiently unbalanced, with playing talent concentrated in a few teams, perennial cellar dwellers would be unable to attract fans and even the fans of dominant teams would lose interest in the sport. As the Yankees won the pennant each year from 1950 to 1958, the attendance of the American League declined. The financial viability of the league and each of its teams requires that MLB preserve competitive balance.

In contrast, economists argue that if reserve clause players may be exchanged via trades or sales, owner profit incentives will prompt migration of talented players to large-market teams just as they would under free agency. Under the reserve clause, owners reap the financial rewards for player transfers; under free agency, players reap the rewards. Economists see the reserve clause as a ploy to transfer wealth from players to owners but not as a scheme to preserve competitive balance. The invariance principle first presented by Rottenberg (1956), which is representative of the principles of the Coase (1960) theorem, states that a change in property rights (reserve clause to free agency) affects only the distribution of wealth (owner vs. player) but has no impact on the allocation of resources (competitive balance).[2] El-Hodiri and Quirk (1971) formally demonstrate this principle in the theoretical context of a professional sports league. The Coase theorem requires an absence of wealth or income effects and transactions costs for the invariance result to hold but, nonetheless, this is now an empirical issue for MLB. The results, to date, are ambiguous.

Spitzer and Hoffman (1980), Cymrot (1983), and Besanko and Simon (1985) each find that the empirical evidence from the early years of free agency supports the invariance principle. They find no significant changes in roster turn-over rates or competitive balance or that players move to the large-market teams. Quirk and Fort (1992) and Fort and Quirk (1995) argue that their empirical results on competitive balance support the invariance principle.

Alternatively, Daly and Moore (1981) reject the invariance principle, finding that players were more likely to move to large-market teams as free agents than if under the reserve clause. Hylan, Lage, and Treglia (1996) find players to be more mobile under free agency, with the glaring exception of All Star players and Cy Young pitchers, who were less mobile. Maxcy (2002) also identifies more player transfers with free agency but the increase for all pitchers is not significant. The similar results on pitcher mobility by Hylan et al. and Maxcy are an interesting discovery. Another interesting discovery by Maxcy is that more productive pitchers seem to move away from winning teams, perhaps because they have more marginal value to losing teams. Thus, the rejection of the invariance principle improves competitive balance in contrast to the owner's declaration that competitive balance would be worsened by free agency.

The conflicting results on the invariance principle indicate an opportunity for future research. But as Maxcy (2002:158) so appropriately states, "future research on institutional changes in team sports leagues should account for the fact that the world is not perfectly Coasian any more than it is perfectly competitive. Professional team-sport leagues employ a variety of institutional restrictions on their labor markets. Team and individual salary caps, minimum payrolls, and luxury taxes . . . are examples. Studies and policy prescriptions addressing these issues should account for the possibility that transaction costs and income effects may well exist when alternative rules are imposed."

Salary Arbitration

As we have just seen, the reserve clause provides MLB owners with a monopsony, a position from which they are able to retain rights to the talent of a player in perpetuity unless, at their discretion and only their discretion, they wish to trade or sell the player's contract. The reserve clause also enables owners to keep player salaries remarkably low. But, believe it or not, the owners originally suggested that the collective bargaining agreement between owners and players modify the reserve clause to include an option for salary arbitration. After weeks of negotiating over the exact nature of the arbitration process, salary arbitration for players with between three and six years' service and not currently under contract became a reality and was first implemented in the 1974 season.[3]

The procedure agreed upon by the parties is final offer arbitration (FOA). When a player files for arbitration in FOA, the player and owner must submit final salary offers, and an arbitration hearing is scheduled. Player and owner negotiations may continue between the time offers are submitted and the hearing convenes, with the case being withdrawn from arbitration if a negotiated settlement is reached prior to the hearing. The arbitrator is required to select either the player's final offer (Wp) or the owner's final offer (Wo) as the binding salary for one year (i.e., the upcoming season). No compromise between offers is permissible.[4] This FOA process has gone largely unchanged since its 1974 inception.

FOA was chosen because it has the advantage of encouraging negotiations. Since there is no promise of compromise, each party is likely to present reasonable salary offers out of fear that the arbitrator will select the other party's offer. The narrowing of salary positions increases the likelihood of negotiated settlements. The results of the arbitration cases in MLB tend to support this assertion. Approximately 80 percent of all the arbitration cases filed are settled prior to reaching arbitration, and in the last ten years approximately 90 percent of the cases are settled.[5] Coates (2004) examines other structural aspects of MLB filings and hearings and finds that, ceteris paribus, the number of filings significantly increased during the collusion years of 1986–88 and the number of hearings significantly decreased during strike years.

Participants in Arbitration

Who takes the risk of opting for arbitration? Marburger and Scoggins (1996) point out that salary decisions in arbitration occur in February but roster positions are not guaranteed until April. Owners therefore have the opportunity to replace a player that has received a salary increase through arbitration with a cheaper substitute by the time the season begins. They argue that employment risk or the threat of player replacement is inversely related to player quality. Their empirical evidence supports their hypothesis finding that higher-quality (low-risk) players are more likely to file for arbitration and seek an arbitrated settlement than lower-quality (high-risk) players. In a later paper, Bodvarsson and Banaian (1998) no longer find support for this premise. Player performance was found to have no significant impact on arbitration participation although participation was found to increase with player experience, which may act as a player-quality proxy. The continued employment of a player reflects player contributions to the team. A nonproductive player would no longer be employed in the league. Bodvarsson and Banaian also find that non-white pitchers have significantly higher participation rates, but acknowledge the small sample of such players makes this result suspect.

Frederick et al. (1996) also suggest that employment risk affects arbitration behavior, but focus on player positions that are particularly prone to career-threatening injuries. Players with greater exposure to injury are expected to be more conservative in the arbitration process. The authors find limited support for their hypothesis.

Fizel, Krautmann, and Hadley (2002) test the hypothesis that an arbitration-eligible player in MLB is more likely to file for arbitration and proceed to an arbitration hearing if he feels he is underpaid relative to his comparison group. The foundation for their hypothesis is equity theory. Equity is revealed to be a significant determinant of filing but an insignificant determinant of participation in hearings. The authors argue that this result is not surprising in that the decision to file is the choice of only the player and reflects that player's perception of fairness. The probability of proceeding to a hearing, however, reflects both the player's and the owner's sense of equity, which may partially offsetting. These results are related to the work of Marburger and Scoggins (1996). Because equity theory suggests that underpaid players are more likely to file, one would expect the positive correlation between player performance and arbitration participation found by Marburger and Scoggins.

Two other significant determinants of arbitration participation were identified as part of the Fizel, Krautmann, and Hadley (2002) analysis. First, players who once filed and went to an arbitration hearing are likely to repeat their behavior. This may occur because risk-loving players are more willing to gamble with the arbitration process and participate whenever the option is available. Or, as Graham and Perry (1993) argue, the arbitration process may include a "narcotic effect" that relieves both bargaining units of responsibility for the arbitration outcome. As pointed out by Marburger and Scoggins (1996), the owner can release or trade a player that receives as substantial salary increase through FOA, justifying the action on the grounds that the salary is no longer affordable. The owner can then displace the blame to the arbitration system. The player can similarly reduce personal blame and argue that his higher salary is appropriate since the award was made by an objective outsider. Second, the probability of a hearing is directly related to the ratio of salary offers (player/owner). As Farber and Bazerman (1986) suggest, a large difference between the salary offers may reflect reluctance by both parties to compromise during negotiations, making a settlement less likely.

Arbitrator Decisions

In FOA the arbitrator is required to select either the player's salary offer (Wp) or the owner's salary offer (Wo) as the binding salary for the upcoming season. The arbitrator begins the process of resolving the dispute by making a personal assessment of the value of the player (*Wa*). The collective bargaining agreement stipulates that the arbitrator may consider only a specific set of criteria in estimating *Wa*: player performance during the past season, length and consistency of player performance, prior player salary, salaries of comparable players, physical or mental defects of a player, and on-field team performance (including but not limited to team standings and attendance). Other information such as market size, financial position of player and team, negotiating costs, and offers made in prior negotiations are specifically excluded from consideration.[6] The bargaining agreement also dictates that arbitrators may only use salaries of players with comparable experience in developing *Wa*. Farber (1980) argues that an unbiased arbitrator will select the party's offer that is closest to *Wa*. The owner's offer will be selected when $(Wp - Wa) - (Wa - Wo) > 0$, and the player's offer will be selected if the inequality is reversed.[7]

Dworkin (1981) provided the original empirical model and estimates for this arbitrator decision rule. He incorporated the rule into a probit model such that:

$$Decision = \alpha + \beta \left[(Wp - Wa) - (Wa - Wo)\right] + e, \qquad (5.1)$$

where *Decision* = 1 if the owner's offer is selected and 0 if the player's offer is selected. As the difference between *Wp* and *Wa* increases relative to the difference between *Wa* and *Wo*, the player's salary offer becomes more extreme and the probability of the owner winning at the hearing increases ($\beta > 0$).

The interpretation and expected value of α requires discussion. Suppose the salary offers in an arbitration case are equidistant from *Wa* such that $[(Wp - Wa) - (Wa - Wo)] = 0$. According to the arbitrator decision rule, each side should have a 50 percent chance of winning the case. Given the probit specification, the probability of an owner winning the case is measured by the area under the standard normal curve from $-\infty$ to α. One-half of the area under the curve or a probability of 50 percent occurs when $\alpha = 0$. If $\alpha > 0$, owners would have greater than 50 percent chance of winning, indicating arbitrator bias in favor of owners. Conversely, if $\alpha < 0$, owners would have less than 50 percent chance of winning, so the bias would be in favor of players.

The data required to estimate equation (5.1) are readily available except for *Wa*, the arbitrator's estimate of a fair player salary. The selection of arbitrators is an important factor in understanding how to predict *Wa*. Until very recently, a single arbitrator conducted the hearing. The Major League Baseball Players Association and the owners' Player Relations Committee select the arbitrators. An initial list of arbitrators is provided by the American Arbitration Association. The player and owner representatives alternately remove names from the list to select a final panel.[8] Because representatives from both sides can express their preferences in the selection of arbitrators, one can expect each party to veto the choice of predictably biased arbitrators or arbitrators who are expected to make extreme decisions. The selection process retains the arbitrators who will most objectively relate *Wa* to the arbitration-eligible criteria and comparison group as specified earlier. Thus, as Ashenfelter (1987) suggests, arbitrators are likely to be "exchangeable" and produce decisions that are consistent with the decisions of other arbitrators. Marburger (1993) shows that arbitrators may think alike even if they do not overtly attempt to replicate each other. With exchangeability, a common set of weights can be used to describe arbitrator preferences. *Wa* can be approximated by salary models that include as independent variables proxies for the arbitration criteria. Arbitration exchangeability is accepted either explicitly or implicitly in most salary models employed in the MLB arbitration literature, although there has been a variety of performance proxies used in the models (e.g., Burgess and Marburger, 1993; Fizel, 1996; Hadley and Ruggiero, forthcoming).

Dworkin's (1981) estimates for equation (5.1) using cases from the first years of arbitration indicate that extreme offers by players or owners will result in arbitration losses ($\beta > 0$) and that $\alpha < 0$, indicating a bias against owners such that owners would win only 37 percent, not 50 percent, of cases when *Wa* was equidistant from *Wp* and *Wo*. This bias may occur because arbitrators have a different perspective of impartiality than presented in this model. Scully (1978) and Dworkin (1986) argue that impartiality is reflected in offsetting decisions by arbitrators. More specifically, Scully (1978: 447) states that arbitrators may "render one-half of the decisions to players and one-half to owners *without regard to the merits of the case.*" Impartiality is met by a 50–50 won-loss record and not an objective assessment of the arbitration criteria. Frederick, Kaempfer, and Wobbekind (1992) suggest that offsetting decisions may also be made when players participate in arbitration in successive years. If the player won (lost) in arbitration in the prior year, the arbitrator can now decide for (against) the owner in the second year. Again, these judgments neglect the merits of the case. Burgess, Marburger, and Scoggins (1996) refute the assumptions that arbitrators distribute victories between the two sides without considering the merits of the case and show that decisions have significant links to the arbitration criteria. Consistent with this analysis, Fizel (1996) and Fizel (2004) use the Dworkin model and do not find any evidence of bias in favor or against owners or in favor or against all players (in aggregate) using cases from 1985–90 and 1996–2003, respectively. The coefficient β continued to be positive and significant.

Nevertheless, Fizel (1996) uses a reformulation of *Wa* in a version of equation (5.1) to complete a more detailed exploration of the potential for bias:

$$Wa = \alpha[(1 - \theta)f(I) + \theta X]. \tag{5.2}$$

The Farber decision criterion implies that arbitrators make reliable estimates of *Wa* using only the criteria specified as applicable for arbitration decisions $[f(I)]$. Thus, Farber's interpretation of an unbiased arbitrator occurs when $\theta = 0$ in equation (5.2). This interpretation is plausible given arbitrator exchangeability but biased outcomes would result if arbitrators consider information that the collective bargaining agreement dictates as inadmissible (X). Fizel explicitly considers player position, market size of teams, and player ethnicity. Only ethnicity is significant. Although the model continues to indicate no bias with respect to owners or white players, there is significant bias against Latin and Afro-American players. Hadley and Ruggiero (forthcoming) also examine the impacts of player position, teams in large markets, and ethnicity on arbitration results, and they find none of these, including ethnicity, has a significant impact. However, ethnic bias in arbitration was also found by Leonard and Ellman (1994).

Why does the bias exist? Fizel (1996) points out that the salary offers of minority players relative to *Wa* and to owner offers tend to be less extreme than the salary offers of white players. Also, the arbitration bias does not seem to reflect a salary market bias. Thus there is no readily apparent answer. Moreover, the collective bargaining agreement does not permit arbitrators to provide reports on their decisions and identification of arbitrators assigned to each case is not publicly available. Clearly this issue warrants further research.

Pre-Arbitration Negotiation and Salary Offers

Although Farber's (1980) model of FOA is the staple for most of the research on MLB arbitration, it has limitations in its predictions for arbitration offers and outcomes. Here is a brief review of the model. Players and owners develop salary offers knowing that the arbitrator will formulate an estimate of an appropriate award based on the specific criteria outlined in the collective bargaining agreement and select the offer nearest this estimate. Each party recognizes that the submission of a more concessionary offer increases the likelihood of winning. A player must weigh the gain in expected utility from submitting a winning, lower salary offer against loss in expected utility from having his higher salary offer selected (even if less concessionary and winning less probable). An owner must weigh the gain in expected utility from submitting a winning, higher salary offer against the loss in expected utility from having his lower salary offer selected (even if less concessionary and winning less probable). Both parties will select offers that maximize their expected utilities from going to an arbitration hearing. The more risk-averse party will usually submit a more concessionary final offer. The arbitrator then chooses one of the offers, with the more risk-averse party likely to win more cases. In short, final salary offers are submitted and the arbitration decision immediately follows. Overlooked in the Farber model are the continued negotiations that are permitted in MLB after the salary offers are submitted and continuing to the time of a hearing.

Faurot and McAllister (1992) develop a two-stage bargaining model to analyze how continued negotiations between a risk-averse player and a risk-neutral owner may affect salary offers. Salary offers by the player become a starting point in continued negotiations with the team. If a risk-averse player makes a concessionary final salary offer, the level of salary likely to result from a negotiated settlement is reduced, should a settlement be agreed upon before the arbitration hearing. Therefore, they argue that risk-averse players have an incentive to submit risk-neutral offers rather than reveal their willingness to negotiate more concessionary settlements. However, when they assume risk neutrality in an estimation of the impact of the arbitration-eligible criteria on the arbitrator's fair settlement, the estimation does not converge.

Miller (2000a) offers a more formal analysis of the second stage of FOA and then turns to an empirical analysis of the effect of the negotiation period on offer formulations. Miller reemphasizes that the choice of salary offers affects not only the arbitration decision but also the opportunities available for a contract to be negotiated prior to arbitration. He adds that the final offers are not affected by the negotiation stage if both negotiators are risk neutral, but if the parties are risk averse, the more risk-averse party will change his offer while the less risk-averse party may not. Miller finds "weakly significant" results, indicating that position players are risk averse, but behavior that indicates position players to be risk neutral in setting salary offers. Relief pitchers are also risk neutral in setting salary offers. These results along with the risk neutrality of team owners are consistent with the incentives suggested by Faurot and McAllister (1992)—even if risk averse, players should submit risk-neutral salary offers. Only starting pitchers do not produce risk-neutral offers.

Marburger (2004) offers insight into the strategies of players, owners, and arbitrators. Using all FOA filings from 1989 to 2002, he finds that salary offers are a weighted average between the player's previous salary and the average free agent salary. If players seek free agent–level salaries or if owners seek reserve clause–level salaries, the parties are likely to lose, indicating that arbitrators seek outcomes that are a compromise between the free agent and reserve clause markets. Hadley and Ruggiero (forthcoming) find similar results employing an upper and lower frontier for arbitration negotiations. The upper frontier consists of players that earn the highest salary for any given level of performance; the lower frontier consists of players who have the highest performance level of a given level of salary.

Miller (2003) expands to a three-stage model of negotiation, adding the opportunity for the team to trade or keep a player after the setting of salary offers. The model predicts that high-revenue teams are more likely to keep or acquire high-quality players whereas low-revenue teams are more likely to keep or acquire low-quality players, which is not surprising. However, the implication of the model is that final salary offers will be a positive function of team financial conditions, even though the collective bargaining agreement specifically precludes such information from consideration during arbitration. The empirical analysis supports this premise, showing that both player and owner salary offers increase with team revenue and profitability. Although the impact on player and owner was different in magnitude, the offsetting nature of a simultaneous response in both player and owner offers would be consistent with the insignificant effect of team financial condition on arbitration outcomes found by Fizel (1996), described above.

Negotiated Versus Arbitrated Contracts

Burgess and Marburger (1993) investigate whether negotiated contracts differ from arbitration outcomes under FOA. They suggest conflicting theory. Farber (1980) indicates that arbitration decisions are the result of failed negotiations and are therefore apt to be more extreme than negotiated settlements. Faurot and McAllister (1992) and Faurot (2004) argue that the midpoint of risk-neutral offers by player and owner should equal the negotiated settlements if clubs and players have the same expectations regarding the outcome of arbitration. The premise is based on the notion that arbitration criteria, player characteristics, and player performance data are publicly available. Burgess and Marburger find that arbitration decisions fall outside the bounds of negotiated settlements. Arbitration cases won by players are higher than negotiated settlements, and arbitration cases won by owners are lower than negotiated settlements. Burgess and Marburger (1993: 548) conclude "that the bargaining agents retain substantial freedom to negotiate salaries that are not determined solely by arbitrator preferences." This conclusion reaffirms the importance of the research using multistage bargaining models to address FOA in MLB.

Salaries of Arbitration-Eligible Players

The collective bargaining agreement specifies that arbitrators are to give particular attention for salary comparison purposes to the contracts of players with service time not exceeding one year more than the player in question. An arbitration-eligible player with three years of service could be compared to all players with up to four years' service, an arbitration-eligible player with four years of service could be compared to all players with up to five years' service, and so on until the arbitration-eligible player with six years of service could be compared to free agent players. Thus, if one starts with the arbitration-eligible players that can be compared to free agents and works backwards, one has to ask if the salaries of arbitration-eligible players differ from the salaries of free agents with comparable performance and personal characteristics.

Hadley and Gustafson (1991) find that salaries jump once a player obtains FOA rights, suggesting that the mere possession of FOA rights relieves the player of monopsonistic exploitation. Bodvarsson and Banaian (1998) find additional salary premiums for those who file relative to those who do not file. These results reflect the 100+ percent gains in salaries for all players that filed for arbitration in the early 1990s (Fizel, 1994). However, Gius and Hylan (1999) examined the effects of arbitration on salaries prior to the imposition of free agency (1974–75) and found that arbitration eligibility did not significantly change player salaries. Clearly, the important element in all of the recent increases in salaries of arbitration-eligible players is the benchmarking of salaries to free agents.

The first comprehensive salary comparison for the three-tiered MLB labor market came from Kahn (1993). He identified two groups of arbitration-eligible players: those in the last year of arbitration, who would receive direct comparisons to free agents, and all others, who would receive direct comparisons to other arbitration-eligible players but not free agents. All players eligible for arbitration receive higher salaries than reserve clause players who are arbitration-ineligible but those in the early years of arbitration receive less than those in the last year of arbitration. The players in the last year of arbitration sign contracts comparable in value to free agents. A limitation of this study is the use of data during the collusion years of MLB, a time in which free agent salaries were diminished but during which there was an unknown impact on arbitration salaries. Nevertheless, when Marburger (1994) reexamines 1990s' player salaries through the transition from arbitration-eligibility to free agency, his results echo those of Kahn.

Because salary outcomes under arbitration have now been shown to be dependent on salary outcomes of free agency, a comparison of arbitration and free agent salary negotiation becomes relevant. Marburger (1996) examines salary determination for the two markets using 1991 and 1992 players. He finds salary determination for arbitration-eligible players and free agents to be equivalent. Miller (2000b) expands on Marburger's paper by developing a theoretical model that details differences in bargaining strategies for the two markets. Free agent bargaining is dependent on the contribution of the free agent to the value of the team, alternative competitive salaries offered by other teams, and salaries available to the player outside MLB. Arbitration bargaining is dependent on the arbitration criteria identified in the collective bargaining agreement. Using players from 1991 to 1994, Miller confirms that the free agent and arbitration salary negotiations have different structures. As a result, even if players in the last year of arbitration have salaries similar to free agents, the process by which they were determined is different. [9] The conflict between these results merits additional attention. Other than the sample of players and differences in performance measures, the only notable difference in the models is that Miller controlled for sample bias. [10]

Still, there remains a final component of the analysis of the impact of arbitration on salaries. A complete assessment requires that arbitration salary results be compared to MRP. Using the Scully MRP model, Fizel (1994) reports that 77 percent of the players involved in arbitration cases from 1985 to 1990 were paid less than MRP. Zimbalist (1992b) refines the Scully model by including "counterfactual" players in his estimation of MRP. Absent a specific player, he assumes that the roster spot would be taken by a player who exhibits the same performance statistics as the team averages. Zimbalist uses this technique to estimate adjusted player MRPs (which could be negative if a player's stats are below the team averages). He reports that 67 percent of arbitration-eligible players from 1986 to 1989 were paid less than MRP, with salary averages for each year ranging from 50 to 65 percent of MRP. Krautmann, Gustafson, and Hadley (2000) use the Krautmann (1999) model to estimate the MRPs of arbitration-eligible hitters. Specifically, they start with a sample of free agent hitters who signed new contracts between 1988 and 1994. Because these salaries are the outcomes of a free competitive market, they assume that these salaries approximate the players' MRPs. They estimate a salary equation, and use the coefficients to estimate the salary (MRP) that would be paid to the arbitration-eligible players in competitive market. The authors find that, on average, the players who are eligible for salary arbitration have actual salaries that slightly exceed their predicted salaries, implying that these players are paid more than their MRPs. The marked differences provided by these studies indicate that the MRP models have very different assumptions about the operation of the MLB labor market. Additional scrutiny of these assumptions is essential.

Future Research in Arbitration

Arbitration processes have gone largely unchanged since the implementation of arbitration in 1974. As a result, much of the existing literature could be updated to compare different time periods and to reflect structural changes in MLB but outside of arbitration. The time-series analysis of arbitration by Coates (2004) represents another starting point for research. There is also an opportunity to consider aspects of discrimination in arbitration.

Empirical analysis should begin to explicitly control for the differences in arbitration participants by including tests for sample or selection bias. Arbitration includes three groups of players: those that do not file, those that file but do not go to arbitration, and those that file and go to arbitration. Different characteristics within these groups may generate sample bias when any one group is analyzed.

Significant theoretical and empirical insights have been gained through modeling the multistage process of arbitration. Further development of such modeling offers opportunities for additional research.

Finally, a new avenue of research has been created with the advent of the first major structural change in MLB arbitration procedure. Determination of salary arbitration outcomes is now done by a three-person arbitration panel rather than a single arbitrator. Has this change affected offer selection, outcomes, determinants of outcomes, discrimination, and or any other aspect of the arbitration process?

Player Training

Krautmann and Oppenheimer (1996) point out that the lower earnings of reserve clause players, whether arbitration-eligible or not, may not be exploitation. Rather than exploitation, the less-than-MRP earnings may be viewed as the returns to the owners for training their players in the minor leagues. Using Becker's (1971) training model, they examine minor league operations as an owner-investment in players' skills. The return on this investment comes via the reserve clause that allows owners to pay players less than their MRP for the first three years of their MLB career.

Krautmann and Oppenheimer define the surplus from a reserve clause player as the present value of the difference between the player's MRP and his salary over the first six years of his career. Their estimates of this surplus are based on data from Zimbalist (1992a). For an average player, they estimate this surplus at $1.478 million. This is slightly less than the average cost to train a major league player, which they estimate at $1.602 million. They conclude that owners subsidize the average player approximately $124,000 when they fund their own minor league operations.

The Krautmann and Oppenheimer paper challenges the standard interpretation of exploitation found in the literature. They view the surplus (MRP – salary), as a legitimate market return to the owners' investments in training players as opposed to the exploitation of reserve clause players. The reserve clause is simply the mechanism by which this return on investment is realized.

A more thorough analysis of the relationship between exploitation and training is provided by Krautmann, Gustafson, and Hadley (2000). They estimate the surplus of each of the reserve clause players, and then regress this on variables that measure the cost of drafting and training a young player. The regression exhibits significant results, and they indicate that the owners take the largest amount of surplus from the young rising stars. The authors conclude that given the market power of the owners, they take the surplus from the players as it is available. In other words, rising stars exhibit higher MRPs, and therefore a greater amount of surplus is extracted from them. For the average player, it is estimated that the surplus is only approximately 50 percent ($3 million) of the $6 million that it costs to train each MLB player. In qualitative terms, these results are consistent with Mullin and Dunn (2002).

Miceli (2004) takes this argument one step further, suggesting that when players balance the benefits of higher salaries and higher mobility against the need to induce teams to invest in training that increases the players' chances of success in MLB, they may not opt for the conditions/effects of complete free agency. In the context of a principal-agent model of contracting, he goes on to show that the effects of the reserve clause can emerge as part of an optimal contract between players and owners.

Conclusion

The labor market is a small but distinctive component of MLB research. Yet this research is filled with a number of unresolved issues. Together with an eye on the stylized facts of the industry, structural changes, emerging theoretical contributions, and the ever-present abundance of data, many research opportunities are available for the sports economist. Our hope is that this chapter has helped identify and clarify some of the paths available for new discoveries.

Notes

1. Despite excellent compilations of baseball research (e.g., Zimbalist, 1992b; Fizel et al., 1996; Marburger, 1997; Zimbalist, 2003b), the publisher requested that

key issues of MLB baseball be addressed in this text. Although the chapter deals exclusively with the labor market, aspects of the MLB product market are addressed by Krautmann and Hadley, Chapter 9, in their analysis of demand, and by Fort, Chapter 10, in his review of competitive balance.

2. Ronald Coase recently won the Nobel Prize in economics, in part, for this theorem.

3. The minimum service requirement for becoming arbitration-eligible was actually two years beginning in 1974, changing to three years in 1987, and then to the 17 percent most senior of players with between two and three years' service in 1991.

4. The 2003–6 collective bargaining agreement between players and owners specifies that salary offers are to be submitted between January 5 and January 15, and arbitration hearings to be scheduled between February 1 and February 20 (http://us.i1.yimg.com/us.yimg.com/i/spo/mlbpa/mlbpa_cba.pdf).

5. For details, see the arbitration data developed by Doug Pappas for Society of American Baseball Research (SABR) and their Business of Baseball website: www.businessofbaseball.com/data.htm. Also, see Fizel (1994) and Coates (2004).

6. It is important to recognize that these criteria are more akin to marginal physical product than marginal revenue product as explicitly pointed out by Bodvarsson and Banaian (1998:168). Economists may prefer the use of marginal revenue product (Burger and Walters, 2003a), but such models are, by definition, inconsistent with the MLB arbitration decision process.

7. Farber (1980) and Ashenfelter and Bloom (1984) provide the theoretical foundation for this model. Farber and Bazerman (1986) derive this model from minimizing a loss function for arbitrators. Sample (1992) points out that players and agents believe this is the model that arbitrators use in their decisions, and Freedman (2002) provides an example of how arbitrators actually used this model in the 2001 Andru Jones arbitration case.

8. For more details on this and other aspects of MLB arbitration procedures, see Faurot and McAllister (1992).

9. However, Miller finds that salaries for arbitration-eligible players are less than salaries for comparable free agents. Miller did not differentiate between different levels of service time for the arbitration-eligible players.

10. Sample bias probably deserves more attention in the empirical arbitration literature than it has received. For examples where sample bias was explicitly addressed, see Fizel, Krautmann, and Hadley (2002), Miller (2000a), Miller (2000b), and Bodvarsson and Banaian (1998).

6

European Football (Soccer)

Victor A. Matheson

European football, also known as association football in the United Kingdom and soccer in the United States, is unquestionably the world's most popular sport. While baseball may be considered America's national pastime, any objective observer would name soccer as the national sport of most of the countries in Europe, Latin America, and Africa, as well as in much of Asia. The market valuations of the largest football clubs in Europe, such as Manchester United, rival those of the most valuable American sports franchises, such as the New York Yankees and Dallas Cowboys, and earnings from player salaries and endorsements for such soccer stars such as David Beckham and Ronaldo run into the millions of dollars per year.

Despite its worldwide popularity, the sport has perhaps received less attention from academic economists than its international prominence might suggest compared to the "big four" American sports: basketball, football, hockey, and particularly baseball. This chapter reviews the literature in the field of soccer economics with an emphasis on how professional team sports in America differ from the dominant team sport of the rest of the world and on suggestions for future research.

Demand for Football

One of the most commonly asked question facing any sports economist is: What are the determinants of match attendance for individual leagues? This topic has received particular attention in the United Kingdom due to the downward trend in attendance experienced by the English and Scottish leagues following records set immediately after World War II and the sport's subsequent recovery beginning in the 1980s. As shown in Figure 6.1, the trends in soccer attendance differ dramatically from the experi-

Figure 6.1 Major League Baseball (MLB) vs. Soccer (FA) Attendance

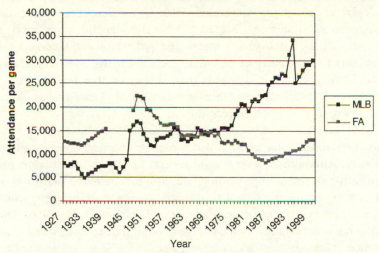

ence of American sports, which have enjoyed reasonably steady growth in fan support.

Hart, Hutton, and Sharot (1975) analyze single game attendances at four top division English clubs between 1969 and 1972 and explain short-run variations in attendance by demographic and geographic factors as well as measures of match attractiveness. High attendances are correlated with larger metropolitan areas and matches involving close geographical rivals. Matches involving teams high in the standings also draw large audiences.

Bird (1982) uses time-series data from 1948 through 1975 to estimate league-wide English football attendance based on variables such as ticket prices (including estimated travel costs), time trends, national income, and other variables, such as English success in the World Cup, weather, goal scoring, and hooliganism. Bird's most interesting finding is that income elasticity is estimated at –0.60, indicating that football is an inferior good over the time period examined. This runs counter to the general thinking that professional sports and entertainment are certainly normal goods if not luxury items. In addition, the price elasticity of tickets is estimated at –0.20, implying that teams could increase total revenues by supplying fewer tickets but at a substantially increased price. Bird quite correctly predicts that clubs would eventually exploit the inelastic nature of tickets by moving away from the general admission flat, standing-room terraces common in English football prior to the 1990s to higher-priced all-seated stadiums.

Dobson and Goddard (1992) in fact go one step further by specifically examining the demand for seated versus terrace admission. Based on 795 English league matches in the 1989–90 and 1990–91 seasons, they find that standing attendance tends to vary widely, with matches between nearby geographical rivals and games with teams performing well in recent games drawing high terrace audiences. Seated ticket sales depend more upon past, long-term success. Although not mentioned by Dobson and Goddard, this is perhaps due to the ability of people to plan ahead for their attendance at matches. The disparity in demands may simply be that seated tickets are purchased well in advance, which would explain why seated ticket sales depend on long-term rather than recent form.

Numerous researchers beginning with Neale (1964) have noted the connection between the uncertainty of outcome in sporting contests and their popularity. Although economists in general are loathe to support cross-subsidization of firms, in professional team sports, revenue sharing is often cited as a necessary ingredient to promote competitive balance, which is thought to be crucial in maximizing league profits (Rottenberg, 1956). Jennett (1984) models uncertainty by the inclusion of an independent variable in the estimation of attendances for individual games in the Scottish Premier League (SPL) between 1975 and 1981, which measures the effect that a win would have on the ability of a club to win the championship. In the case where the final game of the season between two clubs will determine the league champion, for this game the variable takes a value of 1, whereas a game played between teams that have both been mathematically eliminated from the running will have a value of 0. Games in which the outcome matters but for which later games in the season may make the result unimportant take values between these two extremes. His pooled results suggest that a game where the league title is on the line would attract over 13,000 additional spectators for a home match and over 7,000 additional fans for an away match versus a match that was meaningless for the championship. The size of the host metropolitan area and the home area unemployment rate are also found to be statistically significant: larger cities draw larger crowds while unemployment reduces the ability of fans to attend games. Indeed, Jennett cites rising British unemployment in the postwar period as a primary factor in declining attendances. Ticket price is not found to be a significant predictor of ticket sales, leading to a conclusion of either model misspecification or the failure of teams to maximize profits. Dobson and Goddard's (1996) examination of attendance in England and Wales between 1925 and 1992 also confirms that unemployment is a strong predictor of match demand while finding that ticket price has only a weak effect on attendance.

As pointed out by Peel and Thomas (1988), Jennett's measure of uncertainty is simplistic in that it assumes a fixed number of wins will be sufficient to win the league championship. Peel and Thomas (1988) propose to use sports betting lines to measure uncertainty. Assuming that betting markets are efficient, in games where two teams are evenly matched, the odds should be even, while long odds will exist in case where one team is a heavy favorite or underdog.[1] Using data from the 1981–82 English season, they find that an increase in the probability of a home team winning the match (as measured by the bookmakers' line) increases attendance and conclude that measures to increase competitive balance may reduce overall league attendance by reducing the probability of home teams winning. It is important to point out that their methodology purports to test the effects of uncertainty on team attendance while actually estimating the effects of expected performance on attendance. They also find that as attendance in lower divisions is examined, the distance between clubs becomes a more and more significant determent to attendance. The implication is that lower division clubs might be best served by organizing into regional leagues where travel is minimized and natural geographic rivalries can be promoted.

Peel and Thomas (1992) extend their previous work by further examining their measure of uncertainty as measured by odds makers. The odds on the game are translated into a percentage chance that a particular team wins and is included in both a linear and quadratic fashion into the estimating equation for attendance. The results suggest a U-shaped relationship between the expected chance of the home team winning and attendance. The authors explain this somewhat unusual result by arguing that collinearity between expected win percentage and other variables such as the teams' current winning percentages makes interpretation difficult, and the home winning percentage also works to predict higher scoring matches. In effect, the results can be interpreted to say that attendance data lead one to believe that fans come to games where they expect that the home team will win in a high-scoring but not too lopsided game. In addition, their new results reaffirmed their previous conclusion that geographic distance is particularly problematic for drawing fans in the lower divisions.

Cairns (1987) further examines Scottish football following the reorganization of its professional leagues in 1975 from two divisions to three divisions organized by playing ability. The smaller number of teams in each division necessarily means competing teams within each division are more closely matched although intra-division attendances diverged following the reorganization.

Forrest, Simmons, and Feehan (2002) focus their attention specifically on the issue of geographical monopoly power in English soccer, incorporating travel costs into demand for tickets. In particular, their inclusion of travel costs leads to price elasticity estimates much closer to unity in comparison with other studies that have examined the connection between price and demand. Their median own-price elasticity of –0.79 compares with Bird (1982), –0.22;

Dobson and Goddard (1995), −0.08; Szymanski and Smith (1997), −0.38; Simmons (1996), −0.40; and Baimbridge, Cameron, and Dawson (1996), who present a demand curve that is actually positively sloped over some range of prices. Since the typical estimates of own-price elasticity suggest an inelastic demand and present owners with the ability to increase total revenues by increasing ticket prices, it is often suggested that football club owners are not profit maximizers (as owners in the big four North American sports are purported to be), but are instead utility maximizers, attempting to maximize wins subject to a budget constraint or a given ticket price (Sloane, 1971).

Other studies, including Baimbridge, Cameron, and Dawson (1996) and García and Rodrígues (2002) simply advance previous studies of attendance demand by including more and more potential predictors, including availability of matches on television, which tends to reduce live attendance, and a host of other estimators, including measures of economic climate, uncertainty, team quality, and current form.

Szymanski (2001) points out that English football has seen a divergence in revenue equality over the past two decades. This observation is echoed by Dobson, Goddard, and Ramlogan (2001), who observe, however, that over longer periods of time, both periods of convergence and divergence can be seen. The recent increase in income inequality has been particularly pronounced between the different divisions of soccer rather than within the particular divisions. If higher revenues lead to higher payrolls and greater on-field success, then matches between teams from different leagues should become increasingly lopsided and less attractive for spectators. The Football Association (FA) Cup, which pits teams from the different divisions against one another, provides a natural experiment for testing this hypothesis. Szymanski (2001) finds little evidence that teams from the Premiership, the top league, have become more dominant in recent years despite their increasingly deeper pockets. Attendance at FA Cup matches in comparison with regular intra-league matches has fallen, however. Adjusting for other explanatory variables, FA Cup attendance has declined from a position where cup matches outdrew league matches by roughly 3,500 fans in the mid-1980s to the current case where league matches actually outdraw cup matches by a small margin. Although the result is interesting, attributing the declining relative attendance to a lack of competitive balance is tenuous without compelling evidence that competitive balance has actually suffered in the wake of increasing revenue inequality.

As the previous studies have shown, researchers are nearly unanimous in their finding that team success is highly correlated with attendance. The question remains, however, as to the direction of causation. In comparing revenue and performance, Dobson and Goddard (1998a) use Granger causality tests to discover that high levels of past revenue lead to current on-field success while past performance has only a limited effect on current revenue. In comparing payroll and performance using similar tests, Hall, Szymanski, and Zimbalist (2002) present an interesting comparison of baseball to English soccer. They conclude that in Major League Baseball performance leads to higher payroll, but payroll does not appear to lead to better performance, a surprising result in and of itself. The situation is reversed in soccer, with high payrolls leading to better performance but performance not causing higher payrolls. To the extent that past revenues lead to higher payrolls, the results of the two studies confirm one another.

Monopsony and Player Salaries

A common thread in the analysis of player salaries in the big four North American sports leagues, Major League Baseball (MLB), the National Basketball Association (NBA), the National Football League (NFL), and the National Hockey League (NHL), is that team owners have a significant ability to join together in holding down player salaries. The established leagues have on occasion faced competition from upstart leagues from the early rivalry between the American League and National League in baseball to the formation of the American Basketball Association and the World Hockey League in the late 1960s and early 1970s, but by and large, they have essentially remained the sole purchasers of athletic talent within their sports. Professional leagues in these sports also exist in other countries, but pay only a fraction of that of their American counterparts. For example, in 2002, the average NBA salary was $4.5 million, with a rookie minimum salary of $350,000. The Spanish ACB league, considered to be the top professional basketball league in Europe, paid an average salary of roughly $250,000 during the same season.

The situation is distinctly different in soccer. The top leagues in England, Spain, and Italy routinely bid against one another for the world's top talent, with clubs in Germany, France, and even Turkey also having made significant player signings. Clubs in numerous countries compete for mid-level talent.

The difference between soccer and other team sports is easily seen in examining U.S. antitrust law. In *Frazie, et al. v. Major League Soccer*, an antitrust complaint brought against Major League Soccer (MLS), the top professional league in the United States, by its players, the U.S Court of Appeals for the First Circuit ruled that the operating principles of the league did not violate the Sherman Act. In formulating its decision the court did not argue that soccer is exempt from antitrust laws (as it did for baseball in the infamous *Federal Baseball Club of Baltimore, Inc. v. National League of*

Baseball Clubs, et al. decision of 1922) nor did it contend that the labor practices of the MLS were not anticompetitive. Instead the court simply argued that due to the presence of unaffiliated minor leagues in the United States as well as the numerous foreign leagues in which American athletes play, the MLS did not have significant monopoly power in the market for soccer talent, even for American soccer talent.

Free Agency and Transfer Payments

As with professional athletes in the United States prior to free agency, European soccer players have generally been considered the property of the club for which they play, and, as in any team sport, the trading of players between clubs is commonplace in soccer. In American sports, however, players are usually traded for other players or for future selections in league drafts, while in soccer, players are most frequently traded for cash settlements known as transfer payments. Players themselves do not share in any of these transfer payments between clubs. Because the amount of the transfer fee, the teams engaging in the trade, and the past performance of the player involved are all matters of public record, transfer payments can be used to analyze bargaining power, racial discrimination, effects on competitive balance, as well as the nature of the system itself.

Although European football leagues have varying rules governing player movement, the English Football League has been most commonly examined in the literature. For the first seventy-five years of its existence, the English Football League placed restrictions on player movement, known as the "retain and transfer" system, that nearly exactly matched the "reserve clause" of American professional sports leagues. The retain and transfer system bound the player to a team until that club allowed the player to move elsewhere. A team that released a player who was subsequently hired by another club was entitled to a transfer payment from the new club in compensation (Sloane, 1969).

The strict retain and transfer system was gradually modified to the benefit of the players. Maximum wages were abolished in the early 1960s, and in 1977–78 the "freedom of contract" rule was established. This rule stipulated that players whose current contract with a team had expired were allowed to negotiate with other clubs. Upon expiration of the contract, a player's current club was required to either match the player's previous contract or offer the player a free transfer amounting to the player becoming fully a free agent. If the player's current club offered a contract that at least matched the old contract, the player could still request a move to another team, but the acquiring club would be required to pay the current club a mutually negotiated transfer fee. This setup is essentially identical to the "Rozelle rule" implemented by the NFL in the 1960s. If a transfer fee could not be agreed upon between the two organizations, the matter was brought before the Football League Appeals Committee (FLAC), which served as a binding arbitrator. In other European countries, the transfer fees for out-of-contract players were set by national football associations and were calculated based upon the two teams' match performances as a method of maintaining competitive balance (Feess and Mühlheusser, 2002).

In examining the transfer market under the freedom-of-contract rule, Carmichael and Thomas (1993) analyze the 214 English transfers in the 1990–91 season utilizing a Nash bargaining framework to determine what player and team variables influence the transfer fee paid. The skill of the player, as evidenced by goals scored and league appearances, leads to higher transfer fees and greater bargaining power on the part of the current club. Higher team profits, attendance, winning margin, and rank in the standings by the buying club lead to higher transfer fees after adjusting for player skill, suggesting that rich and successful teams have less bargaining power in the transfer market. On the selling side, the playing division is the most significant variable, with lower division clubs having less bargaining power.

Speight and Thomas (1997a) focus on the arbitration decisions rendered by the FLAC in 164 cases between 1985 and 1990 where teams could not arrive at a mutually acceptable transfer fee. They conclude that roughly 98 percent of the FLAC-determined transfer fee is based upon player and club statistics, with little weight being given to the final offers of the two clubs and little attempt by the FLAC to simply make a compromise between the two offers. Speight and Thomas (1997b) also find that the FLAC awards lower fees than occur under negotiated settlements. This result, however, is highly suspect since the data set for the arbitrated fees and the transfer fees covers different time periods.

Since only a small percentage of players are transferred in any given year, Carmichael, Forrest, and Simmons (1999) examine data from the 1994–95 season in an attempt to determine the factors that make it likely for a player to be transferred. Using a two-stage model, they first address the factors that make a transfer likely and then estimate transfer fees conditional on these probabilities. They find that transfers are more likely among older, more experienced players, when a change in management has occurred, and among players who have been frequently loaned out to other teams as temporary transfers. The transfer received is based upon the age of the player, with a peak transfer payment at the age of twenty-three, and other obvious measures of player skill such as goals scored, league appearances, and international appearances. Each goal scored during the previous regular season added between £21,860 and £32,690 to the transfer payment for the player depending on the player's position. Unlike other, previous studies, Carmichael, Forrest, and Simmons included only individual player variables, and not team variables, in the determination of transfer fees.

Risk and uncertainty are clearly significant components of the transfer market. Although certain aspects of a player's ability are observable through match play and league statistics, other facets of a player, like work ethic and effects on clubhouse morale, are not observable. It is natural to believe that teams attempt to limit their exposure to risk in the transfer market. After examining English League transfers between 1977 and 1994, Carmichael and Thomas (2000) find that certain buying and selling clubs have engaged in long-term relationships involving repeated trades. In addition, intraregional transfers are much more common than transfers involving geographically distant teams. Finally, permanent transfers are often preceded by loan arrangements that allow acquiring teams to "try before they buy," although this method is used with varying enthusiasm by different clubs.

Transfer fee laws in Europe changed dramatically in 1995 when the European Court of Justice ruled in the Bosman case that clubs would no longer have the right to insist on transfer payments for players whose contracts have expired. Jean-Marc Bosman was a Belgian professional player whose team refused to allow him to transfer to any other club upon the completion of his contract by setting an unreasonably high transfer fee. Transfer fees are still allowed among clubs for players whose contracts are not yet expired, and indeed, transfer payments for in-contract players have reached record levels since the ruling. The Bosman ruling ushered in the modern era of free agency continent-wide roughly twenty years after American professional players gained that right.

The effect of the Bosman ruling on football transfers has been widely discussed on a theoretical level. Ericson (2000) argues that it will reduce club investment in player talent and will particularly result in a loss of competitive balance as large clubs free ride on the talent developed by small clubs. Antonioni and Cubbin (2000) and Dilger (2001) challenge this claim by asserting that teams can counter any detrimental effects from the loss of transfer fees for out-of-contract players by simply signing players to longer term contracts or by selling players before their contracts expire. As a example, Antonioni and Cubbin cite the case of Alan Shearer, who was sold by Blackburn to Newcastle in 1996 for a then record fee of £15 million while still having one year left on his contract.

Feess and Mühlheusser (2002, 2003a, 2003b) assess further modifications to European transfer regulations, known as the "Monti" regime, that would limit the transfer fees that teams owning in-contract players can charge to acquiring clubs. They assert that the post-Bosman regulations led to longer contracts signed between clubs and players and less investment in player training. Changes that reduce the ability of teams to receive large transfer payments for trading away in-contract players would reduce contract length and further reduce player training.

As previously noted, nearly all published research on transfer payments in the post-Bosman era has focused on the theoretical aspects of the ruling. Applied work on the transfer market in the post-Bosman era is certainly an area ripe for future research.

Discrimination

As in other sports, soccer provides a laboratory in which to test the effects of racial discrimination on team performance. If racial discrimination exists, then labor markets are not efficient so that qualified minority players can be found and hired for a lower price than equally skilled white players. Szymanski (2000) examines the performance of thirty-nine clubs in the English soccer league from 1978 to 1993 and compares their success with their payroll. Teams with higher proportions of black players fared better in the standings, at a statistically significant level, than teams with fewer black players. As a rough estimate, a club hiring no black players would need to increase its payroll by 5 percent to maintain its position in the standings.

Preston and Szymanski (2000) follow up this research with an examination of English soccer clubs to determine if the racism found previously is a result of management or fan discrimination. After accounting for team performance, they find little evidence that indicates team revenues or attendances fall as black players gain playing time on predominantly white teams, suggesting that fan discrimination plays little role in the existence of lower salaries for black players. Finally, Reilly and Witt (1995) use a methodology similar to Carmichael and Thomas (1993) to question whether the race of the transferred player has any bearing on the agreed upon transfer price. They conclude that race does not have a statistically significant effect on final transfer prices.

Certainly the race of a player is not the only area in which discrimination can occur. Professional soccer leagues across Europe have gained an increasingly international flavor, and Wilson and Ying (2003) examine five large leagues across Europe and find that players from the Balkans and from Brazil are underrepresented on European teams compared to their contribution to team performance. Their paper, however, merely touches the very tip of questions regarding race and nationality in soccer.

Managerial Efficiency and Pay and Performance

The economics literature is full of studies of sporting production functions, particularly about baseball, beginning with Rottenberg's (1956) seminal ideas, which were subsequently formalized by Scully (1974). The creation of such a function as well as studies of pay and performance and managerial/owner performance in soccer is generally hampered by the lack of individual player data. The natures of the big four North American sports often lend themselves to numerous statistical measures for each player. In soccer, however, the flowing style of the game generates few specific statistical measures aside from goals scored and minutes played. In addition, few plays in soccer are generated solely through individual effort, unlike batting in baseball, for example.

Even the few easily available statistics can be used to analyze players to some extent, of course. Lucifora and Simmons (2003) find, as expected, goals scored, minutes played, and appearances on all-star or national teams are strong, positive predictors of player salary in the Italian Series A League. In addition, they uncover that at the very top of the scoring tables, even a few goals' difference can make a large difference in player salary, leading them to conclude that "superstar effects" are present in Italian football.

Recently, more detailed statistics on English professional league players, including factors such as tackles or passes made and touches on the ball, have become available. Carmichael, Thomas, and Ward (2000, 2001) use this data set, known as the OPTA Index, to calculate a production function for soccer in a manner similar to that used for American sports, particularly baseball. Given the amount of attention paid to production functions in other sports, the limited research completed in soccer leaves room for further investigation.

In English soccer, individual players' salaries are often not public information. Both Szymanski and Smith (1997) and Szymanski and Kuypers (1999) use total team payroll, which is readily available, as a proxy for team talent and find a close correlation between win percentage and payroll. Of course, the extent to which a team over- or underperforms on the field given a specific payroll is a simple measure of management efficiency. The problem with this technique, however, is one of endogeneity as player salaries are often based on player or team performance. Haas (2003a, 2003b) uses input-output tables to determine economic efficiency of clubs in the English Premier League and Major League Soccer in the United States.

Dawson, Dobson, and Gerrard (2000b) examine the English Premier League from 1992 through 1998 to estimate coaching efficiency using either win percentage or league points or standings as the measure of success and team payroll or the cumulative estimated transfer value of the players as the inputs to the production function. The authors use observed transfer prices and player characteristics for players who are traded among teams to estimate transfer values for players who are not traded. The results of their study show that coaching efficiency is only partially correlated with team success so that coaching performance should be measured relative to the inputs available to the coach not simply on the team's winning percentage.

Dawson and Dobson (2002) take this concept one step further by including manager characteristics such as age, achievements as a player, and managing experience into the production function along with player characteristics. They find that managers with a prior affiliation with the club they are managing and managers who have appeared for their country's national team as a player fare better as coaches.

Audas, Dobson, and Goddard (1999) find that managerial turnover in the English Football Association between 1972 and 1997 averaged one change per team every 2.5 years, a rate even higher than that of the NFL, NBA, or MLB. Furthermore, the likelihood of a manager being fired is highly correlated to the team's recent performance, although a manager's past success with a team does serve to improve his chance of retaining his position through a rough period. Audas, Dobson, and Goddard (2002), in subsequent research, attempt to ascertain whether the removal of a manager affects the team's performance. They find that after correcting for mean-reversion, teams that remove a manager in midseason following a string of poor results actually experience even worse results following the manager's departure, leading one to question why these decisions are so frequently made. Similarly, Koning (2003) also finds in the Dutch First Division that firing a coach results in no consistent improvement in team performances, confirming the results of Audas et al. (2002) but contradicting previous findings in the literature regarding other sports.

Again, combining the newly available OPTA data with the questions posed regarding managerial turnover and efficiency seems to be an obvious area for future research. These possibilities only widen as other leagues begin to provide more detailed statistics.

League Structure

Perhaps the most striking difference between American and European sports leagues is that American leagues have traditionally been closed leagues with a fixed number of teams. Europe, on the other hand, has favored open leagues with promotion and relegation. This league structure rewards top performing teams in lower divisions with promotion into the top level of competition, while relegating the teams with the worst on-field performance in the upper competition levels to the minor leagues. Under a closed system, a city can add a team only through expansion, relocation, or the emergence of a rival league, but a under an open promotion and relegation system, a city can gain a top division team simply through providing an economic environment that produces a successful product on the field.

Noll (2002) argues that although promotion and relegation systems are naturally inefficient since high-revenue teams may be relegated to lower leagues due to poor performance or bad luck on the field, promotion and relegation leagues are far more responsive to demographic changes in metropolitan areas and could serve to counter the monopoly power enjoyed by league owners in closed leagues. Although closed leagues have occasionally experienced competition from the entry of rival leagues, open leagues contain all teams within the established hierarchy. Noll's examination of English soccer also finds a great deal of mobility of teams between divisions with the exception of the very top teams, such as Manchester United, Arsenal, and Liverpool. This finding is replicated by Szymanski (2001), who notes that European promotion and relegation leagues have a very strong intra-season competitive balance compared to closed American leagues but very poor inter-season competitive balance.

Both Szýmanski and Noll propose that relegation promotes very intense competition among the bottom half of teams in each division, who make maximum effort to avoid demotion, leading to close races between the teams. On the other hand, fear of demotion limits teams' incentives to engage in measures to promote inter-season balance such as reverse order drafts and revenue sharing, leading to sustained dominance by the teams with the highest revenue potential. For example, whereas home teams in the NFL and MLB share gate receipts with the visitor, there is negligible gate sharing in European leagues (0 percent in England and Germany and 5 percent in Italy). Szymanski and Valletti (2003) further conclude that open leagues encourage teams at the highest level of competition to invest and produce the highest possible level of competition.

The American top soccer division, Major League Soccer, is also a tempting league to study as it is perhaps the largest and most successful single league incorporating a single entity structure, which makes it fundamentally different than either the open structure of large European football leagues or the closed nature of the big four American sports leagues. Szymanski and Ross (2003) examine the theoretical underpinnings of such a league, but again empirical work is lacking.

A final interesting aspect of European soccer in comparison to American team sports is that teams in Europe are frequently publicly owned or controlled by open-membership clubs rather than following the single-owner model that almost exclusively exists in American sports. In examining membership-owned clubs, De Ruyter and Wetzels (2000) consider the altruistic behavior of football club members who pay regular dues or special assessments to promote a club's financial solvency or improve a team's on-field performance.

Roughly half of the teams in the English Premiership, furthermore, have shares that are publicly traded on the London Stock Exchange. The availability of this type of public information on the perceived value of a sports franchise is a rich data source that generally is not available for American teams. Haugen and Hervik (2002) touch upon this potential research area in their estimation of the possible public value of the Norwegian club Rosenborg, and Szymanski and Valletti (2003) examine market capitalization of teams in open versus closed leagues. Along a similar line, Ashton, Gerrard, and Hudson (2003) find that the daily performance of the London Stock Exchange is positively correlated with the success of the English National team. Although scholars have begun to scratch the surface of this topic, overall this potential area for research remains relatively untouched.

Soccer and Economic Growth

Although the economic impact of sports franchises, stadiums and infrastructure, and mega-sporting events has received significant attention in the United States, surprisingly little has been written about the effects of soccer on local or national economies. Baade (1996) covers the topic of sports stadiums in general and finds that the construction of new stadiums or arenas does not lead to an increase in economic activity in these metropolitan areas. His study, as well as those of most other researchers, focuses on the American professional sports landscape. In part this may be due to the fact that over the past decade the United States has experienced a much more significant reformation of its sports infrastructure than Europe. By 2003, 86 of the 120 teams of the big four professional sports in the United States and Canada were playing in facilities constructed since 1990. Although many European stadiums have undergone recent facelifts (for example, permanent seating has replaced open terraces at most English grounds following the Hillsborough disaster of 1989), combined public and private expenditure has not nearly reached the level that it has in America. In part, this may be due to the promotion and relegation system used in European leagues. Cities and private investors may be unwilling to commit significant financial resources to the construction of a new soccer stadium if there is no guarantee that a team will remain in a top division of the league. Certainly the public subsidization of soccer facilities in Europe and other regions is an area that deserves much closer study.

Johnstone, Southern, and Taylor (2000) present a traditional examination of the benefits of the Liverpool and Everton football clubs on the Merseyside economy. Their detailed analysis finds a combined direct expenditure in the 1997–98 season of £55.5 million, with at least £38.5 million staying in the local economy, and 2,000 local jobs depending on the clubs. Like many impact analyses, the study accounts for only gross expenditures and not net expenditures and ignores substitution effects and crowding out.

The economic impact of the World Cup has also been examined by several researchers. Ahlert (2001), using an input-output macroeconomic model, estimates the economic impact of the 2006 World Cup on the economy of Germany, the designated host country. Under a variety of financing schemes for the construction of the necessary infrastructure, he predicts that Germany can expect increased employment over the period 2003–10 of more than 2,400 jobs, annually peaking in 2006 at a gain of 7,300 jobs. According to the model, German GDP will increase by DM 2.9 billion in the year of the event, with cumulative GDP gains over the 2003–10 period of DM 10.4 billion. Kurscheidt and Rahmann (1999, 2002) also use cost-benefit analyses to provide *ex ante* estimates of the impact of the upcoming World Cup in Germany as well as suggestions about how to maximize benefits based upon the use of local funding for facilities and the proper location of venues.

Looking back at the 1994 World Cup in the United States, Baade and Matheson (2004) arrive at a much different conclusion as to the impact of the world's largest sporting tournament. Rather than the $4 billion positive impact as promoted by the event boosters, their analysis finds that the combined economies of the nine host cities experienced cumulative economic declines of $5.1 to $9.3 billion rather than the touted $4 billion expansion. Matheson and Baade (2004) further examine the likely economic impact of a World Cup hosted by a developing nation as will occur in 2010 with South Africa having been selected as the tournament location. Because of the lack of existing infrastructure and the higher opportunity cost of capital in these countries, they argue that mega-events such as the World Cup are likely to be an even worse proposition for poorer nations.

Hoffmann, Lee, and Ramasamy (2002) and Houston and Wilson (2002) examine not the effects of football on the economy, but the effect of the economy on football performance. As in previous studies of the socioeconomic determinants of success at the Olympic Games, Hoffman, Lee, and Ramasamy (2002) find that population, GDP, GDP per capita, host status, and climate all serve as good predictors of national team achievement. In addition, they find that football is particularly ingrained in Latin culture, with South American and other teams with Spanish and Portuguese backgrounds attaining particularly high levels of performance. Houston and Wilson (2002) reveal that population, income, years in the (FIFA), and youth and full World Cup appearances serve as good predictors of world soccer rank. Hoffmann, Lee, and Ramasamy (2002) apply a similar model to women's international soccer and find that success on the women's field is predicted by a fundamentally different set of variables, with Latin culture being significantly less influential in women's football than men's.

The Game Itself

The wealth of statistical data that exists for any organized sport allows scholars to delve into the nature of the sport itself. Gaviria (2000) explores the commonly held notion that soccer is dying a slow death at the hands of conservative, defensive-minded managers. In fact, while playing innovations in the 1960s led to a structural change in scoring that reduced the number of goals scored in the English, Spanish, and Italian leagues by about a goal per game, since that time scoring has remained relatively stable and has even perhaps had a resurgence in the late 1990s.

Palomino, Rigotti, and Rustichini (1999) analyze the distribution of goals throughout a match for 2,885 games in the top professional leagues in Spain, Italy, and England. In a perhaps unsurprising result they find that attacking strategy is dependent on the state of the game, with teams that are behind or tied playing an attacking style of soccer whereas teams that are leading resort to conservative defensive tactics even relatively early in a match.

A couple of papers examine the effects of rule changes within the sport itself on the game. Guedes and Machado (2002) examine the change in the rules that increased the award in the standings for winning from two points to three points while keeping the points for a draw and a loss at one and zero, respectively. Although the intent of the law was to encourage offensive-minded soccer by increasing the awards to winning, their analysis of the Portuguese first division finds that the rule may encourage even more defensive strategies, as outmatched teams try even harder not to lose, an hypothesis echoed by Brocas and Carrillo (2004).

Ridder, Cramer, and Hopstaken (1994) study the effect on scoring and the probability of receiving the dreaded red card, which is shown for particularly egregious violations of the rules by a player during a game and causes the player's team to play shorthanded for the rest of the match. As tactical fouls that deny an opponent an obvious goal-scoring opportunity are penalized with a red card, the immediate benefits of preventing a goal must be weighed against the burden of playing a man down for the rest of the game.

Finally, game theory tells interesting stories about how to take and defend penalty kicks in articles by Chiappori, Levitt and Groseclose (2002) and Palacios-Huerta (2003).

Officiating

Soccer officiating has also received attention from various researchers. Torgler (2004) examines the factors determining referee success at the World Cup and finds that experience at previous World Cups and country origin from

North or South America are significant predictors of success. Sutter and Kocher (2004) find evidence of referee bias in the German Bundesliga taking the form of more penalties being called for home teams than visitors and more added time being awarded in games where the home team is trailing in a close match. Matheson (2004) examines whether "familiarity breeds contempt" when individual referees officiate a particular team repeatedly.

Conclusions and Recommendations for Future Research

Throughout this chapter, areas of potential future research interest have been noted; however, a handful of topics deserve, perhaps, special attention. While students of baseball, hockey, basketball, and American football are limited to studying only a single major league, soccer, with its literally dozens of professional leagues around the world, provides a plethora of untapped data for a scholar of sports economics to explore. The notably different league structures, player markets, and ownership schemes between soccer and the big four North American sports as well as within soccer itself furnish a nearly unlimited source of data for a researcher to compare and contrast. To date, little comparison between the structure of the North American sports and soccer has been done because of a lack of interest in soccer in the United States and because of the embryonic state of the other sports in Europe. Certainly scholars from both sides of the Atlantic have much to learn from one another.

Furthermore, the existence of leagues in multiple countries not only allows for larger data sets, but also can answer questions about whether characteristics of a particular league are symptomatic of the sport or are unique to a particular country or league structure. For example, when comparing the competitive balance of American baseball and European football, it can never be said for certain whether the differences are due to the markedly different ownership structures between the United States and Europe or to inherent differences in the sports themselves. The existence of multiple soccer leagues of the closed multiple-owner and single-entity variety as well as promotion and relegation systems, allows for a better direct comparison of league structures.

Another obvious avenue for future research is the economic impact of soccer on host communities. Unlike the American sports landscape, virtually no comprehensive studies have been done on the economic impact of football franchises and soccer stadiums on European and developing nations' economies. Football franchises are increasingly interested, however, in obtaining public subsidies to improve their infrastructure. The current economists' admonitions against these subsidies rest almost entirely on the American experience and would benefit from a European or Latin American viewpoint.

Next, MLS, the top American soccer league, is perhaps the most prominent example of a "single entity" league structure anywhere in the world, introducing a third type of league structure to the American closed-league, multiple-owner system and the European promotion and relegation model. Everything from competitive balance to player contracts in MLS can be compared to those in traditional leagues. MLS also provides a chance to observe the development of a league where the sport is of secondary interest in a country.

Finally, although the changes in European player transfer rules have been extensively analyzed from a theoretical standpoint, little empirical work has been done since these changes have taken place. Sports economics in general has always benefited from its easy access to data, and recent information on transfer payments will allow an important check on the theoretical findings.

Note

1. The efficiency of betting markets is a common research topic in the field of the economics of gambling. Football betting data in particular have been examined by, among others, Pope and Peel (1989), Forrest and Simmons (2000), Kuypers (2000), Cain, Law, and Peel (2000), and Goddard and Asimakopoulos (2004).

7

Female Intercollegiate Athletes and Women's Athletics

Brad R. Humphreys

More than a decade ago, Lawrence Kahn (1991: 412) stated in his comprehensive survey of discrimination in sports, "Unlike black and white athletes, male and female athletes seldom work for the same employer in professional sports. Thus there are few opportunities in sports to study the issue of gender discrimination." Kahn was only partially correct in his assessment, and sports have changed considerably in the intervening years. Even at the time, both males and females were coaching men's and women's sports at the collegiate level and male and female jockeys were competing for mounts in professional horse racing (see Ray and Grimes, 1993). Since then women's team sports have become much more visible at the collegiate level and professional leagues have appeared in both basketball and soccer in North America and Europe. Gender equity issues at colleges and universities in the United States have become a prominent area of public policy debate. The landscape has changed dramatically in terms of the economic issues related to gender and discrimination.

This chapter critically reviews the economic research on female intercollegiate athletes and women's athletics. Although economic research in this area has increased in recent years, in part due to the events mentioned above, a number of important research questions remain unanswered and a number of promising areas for economic research still remain unexamined.

As might be expected in an area where males and females compete for scarce resources, issues related to gender equity and discrimination dominate the literature, with Title IX—a 1972 statute mandating equal opportunity for all individuals in federally funded educational activities—receiving the lion's share of attention. Despite this attention, two key research questions related to Title IX remain unanswered: (1) is there an economic basis for legislating equality of opportunity in intercollegiate athletics; and (2) what was the overall impact of Title IX on opportunities in intercollegiate athletics for all college students? The first question has received almost no attention in the literature, and the single related study reports no evidence supporting the statute. The second question has spawned a larger literature, but no consensus has emerged regarding the impact of Title IX on opportunities for male college students.

This area is also well suited to comparative studies of economic behavior. Colleges and universities typically sponsor both men's and women's teams in a number of sports—basketball, soccer, swimming, lacrosse, and track and field, among others—and although some research has focused on coaches' salaries across and within these sports, important topics such as comparative studies of competitive balance, managerial/coaching efficiency, and the analysis of the gender gap in athletic performance still remain largely unexamined.

The emergence of women's team sports—in particular college basketball and professional basketball and soccer—provides an interesting setting for studying the effects of organizational structure on economic performance and industrial organization. Economists know relatively little about the effect of different organizational forms on firms' behavior or their effect on industry structure in markets containing firms with different organizational forms and goals. Women's basketball and soccer now include for-profit professional teams and not-for-profit college teams. Studying the organization of teams and leagues and the outcomes in these leagues can provide insight into economic behavior in this setting as well as in the hospital, publishing, social service, and other industries that contain both for-profit and not-for-profit firms.

Title IX: The 600 Pound Gorilla

Even a cursory review of the literature on the economics of female intercollegiate athletes and women's athletics reveals that the vast majority of academic research focuses on the effects of Title IX of the Education Amendments of 1972 on university athletic departments and college athletes. Broadly defined, Title IX prohibits discrimination on the basis of gender in any educational program or activity receiving federal financial assistance. This law, although directed at gender discrimination in federally funded educational programs, has been interpreted to apply to all athletic programs at colleges and universities, even if these programs do not receive any direct federal financial assistance. The implementation of Title IX focuses on three specific areas of intercollegiate athletics:

1. Equal opportunity for females and males to participate in intercollegiate athletics
2. Equal access to athletic scholarships for female and male athletes
3. Equal provision of practice time, support, travel, publicity, and so on for female and male athletes.

Looking beyond the issue of measuring compliance with Title IX—an issue addressed in detail below—it is interesting that the *economic basis* for Title IX lies in the lifetime benefits accruing to participants in education, or in this particular application, to participants in intercollegiate athletics. By denying females equal participation in intercollegiate athletics, colleges and universities were restricting females' access to a collegiate experience that would provide them with economic advantages in the labor market after graduation. This viewpoint implies that participation in intercollegiate athletics can be viewed as a form of human capital investment.

The Economic Basis for Title IX

Given this economic rationale, it is surprising that economists have paid so little attention to this key assumption underlying the statute. Does participation in intercollegiate athletics lead to any observable economic benefits to either males or females? These economic benefits might be detectable in three areas: increased academic success of participants in intercollegiate athletics, higher graduation rates, and increased lifetime earnings. Of course, females experienced economic damages in the form of reduced access to athletic scholarships before the implementation of Title IX, but the legislation has a much broader aim than simply equilibrating the number of athletic scholarships given to males and females on college campuses.

How large were the economic losses incurred by female undergraduates as a result of reduced access to intercollegiate athletics before the implementation of Title IX? This question gets to the heart of the economic basis for this statute. If there were no economic losses, in terms of lower lifetime earnings or reduced academic performance or graduation rates associated with lower participation in intercollegiate athletics by females, then the primary economic losses would be only the consumption benefits associated with participation in intercollegiate athletics, the restricted access to athletic scholarships, and the benefits associated with improved health and well-being as a result of athletic participation. Arguably, the lost consumption benefits could be partially or fully mitigated by participation in athletics at the club or intramural level, and the health benefits could be partially or fully offset by physical education and coeducational access to fitness centers.

In the absence of benefits associated with earnings, academic achievement, or graduation rates, this leaves only lost access to athletic scholarships as the primary source of economic losses associated with reduced access by females to intercollegiate athletics. Athletic scholarships are important in that they reduce the cost of attending college to recipients and make it possible for some individuals to attend college who would not have otherwise been able to attend because of financial constraints. But a great deal of financial aid was and is available to lower-income families, and the resources used implementing, enforcing, and litigating Title IX could have alternatively financed a large number of need-based scholarships for females. Thus any economic justification for Title IX resides in the economic benefits—increased academic performance, graduation rates, and lifetime earnings—flowing from increased participation in intercollegiate athletics.

No empirical research has attempted to estimate the economic losses experienced by female undergraduates as a result of reduced access to intercollegiate athletics before the passage of Title IX, or after for that matter. Surprisingly, there is very little empirical evidence that females benefit economically, in terms of higher earnings, from participation in intercollegiate athletics. To date, Long and Caudill (1991) have performed the only empirical study of the relationship between participation in intercollegiate athletics and earnings of male and female college students. This study examined a sample of 9,787 individuals who were undergraduates in 1971, prior to the passage of Title IX. In this sample, 15 percent of the males and 5 percent of the females earned varsity letters—a measure of athletic *success* and not participation, although the only measure available in the data—while they were undergraduates. These individuals were surveyed in 1980, six to nine years after graduation. Both the males and females who earned varsity letters had a greater probability of graduating from college, but males who earned varsity letters earned only 4 percent more than males who did not earn letters and females who earned varsity letters had the same earnings as females who did not earn varsity letters. There is no evidence that earning a varsity letter was associated with higher lifetime earnings for women.

Although interesting, this study has several important limitations. First, the students in the sample were undergraduates in the period before the passage and implementation of Title IX, so the results may reflect the adverse effects of reduced participation by females. Second, the six- to nine-year period may not have been enough time for a significant difference in lifetime earnings to appear in the earnings of females, an effect that could be influenced by periods spent out of the workforce by females in prime childbearing and child-rearing years. Nonetheless, the study provides only limited support for an economic basis for Title IX.

Some ambiguity exists in the possible relationship between athletic participation and academic success. On one hand, athletic participation takes time and could reduce time spent by participants on academics, leading to lower academic performance. On the other hand, participating in athletics may increase discipline, organizational skills, and motivation, and thus lead to greater academic success. Also, time devoted to athletic participation may come from nonacademic leisure time, not academic time.

Minimum grade point requirements for participation may also provide additional incentives for academic success to participants in intercollegiate athletics. But these requirements may induce athletes to take easier courses or choose easier majors to remain eligible to compete, complicating the observed relationship between academic success and participation.

It is also possible that participation in intercollegiate athletics leads to higher graduation rates. This is closely related to the link between academic performance and participation. Stronger students will have higher grades, complete more credits per semester, and be more likely to graduate in a timely fashion.

Because academic success is correlated with higher earnings (James et al., 1989; Jones and Jackson, 1990), reduced participation in intercollegiate athletics would cause economic damage to females if participation is associated with greater academic success. The same argument holds for graduation rates, as higher educational attainment is also associated with higher earnings. What evidence supports the idea that participants in intercollegiate athletics have more academic success, or graduate at a higher rate, than other students?

Relatively little research has focused on the academic achievement of athletes, still less has examined gender differences in academic performance among athletes. Maloney and McCormick (1993) examined the academic performance of athletes at a single NCAA Division I institution, but did not distinguish athletes by gender. They found that athletes participating in "revenue" sports (football and men's basketball) performed worse during the semester in which their sport was being played (in season), but found no evidence of lower academic performance by participants in "revenue" sports out of season or by participants in "non-revenue" sports. They also found no evidence that athletes enrolled in easier courses than the student body in general.

Robst and Kiel (2000) examined the graduation rates of males and females at a single NCAA Division III institution, an interesting setting because athletes at Division III institutions are not given scholarships and do not benefit financially from participation. This study found that athletes had higher graduation rates than non-athletes, but that athletes and non-athletes had about the same academic performance in terms of grade point average.

DeBrock, Hendricks, and Koenker (1996) examined graduation rates for football, men's basketball, and women's basketball players at Division I schools over the period 1983–86, using data aggregated to the institution level, not data for individual students. They found that graduation rates for male athletes depended inversely on the success of the individual athletic program, which they interpreted as indicative of professional sports opportunities beyond college. But the overall graduation rates of all athletes depended on the value of a degree from the institution, not on participation in athletics.

Lang and Rossi (1991) conducted perhaps the most detailed analysis of the academic achievement of male and female college athletes. This study assembled a stratified random sample of about eighty athletes at forty-two NCAA Division I institutions that was weighted to be representative of the 56,000 athletes at all Division I institutions. The study considered multiple measures of academic performance rather than a single measure like grade point average and compared the sample of athletes to a larger control group of non-athletes. The study found no evidence that participation in athletics was related to low academic performance, but both female and male athletes were less likely to be outstanding academic performers.

Upthegrove, Roscigno, and Charles (1999) used the data collected by Lang and Rossi (1991) to further examine the effects of participation in intercollegiate athletics on academic performance. This comparative study of the academic performance of male athletes participating in football and basketball and female athletes participating in non-revenue sports found that male athletes were more likely than female athletes to repeat courses and be placed on academic probation. Additionally, male athletes had lower grade point averages than female athletes, even when ability and academic preparation were controlled for. Thus female athletes in non-revenue sports appear to perform better than male athletes who participate in revenue-generating sports, although it is not clear that female athletes perform better than the overall population of undergraduates.

Overall, the evidence that participation in intercollegiate athletics has a positive effect on academic performance or graduation rates is weak. Female athletes had higher graduation rates in several studies at individual institutions, but there is no evidence that participating in intercollegiate athletics leads to greater academic performance among female athletes than in the larger student population.

The lack of evidence that participation in intercollegiate athletics increased the lifetime earnings of females prior to the imposition of Title IX, and the complete lack of research on the effect of participation on the lifetime earnings of females after the imposition of Title IX, coupled with the high profile of

Title IX in the public policy arena, make this a fertile area for future economic research. Athletic departments at colleges and universities continue to cut men's athletic programs and cite Title IX as the primary reason for these cuts. If Title IX imposes large costs on these programs and leads to decreased access to intercollegiate athletics for men, then the economic basis for Title IX and the assessment of the economic benefits accruing to women need additional attention from economists. Longitudinal data on the earnings of individuals are increasingly available to economists and other social scientists. These data sets appear to be well suited to answering such questions.

Organizations and Gender Regulation

Title IX is applied in an interesting organizational setting. Colleges and universities are not-for-profit organizations; some are publicly owned and financed and others are privately owned and partially financed by private funds; some are operated by religious organizations. There is no clear claimant to the residual profits of a university or its athletic department, calling into question the assumption of cost minimization often applied to models of organizational behavior. Further complicating the regulatory setting, intercollegiate athletics is governed by a nonprofit third party, the National Collegiate Athletic Association (NCAA), that operates like a cartel in both output markets and input markets.[1] Although economists have developed a number of economic models of the regulated and unregulated behavior of profit-maximizing firms under a number of different types of industry organization, relatively little theory has been developed to explain how gender equity regulations might affect nonprofit organizations.

Additionally, there is no consensus in the literature on the appropriate way to model the economic behavior of institutions of higher education. Bureaucratic models of public institutions assume rational decision-makers that maximize budget, revenue, or other measures of control. Other approaches include modeling university behavior using a composite utility function or modeling institutions of higher education as profit-maximizing organizations.

Carroll and Humphreys (2000) developed a model of the behavior of nonprofit organizations under a regulation similar to Title IX. In this paper, a utility maximizing athletic director who obtains utility from prestige, total budget, and staff, is subjected to a break-even constraint and a constraint on resources devoted to men's and women's sports. This model predicts that athletic directors will oversupply men's sports in the absence of a Title IX–like regulation, but in the presence of such a regulation athletic directors may either increase women's sports or decrease men's sports. This prediction highlights the unintended consequences inherent in gender regulations like Title

IX, where the regulation requires equality in programmatic offerings or expenditure on both men's and women's sports.

In their empirical analysis, Carroll and Humphreys found that more prestigious athletic departments—those with high expenditure per male athlete, high expenditure per female athlete, or a Division I football program—were more likely to add women's sports and less likely to cut men's sports in response to Title IX, while larger institutions were more likely to cut men's sports. The results generally supported the assumption of prestige maximization in modeling the behavior of athletic directors.

This paper represents the only attempt in the economics literature thus far to model the effects of Title IX on nonprofit organizations. Clearly, additional theoretical work remains to be done in this area. Instead of revenue-maximizing athletic directors, university decision-makers could alternatively be modeled as revenue maximizers, income maximizers, or as profit maximizers. All these approaches have been applied to the behavior of nonprofit organizations in other settings. Furthermore, a potentially interesting principle-agent relationship exists between the president of a university and its athletic director. These two may have different objectives and face different constraints. Little attention has been paid to this interesting principle-agent relationship and the effect and effectiveness of Title IX in such a setting.

The market for intercollegiate athletics also contains a number of interesting features that have not yet been studied by economists. The suppliers in this market are a mixture of public and private organizations that differ significantly in their financing, objectives, and governance. Did public and private universities supply different levels of men's and women's athletics programs before the imposition of Title IX? Did public and private universities respond differently to Title IX? Did exclusive, research-intensive universities respond differently than large public colleges and universities with significant teaching missions? Little research has addressed these interesting and important questions.

The effects of market structure on Title IX have also not been fully explored. Many economists view the NCAA as a cartel in both output and input markets. Although cartel behavior is well understood by economists, little attention has been paid to the implications and effects of the imposition of a gender equality regulation like Title IX on cartel behavior. Are cartel rents redistributed away from universities and toward participants by Title IX? Again, these are open research questions.

Economic Analysis of Compliance and Enforcement

The lion's share of economic research on Title IX has focused on the enforcement of the statute and the related topic of assessing the degree of compliance with the statute. In this literature, the dominant themes have been the extent to which the unintended consequences of the regulation—the tendency of athletic departments to reduce opportunities for males rather than to increase opportunities for females to meet the requirements of the regulation—dominate the intended consequences, and the effect of big-time college football on compliance with the regulation. Football commands a considerable amount of attention because it has many more participants than other intercollegiate sports, has no counterpart female intercollegiate sport, and is the primary revenue-generating sport in most Division I athletic departments.

The sprawling literature on compliance with and enforcement of Title IX is extensive and encompasses many disciplines. It also contains many areas of tension and a number of notable unresolved conflicts. Journals in economics, political science, sociology, law, and sports management have published articles analyzing, documenting, and describing the implementation of the regulation and its enforcement. Zimbalist (1997) points out that the significant increase in participation by females came in the period following the passage of Title IX and that much of the litigation over the legal definition of compliance and the remedies for noncompliance has resulted in few additional gains, implying that much of the current debate misses the point, as the effects of the regulation have already been felt. Two other notable lines of research appear in the literature. The first is that the measures of compliance adopted by the Office of Civil Rights (OCR) of the Department of Education and upheld in court cases have many important flaws. The second is that the presence of a big-time football program greatly complicates the question of compliance with Title IX. I discuss only a few of the most recent articles here. Interested readers should consult the lengthy bibliographies of these papers for additional references.

Zimbalist (1997) surveyed the literature on compliance and enforcement of Title IX. As he points out, the OCR, the agency that enforces Title IX, uses three criteria to determine if an institution is in compliance with the regulation:

1. Does the institution provide participation opportunities for females and males that are "substantially proportionate" to their enrollment rates in the student body?
2. Has the institution demonstrated a history and continuing pattern of program expansion for females?
3. Does the institution "fully and effectively" accommodate the interests of females?

These criteria are applied sequentially, and failure to meet at least one of the three typically results in sanctions. The criteria are also vague enough to leave considerable room for interpretation, resulting in uneven application. In particular, the phrases "substantially proportionate" in the first criterion and "fully and effectively" in the third are not carefully defined and the "continuing pattern of behavior" mentioned in the second is ambiguous. Despite these problems, assessing the degree of compliance at institutions with these criteria has been the focus of a considerable amount of research and a number of court cases.

Rishe (1999) argues that proportional measures of participation opportunities and expenditure adopted by the OCR and used in court cases are inferior to alternative measures; proportional compliance tests compare the male-female composition of the student body at an institution to the male-female distribution of expenditure and participants in the athletic department. Comparing the allocation of resources within the athletic department to the gender composition of the student body holds many things, like the fraction of the institution's budget devoted to intercollegiate athletics, revenues generated by different sports, and the preferences of students for participation in, and consumption of, sports, equal. Because these factors are not equal at every institution, relative measures of compliance are crude and simplistic. Rishe's empirical analysis shows that in the absence of football, most athletic departments would be in compliance with Title IX in terms of proportionality of expenditures and considerably closer to compliance in terms of proportionality of participants in intercollegiate athletics. However, football is not likely to be excluded from compliance tests in the existing environment, clouding the issue even more.

Sigelman and Wahlbeck (1999) also examine compliance with Title IX and its relationship to big-time football. This study concludes that the majority of athletic programs fall far short of the compliance criteria implied by proportionality tests. Like the research by Rishe (1999), this study also concludes that big-time football programs, which typically offer eighty-five full scholarships and consume large portions of the athletic budget for travel, recruitment, and coaching, are the primary barrier to compliance in terms of proportional criteria. Neither study examines the other two compliance tests, a history and continuing pattern of improving participation opportunities for females and "fully and effectively" accommodating the interests of female students, because these criteria are not easy to quantify. It is important to bear in mind that, despite the focus on proportionality of opportunities and expenditure in the literature, this is not the only criterion used to determine compliance.

As an example of the unresolved conflicts in the compliance literature, consider the exchange between Sabo (1998) and McBride, Worcester, and Tennyson (1999) over the extent to which men's sports programs have been harmed as universities adjusted to compliance with the emerging legal standards. As discussed above, Carroll and Humphreys (2000) provide a theoretical motivation for the unintended consequences of Title IX and present empirical evidence that these unintended consequences exist, primarily at institutions with lower spending, in terms of total educational and general expenditures per student. Sabo (1998) surveyed 637 colleges and universities in Division I-A, Division I-AA, and Division I-AAA (71 percent of the institutions in these categories) to determine how Title IX compliance affected both men's and women's sports programs. Sabo concluded that Title IX compliance was not a zero sum game—men's programs were not eliminated in order to meet the proportionality criterion, and consequently, there was no unintended consequence of Title IX. McBride, Worcester, and Tennyson (1999) examined the same data and concluded that Title IX had important unintended consequences. They claim that Sabo's sample was not representative of the universe of institutions, Division I-A was affected negatively, but Sabo's accounting method minimized this impact, and the effect of Title IX on unrealized growth in men's sports programs was ignored by Sabo.

There clearly exists room for additional empirical research on compliance with Title IX. The unresolved debate on the effect of compliance on men's sports could be answered with some data collection and careful empirical research. In terms of compliance with Title IX, the impact of a big-time football program on the proportionality criterion is an empirical question well suited to regression analysis. Given the evidence that many institutions are not in compliance with Title IX in terms of the proportionality criterion, a study of the characteristics of the institutions that have been penalized for not complying with Title IX would provide a great deal of information about how the statute is being enforced. Consider Leeds, Suris, and Durkin (2004) as the initial foray into this area.

Comparative Studies of Earnings and Performance

Intercollegiate athletics is an interesting setting for comparative studies of many types of economic behavior. A large number of colleges and universities sponsor both men's and women's teams in identical or closely related sports. Basketball, soccer, swimming, golf, lacrosse, track and field, and hockey fall into the former category; men's baseball and women's softball fall into the latter. Economists have studied competitive balance, managerial or coaching efficiency, and the gender gap in athletic performance in many other settings. Most of the important methodological issues related to coaching efficiency and competitive balance have been resolved, paving the way for extensions of this research to previously unexamined sports. To date, this rich and varied source of data has not been examined.

Output measures—won-loss records, conference and national championships—are readily available for college sports, as well as extensive data on institutional finances. An increasing amount of financial data from athletic departments is being collected and disseminated. Economists should take advantage of this unexplored area. Does the gender of the head coach affect the efficiency of the coach in women's basketball? Is competitive balance greater in women's soccer than in men's? What about softball/baseball?

A recent paper has already addressed an interesting question in this area. Brown and Jewell (2003), noting the recent growth in participation, prestige, and revenues of women's college basketball, estimated the marginal revenue product of a premium women's college basketball player. The estimated marginal revenue product reported in this paper, approximately $300,000 per year, compares favorably with previous estimates for premium football and men's basketball players. This result suggests that, like football and men's basketball, women's basketball players now generate significant revenues for their institutions and that these revenues are captured, in the form of rents, by the institutions.

The scant literature on comparative economic studies in intercollegiate athletics to date has focused primarily on the earnings of coaches, including the earnings differential between male and female coaches and between the coaches of men's and women's teams. Zimbalist (1999) has discussed the economic issues underlying earnings gaps among male and female college coaches.[2] Among college coaches, the males who coach men's football and basketball teams earn more than the males and females who coach other teams. For example, Humphreys (2000) reported that the median women's basketball coach earned 55 percent of the median men's basketball coach in Division I in the early 1990s. Head coaches' salaries of less visible, non-revenue sports are much lower than the salaries of head basketball coaches.

There are a number of possible explanations for the observed earnings gap between football and men's basketball head coaches and other head coaches of intercollegiate sports teams. Zimbalist (1999) presents a number of possible explanations for this earnings gap, including imperfections in the labor markets for college coaches, a lack of market pressures, and discrimination. Of course the revenues generated by football and men's basketball programs at many universities justify some of this salary differential. Despite the large number of potential explanations for this earnings gap, the public policy implications of the many court cases in this area, and the increasing availability of data, this research question remains open and deserves more attention from economists.

In a related study, Humphreys (2000) showed that female head coaches of women's Division I basketball teams earned about 10 percent more than males, even when ability, experience, revenue differences, and differences in resources were accounted for—perhaps because a good measure of job performance is available for college basketball coaches. This is one of a very few occupations where females earn more than males, an unusual result.

In contrast to this evidence, Cunningham and Sagas (2002) found that female assistant coaches in intercollegiate athletics may be subject to discrimination. This study surveyed several hundred assistant basketball coaches at Division I institutions. The evidence suggests that male assistant coaches had more coaching responsibilities than females, despite the superior qualifications of the females in the survey. In a related study, Whisenant, Pederson, and Obenour (2002) found that male athletic directors at Division I colleges and universities tended to be more successful than their female counterparts. Interestingly, this relationship was reversed at lower level (Division II and III) institutions, where females tended to be more successful than their male counterparts. Based on these results, it appears that the effect of gender discrimination differs across jobs in athletic departments, suggesting a number of interesting areas for future research.

Finally, Scully (2000) explored the concept of diminishing returns in the context of athletic performance. He posits the existence of a "performance function" in individual sports that is analogous to a production function. The concavity property of this function is investigated empirically using results from a number of running and distance events for men from the Olympic Games over the period 1896–1996. He also compares the results from the Olympic Games and the Boston Marathon for men and women over a shorter period. Scully finds evidence of diminishing returns in men's athletics and evidence that women may eventually close the performance gap, at least in track and field events. This setting could easily be extended to intercollegiate athletics. The NCAA keeps extensive records on track and field, swimming, and other events where males and females compete under similar conditions. Furthermore, the intercollegiate athletic setting features quantifiable variation in resources devoted to athletics across institutions. This variation could be exploited to obtain more precise estimates of the rate at which returns diminish in this setting.

Notes

1. Some economists disagree with this position, arguing that the NCAA is best described as a franchise operation, joint venture, or open market. See for example McKenzie and Sullivan (1987).

2. For a recent review of the legal issues in this area, see Gaal, Glazier, and Evans (2002).

8

The Economics of Individual Sports

Golf, Tennis, Track, and NASCAR

Peter von Allmen

This chapter covers sports in which the primary participant competes with little or no interaction between him/herself and any complementary inputs (i.e., teammates). Thus, most research questions revolve around the optimal design of a contest, the economic incentives to perform, and the extent to which they affect the behavior of the participants. Although these individual competitors may belong to a professional association, there is no league of teams as in the National Football League (NFL). These associations, such as the Professional Golf Association (PGA) Tour, govern the organization of play, distribution of gains, participation in playoff contests, and maintenance of monopoly power. The theoretical research most directly applicable to individual sports concerns both the actions of contest organizers (i.e., how to construct an optimal contest under various conditions), and the behavior of individuals in response to incentives. Most of the existing empirical research is concerned with the behavior of participants in response to variation in the total prize pool and the spread of prizes across order of finish. Consequently, I devote much of the chapter to a review of the theoretical and empirical work on rank-order tournaments.

To date, economists have investigated golf, tennis, racing (both on foot and motor), and horse racing, though horse racing is not entirely relevant here given that the horse does the running. Much good work has been done, but many unanswered questions remain at both a theoretical and empirical level. There are many theoretical advances yet to be tested. Thus, even in the absence of further theoretical developments, the economics of individual sports represents fertile ground for the search for empirical verification of labor theories that is simply not possible in other industries. As such, it represents an opportunity to make a contribution that extends well beyond the golf course, race track, and tennis courts. There are really two complementary sets of research questions here. First, how can we use individual sports to test hypotheses about individual behavior in response to incentives? Second, how can we understand the behavior of individuals in such sports in the context of economic theory? The next section reviews the theory that has spawned the first wave of research on rank-order tournaments. The section that follows discusses the current state of the empirical literature in golf, racing, and tennis. The section after that analyzes gender-based research and other research on individual sports. The final section presents ideas and challenges for future research.

Rank-Order Tournaments

The empirical literature on individual sports got off to a decided late start relative to that of team sports, perhaps because it lacked a substantial theoretical platform. Put differently, it did not occur to labor economists that there was much that individual sports could offer standard neoclassical theory of labor. Team sports played in the context of organized leagues can contribute to the industrial organization literature through use of a variety of applied micro theory models that are readily applicable to league and team strategic decisions. Even when it comes to labor market analysis, many playing positions in team sports are nearly ideally suited for standard micro labor models because labor productivity and in turn marginal revenue product are so readily determined. Individual sports such as golf, tennis, and the like have no such luck. So, although the literature on professional and amateur team sports dates back at least to the 1950s, the first published empirical papers analyzing an individual sport did not appear until 1990: Ehrenberg and Bognanno's (1990a, 1990b) analyses of golf. We must begin then, with a review of the theoretical developments that drive the empirical work.

Stating that contestants respond to variations in prize structure is a testable hypothesis, but certainly a valid theoretical starting point assuming contestants maximize expected utility. To stage the best contest, organizers must offer a prize structure that generates profit-maximizing contestant behavior. Thus there are theoretical questions to be answered on many levels. What type of contest maximizes revenue for the organizer? What type of prize structure will generate such a contest? How do changes in assumptions about the quality of contestants (i.e., equal quality or not) affect the optimal prize design? At an empirical level, the most pressing question is whether contestants respond to incentives as theory predicts. With some variety of contest offerings, careful empirics should be able to either confirm or refute theoretical predictions of contest structure. To date, the empirical work makes use of only a portion of the theoretical work on contest design, a topic addressed in the section on the agenda for future research. To begin then, I review only the basic structure of the models as tested to date.

In individual sports, athletes do not compete as members of teams that make decisions aimed at maximizing profits or optimizing attendance and television ratings. Each individual invests in training and competes according to the arguments of his or her own utility function. In return, earnings are not based on the on- and off-field performance of an economic organization that we might call a firm, although the professional organizations to which athletes in individual sports belong, such as the PGA Tour or the ATP and WTA for men's and women's tennis, may in some ways resemble leagues in that they organize contests. Shmanske (2004, especially chap. 9) provides a good a description of how PGA Tour events are organized. Individuals are not bound to specific events (tournaments) in the same way that a member of a baseball team is required to play each game of a season. Thus, we must turn to models designed to describe individual behavior.

Even if economists were to focus solely on individual utility-maximizing behavior, applying the standard labor supply models wherein firms demand labor up to the point where the marginal revenue product is equal to the marginal cost to individual player tournaments is unsatisfactory. In an individual sport such as a running race, labor productivity is not measurable in any meaningful sense because of the nature of the output. Workers (athletes) are not rewarded for running miles in specific times, nor are they rewarded based on average speed. All that matters to a given runner in a given race is that they run even the slightest bit faster than their opponent(s). That is, only rank order of finish matters. Further complicating matters is that tournament sponsors and the economists who want to analyze their behavior have no way to measure effort (e.g., output per hour or piece rate). On the supply side, economists were no better off. They had no way to evaluate labor supply decisions, since hours of work including training time is essentially immeasurable and cannot be compared to a set offered wage in any case.

In the 1980s, this lack of a theoretical base was addressed in a very substantial way. Papers by Lazear and Rosen (1981), Rosen (1981, 1986), Nalebuff and Stiglitz (1983), and O'Keefe, Viscusi, and Zeckhauser (1984) began to set out the conditions under which a contest with highly nonlinear rewards is preferable for the contest organizer. Most importantly, Lazear and Rosen (1981) published their paper describing rank-order tournaments and the conditions under which they might be an efficient form of compensation. This paper was enormously important because it provided the framework for analyzing compensation efficiency in markets where neither output nor marginal product is readily measurable. They note that although measuring input is generally su-

Figure 8.1   **Effort, MC, and MR**

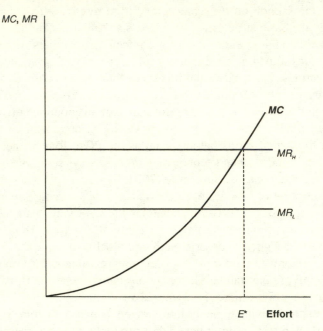

perior as it relates to preventing shirking, when monitoring costs are high, it may be more efficient to measure output. If output too is difficult to measure, a rank-order tournament will be a superior compensation scheme. Quoting Lazear and Rosen (1981: 848), "If it is less costly to observe rank than an individual's output, then tournaments dominate piece rates and standards."

An important extension of this idea appears in Rosen (1986), in which he shows the efficiency of nonlinear rewards in a sequential tournament (such as a single-elimination tennis tournament). He concludes (p. 713), "If top prizes are not large enough, those that have succeeded in achieving higher ranks rest on their laurels and slack off in their attempts to climb higher." Interestingly, nonlinear rewards are required to elicit increasing effort irrespective of the homogeneity of talent. For example, Rosen notes that if there are only a few strong players and the rest are weak, rewards need not be high in early rounds because the promise of higher prizes in later rounds looms. In later rounds however, the talent distribution becomes more equal as weaker players are eliminated, and so organizers must offer a higher prize to elicit the greater effort needed to advance.

The essence of rank-order tournament (ROT) theory is shown in Figure 8.1. Workers compare a predetermined marginal prize (*MR*) to their marginal cost of effort or skill (*MC*), which is assumed to increase at an increasing rate

Figure 8.2   **Finish Position and Prize**

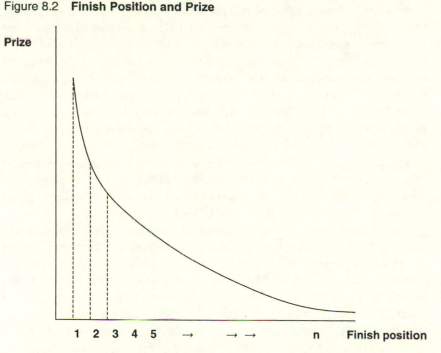

(C′ > 0, C″ > 0). Firms determine the level of effort E^* that workers must elicit to maximize profits. Given the shape of the marginal cost function, firms must offer a relatively large marginal prize (MR_H) to elicit effort from workers. A low marginal prize, such as MR_L, would be less expensive for the firm, but would result in less effort expended by workers. With no way to monitor effort, input-based pay such as hours worked could result in shirking. With little or no way to directly measure output (such as units sold), the most efficient alternative that remains is to set up a prize structure similar to that shown in Figure 8.2, wherein the marginal prize declines sharply as one moves down in the rankings. As we will soon see, prize structures that closely resemble Figure 8.2 are commonplace in individual sports. Nevertheless, the details of precisely how to structure a prize ladder have yet to be explored empirically, as is discussed in the final section.

Also in 1981, Rosen published his paper "The Economics of Superstars" (Rosen 1981), which complements Lazear and Rosen (1981) in that it establishes two additional demand-side properties of contests that support the use of rank-order tournaments in athletic contests. The first is that weaker talent is a poor substitute for stronger talent. "The worse it [weaker talent as a substitute for stronger talent] is, the larger the sustainable rent accruing to higher quality sellers because demand for the better sellers increases more than proportionately" (Rosen, 1981: 846). This claim is readily verifiable in professional sports, even with casual observation. Large throngs of fans follow the lead group at a golf tournament relative to a group of young unestablished players who are unlikely to place even in the top half. Thus, an important element of Rosen's conclusion regarding substitutability is that in a nonsequential tournament (such as a stroke-play golf tournament) too much disparity between the best contestants and the worst in a given contest can decrease overall demand. As discussed in Fullerton and McAfee (1999), organizers have an incentive to ensure a quality contest by limiting the field to invited players only. Even with such restrictions in individual professional sports (other than marathon running) to limit fields, substantially unbalanced winning over the course of a season is a common occurrence, indicating that limiting the field is not a full solution to fostering strong demand.

Second, Rosen notes that technological changes have made it increasingly easy for fans to have access to the very best contestants. He uses the example of a moderately good singer before the days of radio or recorded music who is able to draw a crowd in a local market because consumers there have no access to the very best singers. Once they can listen to a recording of the very best and watch the very best on television, demand for lesser-talented performers may fall dramatically. Note that these two properties reinforce one another when it comes to skewing demand toward the best contestants. From the organizers' standpoint, there is an important task here with the predictions of ROT theory. Players that are the best create disproportionately high demand. On the supply side, offering disproportionately high rewards to players motivates them to play their best. Thus consumers who pay disproportionately high prices to see a tournament of the best players should not be disappointed, unless, that is, the reward structure and talent distribution are such that also-ran contestants quickly give up, leaving fans with a contest in which the winner is apparent long before the end of the contest.

Finally, Rosen makes an observation that demonstrates how valuable sports economics research can be in the search for empirical verification of theory. He notes that (1981: 845) "confidentiality laws and other difficulties make it virtually impossible to obtain systematic data in this field." Although this is true in the corporate world, the professional sports industry has provided fertile ground for this research, as described in coming sections. Thus, in the case of the search to verify ROT theory, the sports industry, chided by some as a less-than-serious undertaking, is uniquely positioned to either verify or refute a well-known theory in a major branch of the discipline.

O'Keefe, Viscusi, and Zeckhauser's (1984) paper is useful when organizing research hypotheses, as it describes four potential functions of a ROT-type contest. First, the contest itself may provide utility in its own right. Simply put, such contests may be fun to watch. Second, they may be the best way to choose the winner when rewards are indivisible (i.e., a single winner must be chosen). Third, contests may be useful in creating an incentive mechanism. Finally, contests can reduce risk when employees and employers are uncertain about the level of effort required. Again we see that the opportunity to meld ROT with individual sports is a winner on all fronts. Each potential benefit of ROT contests is readily apparent in professional individual sports, perhaps most notably in the creation of incentives to increase performance.

Other than differences in contestant ability, there are two potential prize-related drivers of contestant effort in a contest. The first is the absolute level of the prize (i.e., does the winner receive, for instance, $10 or $1,000), and the second is the relative difference between prizes awarded. Much of the empirical work described in this chapter amounts to attempts to reveal and measure the magnitude of the incentive effects of these two elements of ROT compensation schemes. If the absolute magnitude of the prize and effort are positively related, for a given prize distribution scheme we should observe better absolute quality of play in tournaments with larger prize pools. And, all else equal, if competitors respond to ROT contests wherein the distribution scheme is such that the marginal prize is strongly increasing as a player moves up the hierarchy toward first place (as in Figure 8.2), then we should observe better absolute quality of play as the marginal prize increases.

Although increases in marginal prize may increase absolute performance, which in turn increases the benefits of a contest to the organizer, there may be limits to these benefits. As with so many economic concepts, too much of a good thing can be a bad thing. Lazear (1989) described circumstances in which wage compression (more equal wages across competitors) may be more efficient than ROT-style reward profiles in circumstances where highly nonlinear rewards might otherwise seem appropriate. Specifically, too much competition between workers can result in uncooperative behavior that is detrimental to the firm. Workers may attempt to succeed by sabotaging the work of others. In sports, an extreme form of ROT rewards in which winner-takes-all, players may act on the knowledge that there are two ways to finish ahead of a competitor: to speed up oneself, or to slow the opponent down. In competitions where active defense is not within the rules of competition (such as golf), or should only occur within the limits of good sportsmanship (such as racing and tennis), winner-take-all rewards may be inefficient and potentially dangerous. Again sports economics has an opportunity to test a theoretical development that would be almost impossible to test in a corporate environment. The potential for sabotage and its effect on tournament outcomes has been explored in two papers related to auto racing, which are discussed below.

Golf

In discussing the empirical investigations of individual sports, the work of Ehrenberg and Bognanno represents a logical starting point. Their works on golf (1990a, 1990b) stand as the original tests of tournament-theory effects, and so still serve as a benchmark result. They use data from the U.S. and European PGA tours to test the two prize-related hypotheses described above: (1) that the larger the total prize, the greater the effort, and so the lower the total scores we should observe; and (2) in the final round of a tournament, when players who are out of contention for significant prize shares are eliminated, we should observe higher returns to effort (i.e., better play) by players that are closer to the top of the hierarchy. Here they test the ROT theory prediction that as the marginal prize increases, absolute quality of play should increase due to increased effort to win the larger prize.

Econometrically, both tests are straightforward. To test the effect of the total prize on effort, or effort/concentration as they refer to it, they pool data across individuals and firms and estimate the equation:

$$s_{ij} = a_o + a_1 TPRIZE_i + a_2 x_i + a_3 y_j + a_4 z_i + v_j, \qquad (8.1)$$

where s_{ij} is the ith player in the jth tournament. The independent variable of interest is $TPRIZE_i$, and x_i, y_j, and z_i are vectors of control variables for the tournament, player, and opponents respectively. They estimate the model for several samples of players in both papers and find that, all else equal, players do respond to larger prize pools with better play. They find, for example, that increasing the total prize money by \$100,000 in 1984 reduced each player's score by an average of 1.1 over the tournament.

To test the hypothesis that players facing higher marginal prizes will have better absolute quality of play, they estimate final-round scores as a function of each of the three previous round scores, and the rank after the third round.[1] They find that players, especially exempt players who are not in danger of losing their tournament entry privileges, do respond to greater marginal prizes with lower scores. To test for the effects of "bunching" (the relative distance between a competitor and his/her nearest rival above and below) they compute variables that measure the increase in prize money a player would receive if the player improved his/her score relative to competitors in the final round by one two or three strokes. Again they find that players (especially exempt players) respond to the potential for greater returns with greater effort. Thus, in these two papers, they establish both a methodology and a benchmark result that ROT effects are consistent with those predicted by theory. Because the relative spread of prizes across tournaments is fixed in

Table 8.1

Reward Structure in the 2004 Boston Marathon for Finish Positions 1 Through 5

Finish position	Open class	Masters (> 40)	Wheelchair
1	$80,000	$10,000	$10,000
2	40,000	5,000	5,000
3	22,500	2,500	2,500
4	18,000	1,500	1,500
5	14,000	1,000	1,000

Note: Awards in each category are equal for men and women. Prizes in the open division extend (with decreasing marginal spread) through the fifteenth position; the total prize pool for men and women was $225,000. Prizes shown do not include bonuses for achieving record times.

all professional golf tournaments, they are not able to test for the effects of contest design (e.g., winner-take-all versus uniform), or how incentive effects might affect behavior in a sequential-play tournament such as an elimination tournament.

It is also worth noting that Orszag (1994) uses similar methodology but more recent data from a time when the absolute value of prizes was much larger than the prizes in the Ehrenberg and Bognanno data and finds that total prize money is not related to final scores. He hypothesizes that prizes may have grown to the point where players are unable to concentrate and "choke." Given that prize money has continued to grow over the ten years since the data used by Orszag, and top players now regularly make putts worth well over $100,000 on the final days of tournaments, some doubt is cast on this explanation, though the point bears further investigation.

Running

Distance running provides another potential test of ROT theory. Although millions of amateur athletes compete in local races simply for recreation and exercise, elite professionals have the opportunity to earn significant prize money for winning major races. For example, Table 8.1 shows the prize distribution scheme for the 2004 Boston Marathon. Note that for all divisions the prize structure is nonlinear. As a contestant advances through the hierarchy toward first place, prize winnings increase dramatically in both a relative and absolute sense, especially in the open division.

Lynch and Zax (2000) and Maloney and McCormick (2000) use data from a variety of road race distances to test for incentive effects. Although their methodology is different, both papers find support for the hypothesis that improved outcomes (i.e., faster times) are due at least in part to what can be considered supply effects, a possibility not fully considered by Ehrenberg and Bognanno. That is, race times are better when purses are larger not because (or not *only* because) racers have an incentive to run faster, but because faster racers enter richer races. Maloney and McCormick find that both the participation effect and incentive effect are present in their data. Average race times are reduced by 2% when the average prize is doubled (the participation effect), and average race times are reduced by almost 4% when the prize spread is doubled (the incentive effect). Lynch and Zax find that once supply effects are removed, most of the variance in race times has been accounted for, and most marginal prize variables are insignificant.

To further refine estimates of individual behavior, McCormick and Maloney estimate a fixed-effects model with racer dummies. They find that doing so reduces the magnitude of the incentive effect such that it is less than the participation effect. This result is consistent with the Lynch and Zax finding that controlling for runner quality reduces incentive effects. Maloney and McCormick also investigate differences in incentive effects by gender, as discussed later in the chapter.

Motor Racing

Becker and Huselid (1992) apply ROT theory to two forms of motor racing, NASCAR and IMSA, to investigate whether nonlinear payment schemes motivate drivers to increase their performance. If so, we should observe that as the marginal prize increases, drivers increase their performance (effort). Unfortunately, data limitations require that they construct a proxy for absolute performance. Speed-per-car data are not recorded for every participant because NASCAR Winston Cup (now Nextel Cup) races end as soon as the winner crosses the finish line. Thus, they construct an adjusted finish variable:

$$ADJUSTED\ FINISH = (A/F)R, \qquad (8.2)$$

where A is average speed of the winning car, F is the fastest winning speed recorded across all races, and R is the finish position.

Their marginal measure is also not a true measure of marginal prize for two reasons. First, they use the average prize spread in each race aggregated across the top ten finishing positions and the eleventh to twentieth finishing positions. Second, auto racing rewards include a variety of bonus payments for intermediate results such as leading a lap, fastest pit stop, and the like. Becker and Huselid estimate a fixed-effects model that incorporates individual driver dummies, as in the work of Lynch and Zax (2000) and Maloney and McCormick (2000). Despite the data limitations and relatively small marginal prize increases, they find that at the individual race level, incentive effects are present in NASCAR and are subject to diminishing returns. Thus, their NASCAR results indicate that there are limits to incentive effects. The IMSA data show similar incentive effects except without clear support for diminishing returns.

Becker and Huselid focus on the incentives of the pre-set-dollar prize distribution of a single race. However, rewards in racing are multidimensional. As noted above, there are a variety of in-race incentives that may motivate drivers to vary their effort over the course of a race. There are other important sources of revenue that can influence behavior. Von Allmen (2001) provides a more global perspective on winning incentives, and shows how they complicate the optimal reward structure and resulting driver incentives across an entire season. There are four distinct sources of revenue that may impact a driver's incentive in any particular race: individual race winnings; individual race bonuses; revenue from season-long or multi-event rewards that drivers achieve primarily through earning championship points in individual races; and sponsorship revenue, which can best be characterized as a reward for high performance over time. In addition to the revenue effects, there are also cost effects. The marginal cost of creating a winning edge is so great in auto racing, especially given the restrictions placed on the vehicles, that nonlinear prizes could skew future results such that race outcomes become too predictable.

Von Allmen (2001) provides three possible reasons why individual race rewards may not be highly nonlinear. First is the importance of sponsorship. With such substantial season-long rewards and sponsorship revenues that are likely even greater (only anecdotal data exist), there is substantial incentive to remain competitive throughout the season. Keeping one's car on the track provides the sponsor with advertising throughout the event. It follows that as exposure increases, so does the sponsor's willingness to maintain or even increase funding. Second is the sabotage hypothesis. Race organizers may believe that given the risks inherent in auto racing, effort may be pushed beyond the limits of safety if highly nonlinear rewards are offered. The potential for negative externalities in crashes would more than exhaust the rents available and so would be inefficient. Although they do not explore the finding in detail, Becker and Huselid also note that increasing spread in the marginal prizes leads to an increase in caution flags, which may indicate an increase in accidents born of over-aggressiveness. This raises the possibility that, as Lazear (1989) suggests, increasing marginal prizes may be inefficient in some sports. Lazear notes that although increasing marginal rewards can create incentive effects that enhance productivity, in cases where worker productivity is interdependent, competition for wages can lead to reduced cooperation and perhaps outright sabotage. Von Allmen (2001) finds some support for this hypothesis by showing that accident rates per driver mile in winner-take-all events are significantly higher than in races where the reward profile is flatter. The third is the cost hypothesis, which is that given the high marginal cost of winning, race outcomes will be highly correlated, as winners of prior races can afford to invest more in future prizes than previous non-winners.

Depken and Wilson (2004a) use data from the 1949–2001 NASCAR seasons to investigate the sabotage hypothesis and the cost hypothesis. Given data limitations, they are forced to test both hypotheses indirectly. They find that an increase in the concentration of season points leads to a less than proportional increase in season winnings, a condition that supports sabotage behavior but offers no conclusive proof. Their test of the cost hypothesis is whether an increased share of season points causes future dominance. Results are mixed and inconclusive. Clearly there is still work to do to understand the incentive effects of the complex system of rewards in racing, especially in light of the major change in the scoring system in 2004. I return to the subject of efficient contest design in auto racing later in the chapter.

In sum, the empirical literature that investigates the ROT incentive hypothesis should be considered a work in progress. Although several papers find empirical support indicating that athletes respond to nonlinear reward incentives, and that there may be circumstances where this decreases rather than increases efficiency, there is still a lot that is not well understood. In the final section of the chapter, I discuss the gaps in the current literature and their relationship to the broader fields of incentive-based pay, contest design, and gender differences in response to incentives. In the section that follows, I turn to gender- and discrimination-based research in the context of individual sports.

Discrimination in Earnings and Gender-Based Research

The application of established theory related to discrimination and gender is another area in which the sports industry, individual sports in this case, can make a valuable contribution to the economics literature. As usual, the trump card is data. There is a relatively small body of existing work and more importantly substantial research opportunities wherein the availability of data allows for empirical testing that would be difficult or impossible elsewhere. In this section, I review the areas in which prior work exists.

At first blush, it might seem that there is not much to say in a section on discrimination in individual sports. Although there is a substantial racial discrimination literature in the team sports literature, no work has been done using individual sports. The reason is straightforward: athletes in individual sports earn their wages in a fashion that is so transparent and predetermined by finish order that wage discrimination is not only unlikely, it is probably not possible. Prize offerings are typically set in advance for each finish position. No organizer of a legitimate contest could alter the payment scheme *ex post* to reduce the wages of a less preferred group. Although it is possible to limit entry into the contest in the first place, economists have yet to investigate this issue as it relates to race. Gender discrimination also may seem an unlikely fit, given that men and women compete in separate events rather than against one another. There are, however, important exceptions and opportunities that exist.

Ray and Grimes (1993) take advantage of the fact that in thoroughbred racing, men and women compete against one another as equals to investigate whether female jockeys are subjected to gender discrimination in that industry. Using 1988 data, they find that after controlling for performance and experience characteristics, female jockeys have significantly fewer racing opportunities than men. They use a two-equation model in which they estimate the number of mounts (races) as a function of performance variables and a gender dummy, and purse winnings (as a proxy for income) as a function of mounts, performance variables, and gender. There are a number of interesting results.

They find that past performance, as measured by win, place, and show results, does not influence the number of mounts received by male jockeys, but is a significant determinant of mounts for female jockeys. Even more revealing is that the gender variable is significant and negative in the mounts equation, but significant and positive in the purse winnings equation. The first result indicates that, all else equal, women receive fewer opportunities than men. The second indicates that, all else equal, women have higher purse winnings than men. The authors estimate that women should earn about $285,000 more than they do based on their performance characteristics. Given that this appears to fly directly in the face of Becker's predicted outcome for discrimination in a competitive market, an interesting research question is whether the proportion of female jockeys has risen substantially from the 1988 level of 13 percent, and what changes in purse winnings result.

Shmanske (2000) considers whether differences in men's and women's PGA/LPGA are driven by discrimination or demand differences inherent in skill and length of match differences. He estimates the winnings per tournament for men and women using five different skills: driving distance, driving accuracy, greens in regulation, sand bunker shots, and putting. He then uses the results to perform an Oaxaca decomposition to determine the source of the difference in earnings.[2] His results indicate that women actually receive greater returns to overall skill than do men. Thus, he concludes women do not face discrimination in earnings.

It is interesting to note that, in conclusion, Shmanske notes that technically, women are allowed to play in PGA Tour events, but would likely take a pay cut if they attempted to do so. By now we know that since the publication of his paper, Annika Sorenstam did play in a men's tour event (as have a few other women). Despite being the most dominant women's player in recent history, she did not make the cut. However, there simply are not enough data points to test the implications of women playing with men on the tour. That said, a few anecdotal observations are worth mentioning. First, although it is probably attributable to a novelty affect, fan interest in the tournament in which she competed was very keen. Second, Sorenstam's appearance was met with a wide variety of responses from the men on the PGA Tour. While some welcomed her as an equal, others (notably Vijay Singh, who was very outspoken) were highly critical before, during, and after the event, which should be considered a form of employee discrimination. If women continue to play in men's events, it may be possible to test for the presence of employee discrimination and measure the magnitude.

There have been a few papers that investigate the differences in response to incentive effects across gender in individual sports. Here, economists have just begun to test a theory that has received significant attention in the psychology literature. In an important paper, Gneezy, Niederle, and Rustichini (2003) note that although earnings gaps and occupational distribution differences have in the past been attributed to self-selection or discrimination, a third explanation is possible: there is an inherent difference in the way that men and women respond to competitive incentives. They use a series of controlled experiments in which "workers" solve a series of computerized mazes. They find that when payoff for each player is independent of the performance of others, men and women perform equally. However, when the payoff system is changed to a winner-take-all format, the performance of men increases, but women perform the same. If this result holds broadly, then the efficacy of ROT-style compensation schemes in women's tournaments must be called into question. It may be that although nonlinear rewards create the best tournament for men, some alternative scheme could elicit the best performances from women. Such a finding would be especially significant given that women have fought hard to gain equal prize distributions in sports such as tennis.

There are two empirical papers that might shed light on this hypothesis. In what might be considered a preliminary investigation, Coate and Robbins (2001) consider labor force attachment of men's and women's professional tennis players. They find that although they compete for lower prizes than men, women on average compete for as many years and with the same intensity (as measured by the number of tournaments per year) as men.

A more direct test of the hypothesis of inherent differences is found in Maloney and McCormick's (2000) previously discussed paper on competitive running. To capture potential gender effects in their model, they estimate elasticities for men and women separately. They find that while the elasticity of supply based on average prize is larger for women than men (what they call the participation effect), the individual prize spread elasticities are larger for men than women. This latter result supports the hypothesis of inherent differences suggested by Gneezy, Niederle, and Rustichini (2003). Given that so little empirical work exists in an area with clear policy implications, this is clearly a fruitful avenue for further research in terms of optimal contest design. Such research should begin with further attempts to find empirical evidence in the existing data.

Finally, Rishe (2001) takes advantage of the fact that professional golf also maintains a Seniors Tour and tests for the existence of age discrimination. In 1999, average PGA Tour player earnings were 60 percent greater than average Senior Tour player earnings. PGA players appear to be more skilled in crucial areas such as driving distance and accuracy, sand saves, and putting, though as Rishe notes, these could be course effects, contest design effects (there is no cut in the Senior Tour), actual skill differences, or a combination of the three. Rishe uses an Oaxaca decomposition similar to that employed by Shmanske (2000) and finds that earnings are entirely attributable to differential rates of return to skill rather than differences in skill. As he points out, however, this does not imply that the difference is age discrimination. It only shows that the difference *could be* age discrimination. He offers other explanations that seem equally plausible, most notably differences in fan demand created by differences in quality of play, prize magnitudes, and risk preferences. Thus, while Rishe takes an important first step, clearly there is no final answer here.

The Tennis Industry

Four papers by Franc J.G.M. Klaassen and Jan R. Magnus (Klaassen and Magnus, 2001; Magnus and Klaassen 1996, 1999, 2001) investigate a series of commonly held beliefs regarding performance in professional tennis. In the two most recent papers, they develop and test a model designed to ascertain the probability that a given player will win a match, both before the match begins and also once it is in progress. This effort is novel in that, as they say, it is seldom shown and "is the one that viewers want to know above all" (Klaassen and Magnus, 2001: 2). Even if a viewer would rather not know, surely the population of bettors would not only like to know, but would even pay for information. Klaassen and Magnus first establish that each point in a tennis match is not independent of every other point in a match (the probability that a player wins a given point is positively correlated to the outcome of the previous point), but that the relationship is so weak that to assume so is reasonable (2001). They then use this assumption to build their forecasting model, which resides in their program TENNISPROB, which is described in Klaassen and Magnus (2001). Although these papers are much more of a statistical and econometric exercise than an application of theory, the results are interesting in that, in addition to the obvious odds-making application, they could be applied a priori at the application point of a tournament by contest organizers to generate the most evenly competitive field.

Magnus and Klaassen (1996, 1999) test a wide variety of hypotheses that might be taken as stylized facts using data from Wimbledon. The first paper tests seventeen separate hypotheses and finds mixed support. The second investigates the probability of a given player winning the final set of a match. Here they look specifically at the "final" set in a Wimbledon match and test five hypotheses regarding the probability of winning under various circumstances, such as whether the winner of the previous set has an advantage.

Sahota and Sahota (1984) use tennis to develop a model of investment in human physical capital. In contrast to most research on individual sports, they are concerned with player development rather than the performance of polished professionals. They use survey data from nationally ranked players between nine and nineteen years of age from three USTA regional sections to construct a model of parent utility, which includes investments in their children's brains, brawn, and wealth. Although the authors' assumptions are at times questionable (e.g., they use math SAT scores as one of their measures of how well a player might hit a fast-moving ball), and the estimated models have few significant coefficients, their paper poses questions well worth answering. The resources that are required to develop professional athletes in any sport are extraordinary. As the authors point out, there are a number of types of human capital that parents might hope to develop in their children, and resource constraints demand choices. Further investigation into the combination of innate physical ability and investment in training that is likely to produce a successful professional athlete would likely be challenging, but worthwhile.

The Golf Industry

Any study of recreational or professional golf as an industry should begin with Stephen Shmanske's *Golfonomics* (2004). This book, which is a combination of the author's new and previously published research, is divided into two main parts. The first part covers the recreational golf course industry, wherein he considers questions of course location, cart use, course maintenance, and others. Of particular interest in this section is chapter 5, which is based on Shmanske (2001). In this chapter, Shmanske reviews the multifaceted and complex nature of price discrimination at public access golf courses. Discounts from full retail price can include weekday/weekend differentials, senior discounts, resident discounts, junior discounts, twilight discounts, and more. Through a two-consumer model of demand, he demonstrates the welfare effects of second and third degree price discrimination, multi-part pricing schemes, profit-maximizing behavior, and nonprofit models of municipal course management. The results of the empirical model show, as we would expect, that greater variability in prices increases profits. Price discrimination (particularly second degree) increases revenues for profit-maximizing courses yet is harmful to nonprofit courses wherein discounts will transfer more surplus to consumers than a monopolist would. As such, it stands as a solid empirical confirmation of theory. Similar work might be possible with public- or quasi-public-use tennis facilities or bowling alleys. Perhaps even more fruitful would be a pricing study in the recreational skiing industry, wherein price discrimination is at least as complex as golf (prices vary by day of week, holiday/non-holiday, age such as senior rates, and season pass/ day rate). In cases where season passes or one-time fees are an option for consumers, and excludability is possible, further work in this area should also include consideration of the theory of clubs, as in Mulligan (2001).

The second part of the book covers the economics of professional golf, beginning with a description and overview of how professional golf is organized. Of particular note in this section is chapter 10, in which Shmanske develops an empirical model to estimate the marginal productivity of practice. Future research on human physical capital investment of the type suggested by Sahota and Sahota (1984) should attempt to formalize the marginal productivity of practice as is done here.

Future Research: Where Do We Go from Here?

There are a variety of potentially productive avenues for future research in the economics of individual sports. Throughout the chapter several specific areas of need have been mentioned. Here, the focus shifts to larger issues for the research agenda. Stated most broadly, they are: Optimal contest design; the role of sponsorship in athlete incentives; human capital investment in quasi-amateur contests such as Olympic competition; and gender and discrimination issues.

Optimal Contest Design

As Scully (2002: 240) notes, "the specific prize structure in golf has been around for a long time . . . [yet] . . . one cannot assert on theoretical or empirical grounds that it is optimal." Most empirical tests of tournament theory discussed in this chapter find that highly nonlinear pay schemes increase performance by just 2–3 percent. Could performance be improved more with award structures skewed even more toward the winner, such as winner-take-all? A winner-take-all contest could increase the effort of all participants, improving the overall quality of the contest from a fan perspective. It could increase giving-up behavior, especially among weaker competitors, which would decrease the quality of the contest. It would also create incentives for unscrupulous behavior, as suggested by Lazear (1989).

There is an existing literature on contest design, thoroughly reviewed in this volume by Szymanski. In the context of individual sports, contest organizers want to stage events such that they maximize profits, which is the difference between gate, television, and ancillary revenues and expenses, most notably prize offerings. The prize structure of the contest is critical because it affects both the enrollment of quality contestants as well as the behavior of those contestants once enrolled.[3] Contestants expend effort to win prizes such that they maximize the expected utility of participating.

To date, little if any attention has focused on the optimal number of competitors. For example, how did NASCAR decide on the number of cars in a race? Similarly, whereas the PGA Tour reduces the field by half after two rounds, the Senior Tour does not. It is unlikely that much empirical testing lies behind these decisions. We should be on the lookout for rule changes, differences across leagues, and changes in league structure that might represent natural experiments and so provide an empirical window into these questions.

With respect to contestant effort, Szymanski (2003a) describes these possible outcomes in the context of contest literature originally conceived for auctions. Depending on the symmetry of ability and the nature of the contest (simultaneous play as in a stroke play golf tournament or serially as in a repeated match play), optimal prizes range from equal payouts for all finishers to winner-take-all. When contestants are not all of equal ability, as is typically the case, even in professional events, Szymanski notes that "in an asymmetric contest the organizer must decide the appropriate objective. . . . Providing greater incentive for winning effort may reduce the effort of weaker contestants and so reduce average effort" (Szymanski, 2003b: 1143). Nalebuff and Stiglitz (1983) make a similar point when they argue that while increasing the size of the tournament (e.g., having more competitors) can improve incentives and reduce risk, it can also increase the chances that some players will in effect break the contract by supplying no effort. Thus, an important theme that runs through the theoretical literature that has not received the attention it deserves in empirical work to date is that the nature of the prize structure can significantly affect the outcome. The real challenge here may be finding examples of tournaments with wide variation in prize distribution.

Maloney and Terkun (2002) provide an important empirical contribution to the otherwise theoretical literature. They focus on the contest organizer rather than the contestant and show that contest organizers must be cognizant of competing races, and as a result there is substantial variation in the level and spread of the prizes. Some winnings distributions are quite steep while others are much flatter. They find that as the expected prize of a race increases, so does the spread of the prize distribution. For races with lower expected prizes to attract riders, they must deepen the prize pool. Given that many individual sports have competing tours, such as the European counterparts to U.S. tours, it seems that similar analysis may be both possible and revealing.

Sponsorship

None of the existing literature on incentive-based performance includes sponsorship income. The reason is simple—sponsor payments are not generally public information. Yet, unless we stray from the long-standing assumption of declining marginal utility of income, we must acknowledge that our explanations of athlete behavior are incomplete. From a contest design standpoint, this issue may be irrelevant. Given a fixed prize structure, athletes will either try or not. However, it may be erroneous to assume that lack of effort in a given contest is a function of an athlete's ability relative to that of fellow contestants. For an athlete who earns even $10 million per year in sponsorship income (some earn much more), the marginal prize may be very small as a percentage of his or her income no matter how large it is relative to the size of the total prize pool for that event. It may be possible given anecdotal information on sponsor payments to specific athletes to rethink the utility-maximizing model inherent in tournament theory such that the focus is on the value of the marginal prize available to the athlete rather than the value of the prize in absolute terms. Even more valuable (and harder to get) would be time-series data on changes in sponsorship income with changes in performance—a sort of long income function.

Human Capital Investment

As Sahota and Sahota (1984) indicate, the investment in physical human capital required to achieve high-level success in individual sports is extraordinary. Yet, very little is known about the time profile of this investment (must one start hitting range balls at age six?), the financial cost, or the success rates. We have some information about success rates of elite college athletes attempting to transition to professional careers in team sports (it is very low on a percentage basis). We know much less about individuals. Appealing to data on college players may provide some answers here, but such a picture would be incomplete at best. This is especially true given that educational training and athletic training are likely substitutes rather than complements (as in professional baseball).

Gender

Finally, given the work of Gneezy, Niederle, and Rustichini (2003), it seems clear that there is more to learn about gender effects in incentive tournaments. If men and women do not respond equally when confronted with highly competitive environments, then their contests should be designed differently. Such a conclusion would represent a departure (unwelcome?) from the historical push to equalize prize distributions in major tournaments.

Conclusions

Research on individual sports to date focuses primarily on worker response to incentives. The pioneering theoretical work of Lazear and Rosen, combined with the empirical work of Ehrenberg and Bognanno on professional golf, set the stage for additional work in other sports such as foot racing and auto racing. That workers (or male workers at least) respond to nonlinear pay incentives seems well established. Much less work has been done on optimal contest design as it relates to either competitor effort or profit maximization by organizers. Evidence suggests that men and women do not respond equally to incentives in tournaments. Existing evidence indicates that women perform better when prizes are independent of one another, whereas men increase their performance in response to incentives. Further investigation of differences in incentive effects is certainly warranted. Contest organizers may want to discuss with athletes the possibility that although politically difficult, varying the reward scheme by gender may be a good idea.

Although there has been substantial work on the industrial organization aspects of golf, there is no parallel body of work on other major individual sports. In fact, the professional literature is nearly a vacuum in this regard. Given that recreational-level individual sports (golf, tennis, bowling, skiing) are very substantial industries, more research is needed. Just as tournament theory literature uses sports as a vehicle to test theories that may have much broader appeal, the industrial organization literature can benefit from more work similar to that of Shmanske that uses data from other sports industries. Finally, very little attention has been paid to contest design. Although ROT theory seems to hold in those sports in which it has been tested, the focus has almost always been on the competitor rather than the contest organizer. In this regard, we should consider the benefits that might be available from international comparisons in which contest design varies by organization, and from natural experiments in the form of organizational changes.

Notes

1. Ehrenberg and Bognanno (1990a, 1990b) employ an instrumental variables approach correct for simultaneity bias.

2. For a description of this method, see Oaxaca (1973a). The Oaxaca decomposition is commonly used in labor discrimination models in attempt to partial out the sources of wage differentials.

3. Recent theoretical contributions include the work of Fullerton and McAfee (1999), Moldovanu and Sela (2001), Szymanski and Valletti (2004), and Baye, Kovenock, and de Vries (1994, 1996).

The National Football League Conundrum

John Fizel

Studies of professional sports focus primarily on individual player performance in the context of compensation models, production or cost functions, managerial efficiency, or age-performance profiles. Yet, it is the focus on individual player performance that results in a dearth of research on the National Football League (NFL). Individual player performance is straightforward to measure in individual sports such as tennis and golf, and in a team sport such as Major League Baseball where the major confrontation is between an individual pitcher and individual batter. Individual performance metrics have also worked well in analyzing player output in the National Basketball Association. However, any individual player's performance in the NFL is highly dependent on the performance of teammates. Consider a running back's twenty-yard gallop for a touchdown. How much of the success of this play is directly attributable to the skills and tenacity of the running back? What was the role of the offensive line in blocking on the run? Did the particular pass route run by the receiver effectively fake a defensive player out of position? Or, consider the sack of the quarterback by the defensive end. How much of this play is directly attributable to the skills and tenacity of the defensive end? Was the defensive tackle able to prompt a double team by the offensive line that opened the path for the sack? Did the linebacker mow down the running back and eliminate the possibility of an outlet pass? Did the defensive backs have great coverage on the receivers, requiring the quarterback to take extra time before releasing the pass? The National Hockey League (NHL) also has significant joint production in player performance, but the development and use of the plus/minus ratio significantly addresses the player interdependence issue (see Chapter 4 for more on this measure). Moreover, the joint production aspects of NFL plays are much more difficult to disentangle. No measures similar to the plus/minus ratio of the NHL have been created for player performance in the NFL and consequently studies of compensation, production, costs, managerial efficiency, and age-performance profiles are rare for this sport. This is the NFL conundrum!

The objective of this book is to provide surveys of the literature and suggest future research possibilities in given sports. Although the limited scope of NFL research may not warrant a survey chapter, endless research opportunities exist for analysts who creatively address the joint production issues of the NFL or who may gain access to data that NFL teams develop in doing individual player performance assessments. Aspects of team production, efficiency, and costs as well as market structure and institutional issues also warrant attention.

Part III

Issues Across the Sports Industry

9

Demand Issues

The Product Market for Professional Sports

Anthony Krautmann and Lawrence Hadley

The law of demand states that quantity demanded is an inverse function of price. As a pure abstract theory, it is one of the few laws in economics that could be described as universal. But its application and empirical testing in particular industries involves many interesting complications and subtleties. The demand for professional sports provides an excellent case.

Defining Output

What is the product that professional sports teams sell? Although not particularly obvious, the most likely candidates include attendance (quantity of tickets sold) or the team's win percent (quality of the product sold).

In general, firms often compete on the basis of both the quantity as well as the quality of their product. The rules of a sports league establish the number of regular season games, and the seating capacity of the stadium is a long-run-decision. Therefore, the primary short-run decision that a team makes regarding its product is the level of talent embodied in the players so as to create a targeted level of team quality. Fans reveal their willingness to pay by their consumption decision to attend the sporting event, and this decision is affected by the level of quality (winning) embedded in the team. Most demand studies define attendance as the dependent variable and use the team's winning percentage as a shift parameter to control for variations in quality. In other words, fans get utility from quality, which leads to ticket sales and ultimately to revenues.

While a team derives a significant portion of its revenues from ticket sales, it is certainly not the only source. For most sports teams, broadcast revenues constitute an important additional source of revenues. According to the Blue Ribbon Panel (Major League Baseball, 2000), local broadcasting revenues in Major League Baseball (MLB) were identified as one of the primary sources of revenue disparities across teams. So the demand for broadcasts may also be viewed as an additional demand for the product. Since fans value quality, an important issue is the degree to which winning affects a team's broadcast revenues. But most broadcast contracts are long-term and are negotiated before a team's quality is known, thus the link between broadcast revenues and winning is weak at best. Furthermore, although a team's performance over several years may play a role in the final terms of the contract, broadcasting revenues in MLB are much more correlated with the size of the local market than the performance of the team.[1]

In summary, most empirical demand studies define the dependent variable in terms of attendance. The focus is on the short run, so either game-by-game attendance or season attendance is the particular metric of choice. The long-run impact of a new stadium (with the resulting change in seating capacity) on attendance is typically treated as a shift factor, which is controlled by the introduction of binary variables.

Defining Price

Defining and calibrating the price of the product also involves difficult issues. The analyst typically faces a vast array of possible prices from which to choose, ranging from the cheapest seats in remote locations within the park to the luxury boxes that accommodate the high-income fans. As such, analysts are forced to collapse the many prices down into one proxy for price by using one of the following alternatives.

The most common approach is to create a weighted-average (WA) price, where the weights are determined by the proportion of seats in each price category in the stadium (Demmert, 1973; Noll, 1974; Coffin, 1996; Team Marketing, 1991–96). But this definition will underestimate the typical consumer's marginal expenditure because it assigns too little weight to the price of the expensive seats (which are typically sold out), while putting too much weight on the cheap seats (which often go unsold). With current data, we cannot know how many of each type of seats were purchased. Also, there is no way to capture information on discounted prices associated with the preseason sale of season tickets, or on discounts for bulk sales, special groups, or particular games. Thus, using WA to capture a multitiered pricing structure may be flawed to the extent that it does not reflect the prices consumers actually paid.

As an alternative, some analysts have measured price as the team's average revenue (AR), defined as ticket revenues divided by attendance (Siegfried and Eisenberg, 1980; Scully, 1989b). But given the complicated relationship between the multitude of prices and the metric AR, this definition may create difficulties as well. As explained by Coffin (1996), using AR may generate a spurious negative correlation between attendance and price simply because the high-priced seats are typically the first to be sold out. When attendance is high, only the lower-priced seats are available to the marginal fans.

A final alternative is the selection of one of the many prices charged by the team in an attempt to proxy the consumer's marginal expenditure of an available seat (Bird, 1982; García and Rodrígues, 2002; Poitras and Hadley, 2005). Using a common-seat (CS) price assumes that this particular chosen price is the one that a consumer faces for the marginal seat available on game day. What is unclear, however, is whether this definition captures the effect of price on attendance across the entire stadium or just attendance in those seats in that particular price category.

In Table 9.1, we present a sample of these three types of prices for the 1991 through 1996 seasons in MLB. For a weighted-average price, we use the Team Marketing price used in the construction of their Fan Cost Index. For an average-revenue price, we use the gate revenues reported by *Financial World*, and divide it by home attendance.[2] Finally, we use the published price in the Red and Green Books for an "upper deck, reserve seat in foul territory" for a common-seat price. Whereas both the weighted-average and average-revenue prices are highly correlated (this correlation coefficient is over 0.8), the common-seat price is much less correlated with the other two prices (these correlation coefficients are less than 0.4).

Although the appeal of using the sports industry to test economic theory is in the breadth and availability of data, it is ironic that the dilemma of choosing a good proxy for price may never be fully resolved. With multi-tiered prices, it may not be possible to sufficiently proxy price with a single value. Unless teams begin to disclose attendance data within each price category, or begin charging just one general admission price, this errors-in-variable problem will always create doubt regarding any inferences derived from empirical estimates of the demand function.[3]

Inelastic Pricing

Profit maximization dictates that a firm with monopoly power sets its price in the elastic range of demand. Yet a survey of the literature reveals little empirical support for this behavior (Noll, 1974; Siegfried and Eisenberg, 1980; Bird, 1982; Fort and Quirk, 1995; Poitras and Hadley, 2003). Since point estimates overwhelmingly indicate that teams price in the inelastic range

Table 9.1

Different Definitions of Real Price of MLB Seats, 1991–93

Team	1991			1992			1993		
	WA	AR	CS	WA	AR	CS	WA	AR	CS
Baltimore	10.77	9.44	9.51	11.93	10.54	9.84	13.26	11.62	9.56
Boston	14.32	12.13	12.67	14.39	13.30	12.30	13.98	13.23	11.95
Anaheim	11.15	9.95	8.87	9.84	9.98	8.61	9.56	9.92	8.36
Chicago Sox	13.05	11.90	10.14	14.39	12.99	9.84	13.98	13.01	9.56
Cleveland	9.13	11.47	5.70	9.47	11.70	6.15	10.39	10.30	7.17
Detroit	11.41	12.06	8.87	11.07	12.47	8.61	11.23	11.46	8.36
KC Royals	10.52	9.92	8.87	11.32	11.51	9.84	10.99	11.33	9.56
Milwaukee	11.41	12.16	8.87	11.44	10.12	8.61	11.71	12.02	8.36
Minneapolis	10.01	10.07	11.41	10.95	10.66	12.30	10.99	10.96	11.95
NY Yankees	13.31	13.22	10.77	15.13	14.90	11.69	16.01	14.86	12.54
Oakland	15.97	12.02	8.87	12.30	11.86	8.61	12.54	12.24	8.36
Seattle	8.87	9.14	5.70	9.84	10.66	5.54	9.56	9.91	6.57

Texas	10.65	10.47	7.60	10.95	11.01	8.61	10.63	10.67	8.36
Toronto	16.60	14.10	5.07	15.87	13.55	4.92	16.37	14.07	5.97
Atlanta	9.13	9.12	7.60	10.33	9.78	9.84	11.71	10.90	10.75
Chicago Cubs	12.80	12.51	7.60	13.41	13.34	7.38	13.86	13.66	7.17
Cincinnati	11.41	9.14	7.60	8.86	8.43	7.38	9.56	9.17	7.77
Houston	11.53	11.20	7.60	10.21	10.17	7.38	9.92	11.32	7.17
LA Dodgers	10.27	10.06	6.34	11.32	10.86	7.38	10.99	11.27	7.17
Montreal	11.66	14.58	6.97	10.70	10.31	6.77	10.27	10.34	6.57
NY Mets	13.05	12.73	8.24	13.41	13.13	8.00	13.02	12.97	7.77
Philadelphia	11.03	9.40	8.24	10.09	9.69	8.00	9.80	9.36	8.36
Pittsburgh	9.89	9.92	8.24	11.32	11.09	9.84	11.59	10.43	9.56
St. Louis	10.52	10.29	6.34	11.19	10.67	6.77	10.87	10.52	6.57
San Diego	10.77	10.98	6.34	10.46	10.58	8.61	10.39	12.21	8.36
San Francisco	12.29	11.29	10.14	11.07	10.88	10.15	11.11	10.80	8.06
AVERAGE	11.60	11.13	8.24	11.59	11.31	8.58	11.70	11.48	8.54

Sources: Team Marketing.

Note: WA = weighted-average price, obtained from Team Marketing; AR = average-revenue price, defined as gate revenues divided by attendance; CS = common-seat price, defined as the price of an upper deck, reserve seat in foul territory. All prices are in constant 2000 dollars.

of demand, this suggests that we either reexamine the basic objective of team owners or find an alternative explanation for such behavior.

With regard to the objective function of teams, some analysts have focused on the utility that owners receive from controlling a sports team. This approach, termed the "sportsman hypothesis," suggests that the objective of a team owner is to maximize utility rather than profits (DeGennaro, 2003; Ferguson, et al., 1991; Sloane, 1971). Although this hypothesis has received very little empirical attention in the sports economics literature, it could help explain why we find prices in the inelastic range of demand. When looked at more closely, however, such an explanation is not completely satisfying. If owners maximize utility instead of profits, then their pricing decision should be independent of the elasticity. But rather than finding evidence of *both* elastic and inelastic pricing, the literature is unanimous in its finding that teams price in the inelastic range of demand.

Some analysts have proposed that this result is not a violation of profit maximization, but rather a misspecification of the null hypothesis. This argument is that once the season begins, the marginal costs of admitting another fan is essentially zero. In this case, profit maximization coincides with revenue maximization; hence the proper null to be tested is whether teams price at the unit elastic point. Indeed it is the case that most of these empirical studies cannot reject unit-elastic pricing.

Aside from papers that focus on the team's objective, researchers have also developed a number of behavioral models that can generate inelastic prices. One such model focuses on arrangements between local politicians and team owners (Fort, 2004a). According to this argument, owners lower prices into the inelastic range in exchange for special political considerations (especially on the issue of public funding of stadiums). Others have looked at demand from the perspective of habitual consumption (Ahn and Lee, 2003; Quinn and Surdam, 2004). The general idea here is that fan loyalty creates "addictive" or habitual behavior, leading to a dynamic model specification of demand. Maximizing long-run profits leads to first-order conditions that allow marginal revenue to be set below marginal cost, a necessary condition for inelastic prices.

Finally, a recent series of papers have appeared that attempt to explain inelastic ticket pricing by recognizing the importance of other revenue sources. Fort (2004b) argues that teams choose talent to produce wins, which are then sold at the gate *and on television.* Under these conditions, he derives first-order conditions that allow for inelastic prices at the gate. Krautmann and Berri (2004), on the other hand, propose a model that ties gate attendance to concessionary sales. Lowering prices into the inelastic range allows the team to maximize profits by trading off lower gate revenues for additional concessionary revenues.

Figure 9.1   **Upward-Sloping Demand Due to Misspecification**

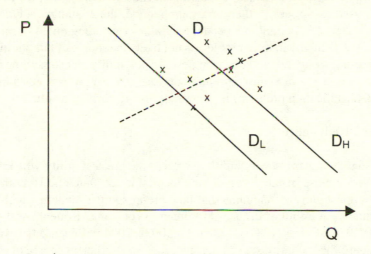

On the whole, the issue of inelastic pricing leads us to one of the following conclusions: owners are irrational; owners are rational, but not profit maximizers; or, owners are profit maximizers, but in a more complicated manner that considers factors other than just ticket prices. All three alternatives have a certain degree of appeal associated with them, backed up by varying degrees of empirical evidence. This topic continues to receive a large share of attention in the literature, and has not been resolved at this time.

Upward-Sloping Demand Curves

The law of demand states that quantity demanded is inversely related to price. Yet a number of empirical studies of demand yield estimates that conclude that attendance is positively related to price. Fort (2003) suggests that this disturbing result is likely a result of a misspecified model. He argues that an estimated demand curve that slopes upward can arise from improperly controlling for shifts in the demand curve or from prices not being appropriately deflated for inflation. To illustrate Fort's argument, consider two demand curves corresponding to a low (D_L) and high (D_H) level of quality. In Figure 9.1 we illustrate how data arising from these two demand curves may yield an estimated demand curve that appears upward sloping. If the analyst fails to control for quality, then fitting a line to the data will yield an upward-sloping demand curve, D. Clearly, this anomaly is the result of an omitted-variables bias.

Although Fort's explanation would result in biased estimates, its ability to explain the upward-sloping demand curve is rather limited—at least as it applies to most of the models appearing in the literature. First, all of the studies used real prices in their analysis. Second, these studies included a large number of important independent variables (including quality), meaning that the omitted-variables problem is not likely the source of this anomaly. As the result, we are left with the troublesome possibility that something else (perhaps the errors-in-variable problem discussed above, or perhaps a more serious identification problem) is generating this disturbing result.

Competitive Balance

Fans want their team to win, but they receive the greatest utility when their team wins a close match. Termed the Uncertainty of Outcome Hypothesis (UOH), this argument maintains that fans prefer sports events in which the final outcome is exciting because of its uncertain outcome (Rottenberg, 1956; Sloane, 1976a; Cairns, 1987; Szymanski, 2003b, 2004a). Because fans value uncertainty, the league must promote and preserve a sufficient degree of competitive balance throughout the league. The literature relating attendance to competitive balance has looked at the UOH from two levels of aggregation: how game-by-game attendance is affected by the closeness of the two opponents, and how league balance affects aggregate league attendance.

The demand literature that estimates game-by-game attendance models is relevant to the competitive balance issue because the quality of the opponents can be easily measured. If the UOH is correct, then attendance should be influenced by the quality of the visiting team relative to that of the home team. In this regard, fans want the home team to win, but they also prefer that the home team beat a quality opponent.

Bruggink and Eaton (1996) estimated a game-by-game attendance model, using Games Behind (GB) the division leader to calibrate the quality of both the home and visiting teams. Consistent with the UOH, they found that GB has a significantly negative impact on attendance, although the implied elasticities were very small—in fact, their imputed elasticity of attendance with respect to GB was less than –0.02.

Rascher (1999) also estimated a game-by-game attendance model, but focused on winning percent (WP) as the measure of quality. Specifically, he argued that fans care about the quality of the home team (measured by the home team's WP), the quality of the visiting team (measured by the visitor's WP), as well as the *ex ante* closeness of the contest (measured by the square of the difference in the two teams' WP). Using data for all MLB games played in 1996, he found that the coefficients on the home team's WP and on the visitor's WP were both significantly positive, while the coefficient on the difference between win percents was significantly negative. This study suggests that fans are sensitive to the quality of both the home and visiting team, and that they value close contests.

Butler (2002) estimated a semi-logarithmic model similar to the Bruggink and Eaton model, except he focused on just inter-league play. In his game-by-game attendance model, Butler used GB for both home and visiting teams. Although the coefficients on GB were negative for both teams (indicating that fans support teams in contention), only the home team's GB was statistically significant.

Rather than focus on the UOH on a game-by-game basis, a number of studies have looked at the impact of competitive balance on demand across the entire league. In the sports economics literature, we find two very different concepts of competitive balance across the league as a whole. The first is intra-seasonal balance; that is, the amount of dispersion in performance (for example, winning percent) across all teams within each season. For any given season, a greater dispersion of team success will result in a greater number of mismatches between contending and non-contending teams. The second concept is inter-seasonal balance, which focuses on how teams perform across many seasons (especially in regard to the turnover rate of playoff-bound teams). The lower the turnover rate, the greater the number of fans who believe that their team has no chance to make the playoffs in the foreseeable future. Without any legitimate hope of their teams making it to the playoffs, fans lose interest in the game and league attendance suffers.

Many of the studies on competitive balance have focused on how intra-seasonal balance affects league demand (Noll, 1974; Bruggink and Eaton, 1996; Coffin, 1996). Although researchers usually find that league attendance is negatively related to this type of balance, these results may be questioned given the failure to control for inter-seasonal balance. Humphreys (2002) included a variable that simultaneously captures both intra- and inter-seasonal balance, and he finds that attendance falls with either type of imbalance. A recent paper by Krautmann and Hadley (2004) included separate measures for inter-seasonal and intra-seasonal balance. Although they found that only inter-seasonal balance was significant, its impact was quite low. They estimate that improving inter-seasonal balance by one standard error increased attendance by less than one percent.

Related to the issue of inter-seasonal balance is the growing body of literature dealing with the competitive advantage of large-market teams over their small-market counterparts. For the most part, this view is ultimately concerned with the externality associated with the free-market allocation of talent across teams from differing market sizes. If market forces tend to agglomerate talent in the large-market teams, then inter-seasonal balance will suffer.

Studies dealing with the effect of market size on the demand for talent suggest that large-market teams have a significant advantage over small-market teams.[4] For example, Burger and Walters (2003b) found that the marginal value of a player in New York City (the largest market) is almost six times larger than in Milwaukee (the smallest). Solow and Krautmann (2004) and Gustafson and Hadley (2004) came to similar conclusions, although these estimates imply a smaller advantage for large-market teams. The implication of these studies is that the league has an incentive to override the free market allocation of talent by pursuing policies that redistribute revenues to small-market teams.

New Stadiums, Public Money, and Demand

It is well documented in the sports economics literature that playing in a newly constructed home stadium has a strong impact on attendance. This effect can be traced back to Demmert (1973) and Noll (1974), or more recently to Coffin (1996), Bruggink and Eaton (1996), Rascher (1999), Poitras and Hadley (2005), Leeds (2004), and Solow and Krautmann (2004). These studies all document a significant, positive relationship between attendance levels and a new stadium. Across the literature, this is an effect that is unanimously documented.

There are, however, two related issues that are disputed. First, does a new stadium generate extra revenues sufficient to pay for the costs of construction? Several papers have answered this question in the negative (Coffin, 1996; Leeds, 2004). But these papers do not model any revenue effects beyond the stadium's first few birthdays. Poitras and Hadley (2005), on the other hand, developed a dynamic model that allows for revenue effects over the life of the stadium. The point here is that a new stadium is forever preferred to an old stadium simply because there will always be thirty to forty years' difference in the vintages of the two stadiums. In contrast to other studies, Poitras and Hadley find that newly constructed stadiums can generate sufficient additional revenues to pay for themselves without public subsidies. The normative conclusion reached here is that new stadiums should be financed privately by the MLB teams involved.

Regardless, the majority of new stadiums are financed with taxpayers' money. Is this justified? Perhaps the benefits accruing to the local economy generated by a new stadium are sufficient to justify the generous subsidies that governments typically bestow on team owners. Contract research, typically commissioned by MLB owners, often purports to find substantial economic benefits to a local economy from a new baseball stadium.[5] Not surprising, the assumptions made to generate these results are typically quite optimistic and/or biased in the direction of grossly exaggerating the economic impacts of a new stadium. The academic literature, on the other hand, typically concludes that net benefits to the local economy are negligible. Although it is easy to document the increased revenues going to local businesses, most of this spending comes from local residents. As such, other entertainment spending is likely to be substituted in place of those generated by the presence of a MLB team (Baade, 2000; Baade and Sanderson, 1997; Siegfried and Zimbalist, 2000).

A professional sports franchise is a local monopoly (or at best, a duopoly) that uses its market power to extract rents from both fans as well as local taxpayers. Extracting rents from taxpayers is typically achieved by threatening to leave if local taxpayers reject its demands for subsidizing a new stadium. The reality is that empirical estimates of demand suggest that the benefits accruing to owners from playing in a new stadium may be more than sufficient to privately finance the construction. Yet the political backlash from losing an endearing franchise, especially if there are no acceptable replacements, precludes most local politicians from allowing this to happen.

A Simple Demand Function

To illustrate a number of the issues discussed above, we estimated two different model specifications of the demand function in MLB. The simplest is the linear function, given by:

$$Q_t^D = \alpha + \beta_1 \, POP_t + \beta_2 \, INC_t + \beta_3 \, WP_t + \beta_4 \, WP_{t-1} +$$

$$\beta_5 \, AGE_t + \beta_6 \, AGE_t^2 + \beta_7 \, P_t + \sum_{i=1}^{5} \delta_i \, D_{it} + \varepsilon_t, \qquad (9.1)$$

where Q_t^D is regular-season attendance, POP_t is metropolitan population (in thousands), INC_t is real metropolitan income per household, WP_t and WP_{t-1} are winning percentage in seasons t and $(t-1)$, AGE_t is the age of the stadium, P_t is one of the three real prices (WA, AR, or CS), and D_{it} are five different dummy variables for the 1991, 1992, 1993, 1995, and 1996 seasons.[6]

If large-market teams draw more fans, then we would expect $\beta_1 > 0$. If baseball attendance is a normal good, then we would expect $\beta_2 > 0$. If fans respond positively to their team's performance, then we would expect $\beta_3 > 0$ and $\beta_4 > 0$. If attendance falls with stadium age, but at a diminishing rate, then we would expect $\beta_5 < 0$ and $\beta_6 > 0$. If the law of demand holds, then we would expect $\beta_7 < 0$. Finally, since fewer games were played in 1994 (the year of the omitted dummy variable), we would expect the prior seasons (1991–93) to have greater attendance than 1994; hence, we would expect $\delta_1 > 0$, $\delta_2 > 0$ and $\delta_3 > 0$. The coefficients for the 1995 and 1996 dummy variables would reflect how quickly fans began returning to the game after the players' strike of 1994. As an alternative, we also considered a log-linear

Table 9.2

Descriptive Statistics for Demand Analysis

Variable	Mean	Standard error	Minimum	Maximum
Q^d	2,051,000.00	687,010.00	910,000.00	4,060,000.00
Real income	28,265	3,898	16,694	36,782
Metro population (1,000s)	6,489.8	5,260	1,709	19,876
Winning percent	501	66	327	694
Stadium age	28.94	21.67	1	85.0
Stadium age squared	1304	1999	1	7225
Weighted-average price	12.02	2.03	8.80	16.99
Average-revenue price	11.90	1.92	8.43	20.83
Common-seat price	8.63	2.00	4.92	15.40
D91	0.17	0.37	0	1
D92	0.17	0.37	0	1
D93	0.17	0.37	0	1
D95	0.17	0.37	0	1
D96	0.17	0.37	0	1

Note: Q= Number of tickets sold.

(that is, Cobb-Douglas) functional form for the demand function, given by:

$$\ln\left(Q_t^D\right) = \alpha + \beta_1 \ln(POP_t) + \beta_2 \ln(INC_t) + \beta_3 \ln(WP_t) +$$

$$\beta_4 \ln(WP_{t-1}) + \beta_5 \ln(AGE_t) + \beta_6 \ln(P_t) + \sum_{i=1}^{5} \delta_i D_{it} + \varepsilon_t , \qquad (9.2)$$

We used the 1991 through 1996 seasons to estimate equations (9.1) and (9.2). Table 9.2 presents the summary statistics of the variables. The OLS estimates of the linear demand function using all three specifications of price (WA, AR, and CS) are presented in Table 9.3. Table 9.4 reports the OLS estimates for the log-linear functional form. Except for the 1995 season (which also lost about 10 percent of its games), all the seasons had significantly greater attendance than the 1994 strike season. Consistent with the study by Schmidt and Berri (2003), we find that fans began returning to the game within a year after the 1994 strike. As noted by Poitras and Hadley (2005), attendance falls, but at a diminishing rate, as a stadium ages. Consistent with the large-market versus small-market literature, attendance rises with metropolitan population. Finally, real income was never significant in any model specification.

Tables 9.3 and 9.4 highlight the fact that the manner in which price is defined can have a dramatic effect on the robustness of the estimates. For example, note the estimated coefficients on the price variables. *Only when price is defined according to the common-seat criterion is the estimated co-*

Table 9.3

Linear Demand Function: OLS Estimates of Equation (9.1)

Variable	Coefficient	Coefficient	Coefficient
Constant	−437,381	−804,470	−1,107,800*
Real income	−1.47	11.75	−13.09
Metro population	26.97***	23.53***	16.28*
Winning percent	3,786.34***	3,942.3***	3,693.0***
Winning percent$_{t-1}$	2,232.30***	2,360.7***	1,526.1***
Stadium age $_{t-1}$	−40,384.8***	−39,063.4***	−23,877.7***
Stadium age squared	417.20***	407.25***	225.15**
Average-revenue price	**−33,764.2**	—	—
Common-seat price	—	**−64,444.1*****	—
Weighted-average price	—	—	**66,659.3****
D91	503,305***	479,250***	611,423***
D92	453,098***	456,769***	552,569***
D93	705,849***	710,529***	777,953***
D95	59,145	71,551	64,221
D96	448,999***	463,810***	399,391***
R^2	0.52	0.54	0.53
Number of observations	156	156	156

*** Significant at 1% level
 ** Significant at 5% level
  * Significant at 10% level (one-tailed test)

Table 9.4

Log-Linear Demand Function: OLS Estimates of Equation (9.2)

Variable	Coefficient	Coefficient	Coefficient
Constant	3.723*	2.548	4.981**
ln(Real income)	0.055	0.158	−0.062
ln(Metro population)	0.114***	0.108***	0.086***
ln(Winning percent$_t$)	0.956***	0.977***	0.937***
ln(Winning percent$_{t-1}$)	0.573***	0.598***	0.444***
ln(Stadium age)	−0.086***	−0.082***	−0.071***
ln(Average-revenue price)	**−0.073**	—	—
ln(Common-seat price)	—	**−0.148***	—
ln(Weighted-average price)	—	—	**0.343****
D91	0.251***	0.240***	0.289***
D92	0.238***	0.236***	0.272***
D93	0.357***	0.356***	0.382***
D95	0.018	0.021	0.021
D96	0.222***	0.228***	0.209***
R^2	0.54	0.55	0.56
Number of observations	156	156	156

*** Significant at 1% level
 ** Significant at 5% level
  * Significant at 10% level (one-tailed test)

efficient on price significantly negative. In fact, when using the weighted-average price, the coefficient is significantly positive! Although this direct effect of price is not uncommon in the literature, it is certainly inconsistent with the law of demand.

Since it is the only specification that yields significantly negative coefficients, we used the estimates on the CS definition of price to calculate the own-price elasticity of demand.[7] The log-linear model assumes constant elasticity, so the coefficient on CS price in Table 9.4 implies an own-price elasticity of −0.148. Not only do we reject the null of elastic pricing, but we also reject the null of unit-elastic (that is, revenue-maximizing) pricing. For the linear model, the elasticity depends on the values of all of the variables in equation (9.1). To see if the elasticity changed across the sample period, we calculated this elasticity in both the 1991 and 1996 seasons using season-specific mean values for the right-hand side variables. For 1991, this elasticity was −0.24, while in 1996 it was −0.27. Again, these estimates lead us to reject elastic pricing.

Concluding Remarks

This survey of the demand for sporting events has covered a number of issues, some theoretical, others purely empirical. To summarize, the following conclusions and/or assertions are posited:

Fans get utility from the excitement of the game. This determines their willingness to pay, and hence their desire to attend ball games. Thus, teams provide their fans with entertainment services, which they sell in terms of tickets to the game.

The difficulty in identifying the effect of price on demand arises from the multitiered pricing policies pursued by teams. It is certainly not clear which definition of price is "best," but in our empirical model, the common-seat specification is the only definition that gave us negative and significant coefficients on price.

There exists (near) unanimity across the literature in finding that teams price tickets in the inelastic range of demand—our empirical model yielded inelastic results as well. In addition, our results rejected unit-elastic pricing as well. Given the pervasiveness of these results, perhaps sports economists should lean toward models that predict such pricing behavior.

Equally disturbing from a theoretical point of view is the frequency with which sports economists find positive price effects on attendance. When we estimated demand using the weighted-average price, we got positive and significant coefficients on price as well. Although we cannot explain this anomaly directly, it is possible that these results arise from using a single measure of price to represent the prices fans actually face.

Fans demand excitement at the game. Although a more direct test of the Uncertainty of Outcome Hypothesis is possible when estimating the demand for specific games or across the league as a whole, we found that large-market teams enjoy an advantage over their small-market counterparts, which can lead to problems of inter-seasonal imbalance over time.

Finally, the added drawing power of a team playing in a new stadium suggests that teams may be more capable of privately funding their own stadiums, rather than asking taxpayers for a subsidy.

Notes

1. Using the *Financial World* data from 1990 through 1995, the correlation between media revenues and market size (population) was about 0.7, while the correlation between these revenues and winning percent was only about 0.2.

2. Prices are reported for just the 1991 through 1996 seasons because Team Marketing began constructing their Fan Cost Index in 1991, and *Financial World's* survey of gate revenues ended in 1996.

3. If anything, teams are increasingly complicating the task of estimating the relationship between price and quantity demanded given the growing trend to price discriminate by charging higher prices for "premium" games.

4. The winning percentage of large-market teams in MLB during the late 1990s was about 40 points higher than that of small-market teams (Solow and Krautmann, 2004).

5. Two examples of team-generated studies of the positive economic effects of new stadiums were conducted by the San Francisco Giants (1994) and the Cincinnati Reds (1996).

6. Since the 1994 season corresponds to the omitted dummy variable, the five seasonal dummy variables represent attendance deviations from the 1994 season. This should control for the effects of the 1994 strike.

7. Of course, the AR price also gave a negative, but insignificant, coefficient on price. Using it to calculate the elasticity gave an even smaller value to the elasticity (that is, for the log-linear model, this elasticity is only -0.073).

10

Competitive Balance in North American Professional Sports

Rodney Fort

The Issues

Only labor issues occupy as much space in the sports economics literature as competitive balance. With apologies to world sports fans (football, rugby, and cricket), this review is limited to competitive balance in the four main North American pro sports leagues—Major League Baseball (MLB), the National Basketball Association (NBA), the National Football League (NFL), and the National Hockey League (NHL). There is just as large a literature on world sports, pursuing the same interesting competitive balance topics (and more), but there is enough about North American leagues to generate a lengthy review.

The chapter opens by presenting competitive-balance measurements to date under the characterization of the three primary elements of competitive balance suggested first by Sloane (1976a), and then explicitly detailed by Cairns (1987): game uncertainty (GU), playoff uncertainty (PU), and consecutive-season uncertainty (CSU). In addition to conforming to a well-known characterization, identifying these three dimensions of competitive balance also lays bare a few controversies that have needlessly (in my opinion) arisen in the literature. The first section of the review concludes with these controversies and points out why they really need not have happened at all.

The chapter moves on to present two additional lines of inquiry in the competitive-balance literature (Fort and Maxcy, 2003): analysis of competitive balance (ACB) and analysis of the uncertainty of outcome hypothesis (UOH). Many are interested in how competitive balance has behaved over time, the point of the ACB literature, as well as its impact on fan demand, from the UOH literature, as aids to policy analysis. But they both also shed light on two of the most important topics in sports economics, first introduced by Rottenberg (1956).

Rottenberg's invariance principle (IP) states that some policies imposed by leagues (e.g., the draft and the reserve clause) will have no impact on competitive balance at all and will only redistribute the value created in the league between players and owners. The ACB literature informs this hypothesis by showing whether competitive balance has remained invariant to these types of changes, as Rottenberg suggests, or not. In addition, the ACB literature has shed light on the impacts of macroeconomic situations, racial integration, expansion, and the growing role of media on competitive balance.

Rottenberg's "other hypothesis" is actually an explicit statement of the UOH. If competitive balance declines enough, then the league will suffer economically. In the limit, as larger-revenue teams come to dominate play, only fans of those teams will stick with the league. Even the overall value to the remaining large-revenue clubs is smaller than if there were more balance and broader appeal. By including measures of competitive balance in demand estimation that capture its three main elements—GU, PU, and CSU—along with the rest of the determinants of demand, the UOH literature has directly examined this hypothesis about fan preferences.

This chapter concludes with thoughts about where future analysts can take the ACB and UOH lines of inquiry. Since the literature has almost exclusively covered baseball, our knowledge of competitive balance and its impacts on fans in other sports is extremely limited. In addition, the focus of the ACB literature is heavily on GU so that little is known about PU and CSU. Further, the UOH literature covers only attendance even though the demand for broadcast games is an increasingly important factor in the overall appeal of North American pro sports. Finally, while much is bandied about on the topic, actual analysis of the optimal level of competitive balance is completely absent from the literature.

Competitive-Balance Measurements

There are many measurements of competitive balance. And there have been arguments about their relative efficacy. In this section of the review, the measurements of GU, PU, and CSU are presented. The section concludes by observing that the arguments over relative efficacy actually were confusion about the distinctions between the three main elements of competitive balance.

Measures of Game Uncertainty

There are two types of GU variables. The first type measures the dispersion of winning percentages. These are the first four variables in Table 10.1, along

Table 10.1

Measures of Game Uncertainty (GU)

Description and References

Measures of winning percentage dispersion

1. *Ratio of actual standard deviation of winning percent to the standard deviation in a hypothetically balanced league*
   MLB: Scully (1989b), Balfour and Porter (1991), Quirk and Fort (1992), Fort and
         Quirk (1995), Vrooman (1995), Sherony, Haupert, and Knowles (2001),
         Humphreys (2002), Fort (2001, 2003), Schmidt (2001), Maxcy
   (2002), Schmidt and Berri (2003, 2004), Lee (2004a)
   NBA: Noll (1988), Quirk and Fort (1992), Fort (2003)
   NFL: Quirk and Fort (1992), Fort and Quirk (1995), Fort (2003), Schmidt and
         Berri (2004)
   NHL: Quirk and Fort (1992), Fort (2003), Schmidt and Berri (2004)

2. *Likelihood that the winning percents of the top and bottom 20% of teams occur in the "idealized" normal distribution*
   MLB: Fort and Quirk (1995), Lee (2004a)
   NFL: Fort and Quirk (1995)

3. *Herfindahl-type concentration of winning percent of the teams at the top or bottom of the standings*
   MLB: Eckard (2001a), Humphreys (2002)

4. *League-wide Gini coefficient of winning percents*
   MLB: Schmidt (2001), Schmidt and Berri (2001)

Measures of game closeness

5. *Relative quality of the home team, by winning percents or league standing at time of game*
   MLB: Demmert (1973), Hill, Madura, and Zuber (1982), Fort and Rosenman
         (1998, 1999)
   NHL: Jones (1984)

6. *Probability home teams will win, based on betting odds*
   MLB: Knowles, Sherony, and Haupert (1992)

Note: Some references listed under (1) actually used only the standard deviation of winning percent.

with brief descriptions (in all descriptive tables, variables are listed in order of their original appearance in the literature). Typically, ties count as half a win. Each of the measurements has distinctive strengths and weaknesses.

For example, in the NHL the dispersion in winning percent has limited appeal as a measure of GU, since season points, not winning percentage, determine final standings. For games ending in regulation time, every hockey game is worth two points. The winning team collects both points, the losing team none. But in the event of a tie at the end of regulation time, each team receives one point and then they proceed to overtime, where either team can secure a second point by winning. So, the usual game is worth two total points, but overtime games carry a total of three points. For the NHL, the dispersion of points would be a more representative measure than the dispersion of winning percentages.

As another example, the standard deviation is an intuitive measure of dispersion and is heavily used in ACB analysis. But if fans are insensitive to changes around winning percents of 0.500, but are sensitive to changes in the relative extremes of the winning percent distribution, then the second and third measures of dispersion, which focus on the behavior in the tails of the winning percent distribution, may be more appropriate for UOH analysis. Another strength of second and third measures listed in Table 10.1 is that they facilitate analysis of both the upper and lower tails of the winning percent distribution.

For a final example, Utt and Fort (2002) point out the pitfalls of the Gini coefficient of league-wide winning percents as a measure of GU. First, this type of Gini coefficient must be adjusted for the zero-sum nature of league play. Unlike, say, income, it is theoretically impossible in a league of more than two teams for one team to have "all of the winning." Additional complexities involving unbalanced schedules, inter-divisional play, and inter-league play in Major League Baseball (MLB) must be overcome before winning percent Gini coefficients can meaningfully represent GU.

The last two variables in Table 10.1 measure the expected closeness of games in the eyes of fans of the home team. They measure GU both over a season and on a game-by-game basis. This type of GU measurement has proven particularly insightful in the UOH line of the literature covered in a subsequent section of this review.

Measures of Playoff Uncertainty

The two types of PU measures, and brief descriptions, appear in Table 10.2. The first type (the first three variables) is designed to capture whether a team is in contention for the playoffs as the season progresses. Again, the variables are listed in temporal order of their introduction. The first and third variables directly cover the closeness of the race for the playoffs while the second gets at playoff contention by measuring how far the season has progressed.

The second type of PU variable (items 4 through 6 in Table 10.2) provides an *ex post* measure of the concentration of championships. These variables have proven quite useful in examining PU over time. Note here that the Gini coefficient of the concentration in championships for a given league is completely appropriate since one team could, hypothetically, win the championship every single season.

Table 10.2

Measures of Playoff Uncertainty (PU)

Description and References

Measures of playoff contention

1. *Games back, as a measure of closeness of pennant race*
   MLB: Demmert (1973), Canes (1974), Noll (1974), Hunt and Lewis (1976), Hill,
         Madura, and Zuber (1982), Whitney (1988), Baade and Tiehen (1990),
         Domazlicky and Kerr (1990), Butler (2002), Schmidt and Berri (2004)
   NHL: Jones (1984)
2. *Month of the observation, a measure of depth into the season and knowledge*
   of playoff possibilities
   MLB: Whitney (1988), Fort and Rosenman (1998, 1999)
3. *End of season winning percent difference between top and bottom teams*
   MLB: Lee (2004a)

Measures of championship concentration

4. *Years per championship*
   MLB: Quirk and Fort (1992), Fort 2003
   NBA: Quirk and Fort (1992), Fort 2003
   NFL: Quirk and Fort (1992), Fort 2003
   NHL: Quirk and Fort (1992), Fort 2003
5. *Gini coefficient of championship concentration, normalized on league years*
   MLB: Quirk and Fort (1992)
   NBA: Quirk and Fort (1992)
   NFL: Quirk and Fort (1992)
   NHL: Quirk and Fort (1992)
6. *Championship domination by larger market teams*
   MLB: Fizel (1997)

Measures of Consecutive-Season Uncertainty

Variables used to measure CSU are in Table 10.3 and, as before, in order of
their introduction to the literature. The first variable listed is a simple correlation of success across years, while the remaining variables are more complex measures capturing winning percent dispersion between seasons. The
second variable measures this phenomenon for a given team, while the third
is for a league as a whole.

The Relative Efficacy of Competitive-Balance Measures

With so many measures to choose from, it should come as no surprise that
there have been disagreements in the literature about their relative efficacy.
Sometimes, the argument ends up to be a matter of computational confusion,
as in the interchange between Eckard (2003) and Humphreys (2003). But
sometimes the issues are larger and so are the disagreements.

Table 10.3

Measures of Consecutive-Season Uncertainty (CSU)

Description and references

---

1. *Correlation between this year's winning percent and last year's winning percent*
   MLB: Butler (1995)

2. *Sum of the cumulative variance and the time variance of winning percents for each team (an ANOVA approach)*
   MLB: Eckard (2001a)

3. *Ratio of standard deviation of winning percent averaged across teams to standard deviation of winning percent averaged across a specified number of seasons*
   MLB: Humphreys (2002)

An interesting example occurs in a symposium entitled "Competitive Balance in Sports Leagues" (*Journal of Sports Economics,* vol. 3, no. 2, May, 2002). In the introduction to the symposium, Zimbalist (2002: 112) claims that there is a best way to measure competitive balance, namely, "the one to which the consumers show the greatest sensitivity." Zimbalist (2003a: 161), in response to Fort and Maxcy (2003), states that he really meant, "if one were choosing among several measures, the best from the group would be the one to which fan behavior showed greatest sensitivity." So be it.

Fort and Maxcy (2003) suggest that Zimbalist's (2002) claim is fine for the UOH literature, but misses the essential point that UOH analysis is not the only way to discover economically interesting things. There remains the examination of league actions designed to alter competitive balance in the ACB literature as well. The behavior of the many different types of GU, PU, and CSU variables over time generates insight for ACB analysts. So, as noted in the introduction to this review, careful attention to the UOH/ACB distinction, as well as the GU/PU/CSU distinction, explains this disagreement.

Humphreys (2002), in his article in the same symposium, argues that his invention (the third variable in Table 10.3) contributes more to the explanatory power of a cross-section, time-series model of MLB attendance than either the first or third variables in Tables 10.1. He argues that this is because those variables in Table 10.1 pertain to a given year and do not capture variation across years. Humphreys (2003: 81) puts his analysis in the following context: "My goal was to redirect the focus of research on competitive balance towards the economic issues associated with competitive balance and away from the technical issues related to the measurement of competitive balance that have dominated this literature in the past." But, again, adherence to the ACB/UOH and PU/GU/CSU distinctions reveals this criticism and claim to be groundless.

First, as just argued, the UOH line of inquiry pushed by Humphreys is not the only productive one; the ACB line also investigates "economic issues associated with competitive balance." Second, as outlined in the subsequent section on UOH analysis, there has been plenty of attention to the impact of competitive balance on fan demand (at least in baseball)—eighteen studies over roughly thirty years (just on North American sports leagues). Finally, if one seeks to capture the three dimensions of competitive balance in an attendance model, then variables must be used to cover all three in any attendance-demand model. If anything, Humphreys' approach suffers by including only variables that cover GU and CSU, and then only one at a time, when both variables, plus a variable to cover PU, belong in the regression. Since this is all relative to the UOH, and a matter of unobservable fan preferences, it may end up that some or none of the dimensions of competitive balance influence attendance. But they must be empirically analyzed together in order to make that determination.

Ultimately, as always, working to reduce confusion gently nudges analysts in the right direction. The first lesson from Zimbalist (2002) and Humphreys (2002) is to carefully determine whether the analysis is of the ACB or UOH variety. Measurements useful for ACB may not generate the most precise insights in the UOH context and "the best" UOH variable, used alone, needlessly limits insights into ACB analysis. And, in UOH analysis, the data inform us best about competitive balance when variables are included to cover all three of its elements—PU, GU, and CSU.

ACB Findings

ACB work on GU has used variables 1 through 4 in Table 10.1 (the problems with using the last variable have already been listed). In addition, there have been recent ACB time-series approaches on the behavior of GU. ACB work on PU has employed variables 4 through 6 in Table 10.2. Rather than itemize the ACB findings on GU and PU, it is straightforward to produce updated results for each of the four major North American sports leagues. However, ACB works on CSU are fewer in number, using variables 2 and 3 in Table 10.3. This section of the review concludes with a look at what ACB analysis can tell us about the only coherently examined league, MLB.

ACB and Game Uncertainty

An update for all leagues using just variable 1 from Table 10.1 appears in Table 10.4. As this measure increases, GU declines. Turning first to MLB,

Table 10.4

Analysis of Competitive Balance and Game Uncertainty
(Variable 1, Table 10.1)

Decade	MLB-AL	MLB-NL	NBA	NFL	NHL
1901–9	2.55	3.28			
1910–19	2.71	2.36			1.34
1920–29	2.40	2.31		1.96	1.79
1930–39	2.79	2.37		1.70	1.63
1940–49	2.29	2.50	2.58	1.85	1.91
1950–59	2.52	2.06	2.18	1.52	2.04
1960–69	2.01	2.18	2.90	1.68	2.00
1970–79	1.96	1.84	2.39	1.62	2.64
1980–89	1.75	1.69	2.72	1.52	2.02
1990	1.45	1.45	3.15	1.62	1.69
1991	1.54	1.56	2.86	1.74	1.87
1992	1.61	1.68	2.89	1.65	1.72
1993	1.39	2.37	2.87	1.28	2.66
1994	1.72	1.82	3.21	1.40	1.87
1995	2.12	1.54	2.92	1.22	1.54
1996	1.77	1.42	3.10	1.47	2.09
1997	1.58	1.49	3.46	1.46	1.41
1998	2.06	2.24	3.43	1.71	1.74
1999	1.93	2.01	2.88	1.49	1.75
1990–99	1.72	1.76	3.08	1.51	1.83
Pre-stoppage	1.50	1.76	3.06		1.96
Post-stoppage	1.83	1.79			1.75
2000	1.37	1.76	2.92	1.58	1.88
2001	2.41	1.65	2.85	1.63	1.95
2002	2.69	2.06	2.50	1.32	1.66
2003	2.48	1.78	2.27	1.54	1.69
2004	2.11	2.20	2.65		1.73
2000–2004	2.21	1.89	2.63	1.52	1.78

Sources: All calculations (ties count as half a win) are from final standings at baseballreference.com, basketballreference.com, pro-footballreference.com, and (hockey) USAToday.com.

Notes: MLB: Scully (1989b) 1980–84. Calculations reflect MLB strike of 1994 and the NBA lockout of 1998.

for both the American League (AL) and National League (NL), over the entire tabled time period, GU has increased (variable 1 fell by 13 percent in the AL and by 42 percent in the NL). But the most recent data in Table 10.4 show that GU appears to be decreasing of late. Indeed, in the AL, by this measure, GU has climbed back to nearly its historically high levels in the 2000s. And although the AL has almost always had less GU than the NL, the reverse is true over the last five years in Table 10.4.

Since the National Basketball Association (NBA) began play in 1947, over the entire period in Table 10.4, GU in the NBA has remained virtually unchanged. The NBA has been the league with the lowest level of GU in every decade except the 1950s, when the Yankees ran roughshod over MLB's AL. But there has been a slight increase in GU in the NBA, albeit ever so slight in the 1980s and 1990s.

Except for its earliest two decades in Table 10.4, the National Football League (NFL) has had the highest level of GU of all pro sports leagues. On top of that, GU has increased 23 percent since the league's inception in 1922. Notice that GU did not show substantial increases with the institution of the salary cap in 1994. And the larger increases in GU occurred after extensive revenue sharing was already in force. Rather than being the result of conscious policy, this suggests some other explanation, like the revenue base of NFL markets gradually equalizing over time.

Turning finally to the National Hockey League (NHL), the data in Table 10.4 show the league had quite a low level of GU up to the 1970s. Indeed, measured overall, GU has declined a full 33 percent since the NHL began play in 1918. But such a conclusion misses the increases in GU that have occurred since the 1970s, when GU was at its historically lowest level. Since the 1970s, GU has improved 33 percent in the NHL. Indeed, through the 2000s, the NHL enjoys GU only marginally lower than in the NFL.

ACB time-series analysis of the behavior of GU is quite recent and has only covered MLB. Figure 10.1 is a schematic of this time-series approach. By and large, the ACB time-series approach has failed to reject that the GU time series is nonstationary, measured by variables 1 and 4 in Table 10.1 (Schmidt, 2001; Schmidt and Berri, 2002, 2003). The exception is Lee and Fort (2005). Using ordinary unit root tests (on variables 1 and 2 in Table 10.1), they replicate the previous findings, but then reject nonstationary GU time series using unit root testing *with break points*. The break points occur in interesting ways coincident with the Great Depression, early team relocations and expansion, and the integration of MLB. However, there are no break points after 1937 in the NL or after 1962 in the AL. More details on this are at the end of the section.

ACB and Playoff Uncertainty

For PU, variable 4 from Table 10.2 is calculated and displayed over time in Table 10.5, again for all four major North American leagues. The data strongly indicate that titles are heavily concentrated in all leagues so that PU is low. It is always a judgment call on just what constitutes larger- and smaller-revenue markets, but it also appears that titles typically go in favor of large-revenue market teams. Teams in New York and Los Angeles have the lowest years per title in all leagues except hockey, and the larger-revenue

Figure 10.1 **Time-Series Approach Schematic**

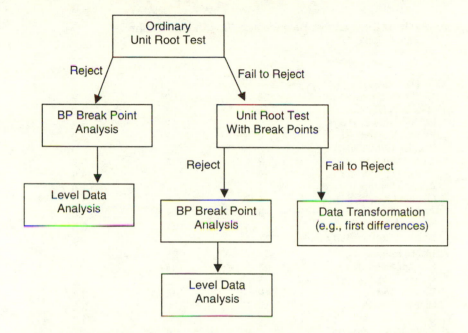

market Canadian cities of Ottawa and Montreal dominate that league. Interestingly, while U.S. teams typically dominate the top spots in reported revenues, they do not rank among the top for hockey championships. It is also worth noting that teams at the higher end of reported revenues can change over time, explaining Seattle and Atlanta in the MLB list. From Table 10.5, it is clear that championships have always been concentrated, and dramatically so in MLB and the NBA. Low PU is a fact of life in North American leagues.

ACB and Consecutive-Season Uncertainty

To date, all of the ACB analysis of CSU concerns MLB. Using variable 2 in Table 10.3, Eckard (2001a) shows that CSU in the NL has fallen from 1995–99 relative to prior periods, but not markedly so. But CSU clearly fell in the AL over 1995–99 relative to prior periods. Humphreys (2002) uses variable 3 in Table 10.3 and finds that, generally, CSU has increased in MLB. Examination of Humphreys' table 2 shows the same middling decrease in CSU in the NL, and the same striking decrease in CSU in the AL, found by Eckard over the period 1995–99.

As a minor contribution to this review, since the work on this variable is the most dated, variable 1 in Table 10.3 for MLB is calculated and displayed

Table 10.5

Analysis of Competitive Balance and Playoff Uncertainty
(Variable 4, Table 10.2)

League / Teams	Titles	Years	Years/Title
MLB (12 teams)			
New York Yankees	39	102	2.6
New York Giants	15	57	3.8
Los Angeles Dodgers	9	47	5.2
Florida Marlins	2	12	6.0
Brooklyn Robins/Dodgers	9	57	6.3
Milwaukee Braves	2	13	6.5
St. Louis Cardinals	16	104	6.5
Arizona Diamondbacks	1	7	7.0
Oakland Athletics	6	44	7.3
Atlanta Braves	5	39	7.8
Baltimore Orioles	6	51	8.5
Boston Pilgrims/Red Sox	11	104	9.5
NBA (14 teams)			
Los Angeles Lakers	22	44	2.0
Minneapolis Lakers	6	12	2.0
Boston Celtics	19	58	3.1
St. Louis Hawks	4	13	3.3
Chicago Stags	1	4	4.0
Syracuse Nationals	3	14	4.7
Washington Capitols	1	5	5.0
Philadelphia Warriors	3	16	5.3
Chicago Bulls	6	38	6.3
Philadelphia 76ers	6	41	6.8
New York Knicks	8	58	7.3
Washington Wizards	5	41	8.2
Rochester Royals	1	9	9.0
Detroit Pistons	6	56	9.3
NFL (20 teams)			
New York Giants	17	71	4.2
Dallas Cowboys	10	44	4.4
St. Louis Rams	2	9	4.5
Cleveland Browns	11	54	4.9
Boston Redskins	1	5	5.0
Denver Broncos	6	34	5.7
Green Bay Packers	12	71	5.9
Oakland Raiders I	2	12	6.0
Baltimore Colts	5	31	6.2

(continued)

in Table 10.6. CSU increases in the 1980s and 1990s but declines in the 2000s in both the AL and NL. Further, CSU is lower in MLB in the late 1990s than it was in the early 1990s. All in all, a coherent picture is painted of a recent decrease in CSU in MLB.

Table 10.5 *(continued)*

League / Teams	Titles	Years	Years/Title
Chicago Bears	11	71	6.5
Miami Dolphins	5	34	6.8
Tennessee Titans	1	7	7.0
Washington Redskins	10	71	7.1
Buffalo Bills	4	34	8.5
New England Patriots	4	34	8.5
Minnesota Vikings	5	43	8.6
Carolina Panthers	1	9	9.0
Cleveland Rams	1	9	9.0
Oakland Raiders II	1	9	9.0
Los Angeles Rams	5	49	9.8
NHL (17 teams)			
Ottawa Senators I	8	18	2.3
Montreal Canadiens	27	88	3.3
Detroit Red Wings	22	79	3.6
Toronto Maple Leafs	22	88	4.0
Edmonton Oilers	6	26	4.3
Boston Bruins	17	81	4.8
Colorado Avalanche	2	10	5.0
Montreal Maroons	3	15	5.0
Philadelphia Flyers	7	38	5.4
New Jersey Devils	4	23	5.8
Dallas Stars	2	12	6.0
Hamilton Tigers	1	6	6.0
New York Islanders	5	33	6.6
Calgary Flames	3	23	7.7
Chicago Blackhawks	10	79	7.9
New York Rangers	10	79	7.9
Carolina Hurricanes	1	8	8.0

Sources: From final standings at baseballreference.com, basketballreference.com, pro-footballreference.com, and (hockey) USAToday.com.

Notes: Years refers to continuation of franchises that may include team changes over time such as Brooklyn Robins/Dodgers, Baltimore/Capital/Washington Bullets/Washington Wizards, Ft. Wayne/Detroit Pistons, Ottawa Eagles/Senators I, Detroit Cougars/Falcons/Red Wings, and Toronto Arenas/St. Patricks/Maple Leafs.

AL and NL league champions in MLB and division champions in all other leagues. NFL calculated relative to 2003. MLB, NBA, and NHL calculated relative to 2004. Only teams winning less than every ten years are shown.

ACB Implications for League Policy

Based on UOH logic, but without analysis, team owners have argued that particular policies must be put in place to enhance competitive balance. For

Table 10.6

Analysis of Competitive Balance and Consecutive-Season Uncertainty in MLB (Variable 1, Table 10.3)

Year	Variable 1	
	American League	National League
1900s	0.39	0.74
1910s	0.54	0.55
1920s	0.67	0.70
1930s	0.78	0.62
1940s	0.59	0.69
1950s	0.80	0.65
1960s	0.57	0.63
1970s	0.63	0.62
1980s	0.39	0.40
1990s	0.39	0.26
1990a	0.26	0.17
1990b	0.53	0.36
2000s	0.67	0.54
Average	0.58	0.58

Note: 1990a is before the strike, and 1990b is after the strike. The lower is variable 1, the greater is consecutive-season uncertainty, and the greater is competitive balance.

example, leagues held steadfast to their argument that the reserve clause was necessary to enhance balance. And the same logic has been invoked for compensation requirements after the end of the reserve clause, the reverse order of finish draft, local revenue sharing, salary caps, and competitive-balance taxes (the so-called luxury tax).

ACB can inform this debate, albeit in a limited fashion. Although some of the work cited above covers the other North American Leagues, and the updates in Tables 10.4 and 10.5 help, only MLB has a comprehensive treatment that includes some ACB analysis of all balance dimensions and the application of modern time-series techniques. So the following synopsis and application to policy is restricted to MLB.

Here is the synopsis for all three dimensions of competitive balance. From its earliest days to the present, GU has increased in MLB, especially since the 1960s. But GU appears to be decreasing of late. The AL has almost always had less GU than the NL. The time-series perspective also indicates that all of the major regime changes in GU occurred prior to 1962. After that, there has been a trend in greater GU over time. There has never been very high PU, and larger-revenue teams typically dominate. In addition, GU has decreased in the 1990s relative to the 1980s, but appears to be rising a bit most recently. Finally, CSU has generally increased in MLB but there is evidence of a recent decline, and more so in the AL than in the NL.

Turning to MLB attempts to alter balance, the reverse order of finish draft was in place for 1965, the reserve clause reigned until 1975, compensation requirements were imposed in the earliest form of free agency, and extensive local revenue sharing and a competitive-balance tax were introduced in 1996 and expanded in 2001. There were also early and later expansion episodes that could be predicted to have reduced competitive balance and a veritable explosion of television broadcasting in the early 1980s may have done the same.

But the synopsis of ACB findings suggests the following about these efforts by MLB to enhance competitive balance. While it is true that GU has increased since the 1960s, time-series analysts detected no real regime change. So, if the draft enhanced GU, it did so only by contributing to a consistent trend over time. And nothing about the behavior of either PU or CSU appears coincident with the imposition of the draft—PU is unchanged and CSU was generally increasing anyway.

The synopsis also suggests that the reserve clause was not essential to the maintenance of competitive balance in MLB. Before and after the end of the reserve clause, there was a steady increase and no regime change in GU, PU held steady, and CSU generally increased. And the same can be said of compensation requirements since the steady improvement continued apace after they were ended.

Finally, although improvements in competitive balance are consistent with the intent of local revenue sharing and competitive-balances taxes, the rocky behavior of competitive balance in the 1990s, along all three dimensions, casts some doubt on their efficacy in the particular decade where both techniques were increased pretty dramatically. Much more work remains to be done here, especially expanding the analysis to other leagues.

Competitive Balance and Attendance Demand

UOH analysis attempts to discover the impact of the elements of competitive balance on fan demand. In addition to the usual economic determinants, like cost of attendance (including travel cost), income, price of other goods, and population, preference variables including stadium age, the level of quality of the home team, GU, PU, and CSU have been included in demand analysis. In this section, the UOH work is reviewed not on a finding-by-finding basis, but from the perspective of pursuing good science. Using this perspective suggests that it is too early to make much of UOH findings, particularly as to how they affect competitive balance policy.

Let us be clear up front. From the pioneering work of Demmert (1973) and Noll (1974) onward, neither the season-level analysis of North Ameri-

Table 10.7

The Uncertainty of Outcome Hypothesis Line of Inquiry

Description and References

1. Game uncertainty
  MLB: Demmert (1973), Hill, Madura, and Zuber (1982), Knowles, Sherony, and
        Haupert (1992), Fort and Rosenman (1998, 1999), Schmidt and Berri
        (2001), Humphreys (2002), Lee (2004a)
  NHL: Jones (1984)

2. Playoff uncertainty
  MLB: Demmert (1973), Canes (1974), Noll (1974), Hunt and Lewis (1976), Hill,
        Madura, and Zuber (1982), Whitney (1988), Baade and Tiehen (1990),
        Domazlicky and Kerr (1990), Fort and Rosenman (1998, 1999), Butler
        (2002), Lee (2004a), Schmidt and Berri (2004)
  NHL: Jones (1984)

3. Consecutive-season uncertainty
  MLB: Humphreys (2002)

can league attendance demand at the team and league level (Siegfried and
Eisenberg, 1980; Jones, 1984; Domazlicky and Kerr, 1990; Baade and Tiehen,
1990; Coffin, 1996; Kahane and Shmanske, 1997; Schmidt, 2001; Schmidt
and Berri, 2001; Humphreys, 2002; Schmidt and Berri, 2002, 2003, and 2004),
nor the game-by-game analysis of demand within a season (Hill, Madura,
and Zuber, 1982; Knowles, Sherony, and Haupert, 1992; Welki and Zlatoper,
1994; Butler, 2002; Marcum and Greenstein, 1985; Bruggink and Eaton,
1996; Fort and Rosenman, 1998, 1999) includes all three dimensions of competitive balance. To date, there has been only an incomplete inclusion of the
UOH in attendance demand analysis. (The works that have included any
variables aimed at capturing the UOH are in Table 10.7.)

As if this were not enough, the following is also true. Only the works of
Schmidt and Berri (2001, 2004) analyze the time-series behavior of attendance in North American pro sports leagues beyond a correction for serial
correlation or the inclusion of time-trend dummy variables (we exclude from
this observation, of course, those works estimating game-by-game attendance
demand in a single season, just listed). In terms of this shortcoming in the
literature on North American leagues, the following lesson from the evolution of UOH analysis in Rugby League proves informative.

Burkitt and Cameron (1992) estimate the demand for British Rugby
League, 1966–90, paying no attention at all to the time-series behavior of
attendance. Davies, Downward, and Jackson (1995) pointed out that ignoring time-series behavior in sports data could lead to spurious correlations
posing special problems for policy prescriptions. Examining the time-series
behavior of Rugby League attendance, Davies et al. find that there is no

long-term relationship between attendance and success in Rugby League, results are heterogeneous across clubs so that pooled attendance analysis is faulty, and attendance drives success, rather than vice versa. Jones, Schofield, and Giles (2000) then extended this examination of Rugby League to a longer time series with more teams, fine-tuning the analysis.

The lesson from the Rugby League example is that time-series details in the data deserve attention before moving to any analysis of annual attendance demand. But nearly none of the work to date does so. Thus, there are two significant shortcomings in the UOH line of inquiry into competitive balance. There is no complete inclusion of all three dimensions of competitive balance, and the results of annual attendance modeling are suspect (biased coefficient estimates and spurious correlations). Thus, rather than spend much time on what that work found about the UOH, the rest of the section presents what the limited UOH time-series analysis of attendance has found. In this case, once again, the work is only on MLB.

As with ACB time-series analysis of GU in the last section (referring back to Figure 10.1 may be helpful), Schmidt and Berri (2001, 2004) fail to reject nonstationary attendance time series using ordinary unit root tests. For nonstationary attendance, the use of level data (as with annual attendance regressions) can produce biased coefficient estimates, spurious correlations, and, hence, unreliable inferences. Because all of the works in Table 10.7 use this type of data, the Schmidt and Berri finding undoes all inferences emanating from this literature.

Schmidt and Berri proceed to take first differences and analyze the impact of GU on attendance demand. Technically, this approach is valid but it does produce limited insight about the determinants of demand. For example, demand elasticities are not forthcoming from first differences. But this is not a fatal flaw, and clearly this work moves UOH in the correct technical direction.

Consider the technique adopted by Lee and Fort (2005) in their ACB time-series analysis of GU, which assumes that the attendance time series is stationary within breaks. If this assumption is true, then some or all of the works cited in Table 10.7 may be redeemed. Applications in Table 10.7 that have data within stationary subsamples no longer suffer the spurious correlation problem (although none of them includes all three dimensions of competitive balance). In addition, the regressions now can produce elasticity estimates for the determinants of fan demand. Only more UOH time-series analysis will determine if the assumption of stationary subsamples is appropriate.

Conclusions

For the review of competitive balance offered in this chapter, it has proven insightful to organize the literature around the three dimensions of competitive balance—GU, PU, and CSU. Doing so helps to clear up some of the confusion in the literature about the relative efficacy of competitive-balance variables. Further, organizing the review on these three dimensions of competitive balance helps relate ACB and UOH results to actual choices leagues make to alter competitive balance. Such organizational methods also help to emphasize that measures of all three dimensions will help capture the multidimensionality of competitive balance.

Results in the ACB literature, along with the actual changes in competitive-balance policy in MLB, suggest that the draft may have had some impact on competitive balance, but none of the other policies (the reserve clause, compensation requirements during free agency, and perhaps extensive local revenue sharing and competitive-balance taxes) has had any effect on competitive balance. Results in the UOH literature are insufficient to generate insights into policy choices by North American pro sports leagues.

This all suggests a couple of important deficiencies in the competitive-balance literature. First, the ACB literature is predominated by the analysis of MLB and the UOH literature is only about MLB. Although there remains much to learn about MLB (especially from the UOH perspective), we know next to nothing about what the analysis of other leagues may provide. Second, the application of time-series analysis to UOH has only just begun and not that much more has been done in the ACB literature. The results of future time-series work will determine judgments of past and future attendance regressions on annual data.

There are also a couple of missing elements in the analysis of competitive balance. All of the published demand studies I could find pertain to gate attendance. But broadcast games are an increasingly important factor in the overall appeal of North American pro sports. Future efforts could investigate the role of the UOH in fan demand for broadcast games.

Finally, we come to the elephant in the living room. I find nothing published on the optimal level of competitive balance, so there is no benchmark to compare to actual outcomes. Without knowing something about the optimal level of competitive balance, how can ACB inquiry judge whether changes in competitive balance are improvements or not? Although it is interesting to know how the UOH fares as a determinant of demand, what are the policy implications of UOH? For example, suppose one finds that increasing GU, PU, or CSU leads to increased attendance. From the standpoint of welfare analysis, it also is important to know whether doing so will move the league closer or farther away from the optimal levels of these competitive-balance dimensions. From the perspective of fan welfare, the determination of this benchmark seems a critical missing element in the analysis of competitive balance.

Part IV

Econometrics and
Theory in Sports Economics

11

Team Sports Efficiency Estimation and Stochastic Frontier Models

Young Hoon Lee

In recent years, there has been considerable interest in team efficiency (or managerial efficiency) in the professional team sports industry. Unlike many industries, where firm-level data on inputs and outputs are often unavailable, data on the input and output performance of the professional team sports industry are widely reported. Therefore, the professional team sports industry offers almost a unique opportunity to estimate production functions and team efficiency at firm level.

Output in professional team sports is conventionally measured in terms of team success as exhibited in winning performance. Inputs into the production process are reflected by player talent. Interaction between players is essential to team performance, and good managers will select teams and strategies that can exploit the teamwork. Team or managerial efficiency is determined by how well the manager transforms given player talent to winning performance. Therefore, production frontier or cost frontier models have been applied to empirical studies.

This chapter discusses the various methodologies for estimating team or managerial efficiency that have been applied previously by reviewing the literature on sports team efficiency while also discussing the available methodologies by reviewing the recent development of the stochastic frontier literature. The objective of this chapter is not to be exhaustive, but to offer a significant discussion on econometric methods for estimating efficiency in the sports team industry. Therefore, we will concentrate on the estimation of production frontiers and the measurement of efficiency for professional team sports teams.

Although there have been numerous studies of sporting team or managerial efficiency, very little attention has been paid to the peculiar economics of the industry (Neale, 1964). The output of a sports team is a joint product with rival teams. The total amount of output is fixed by this nature of the professional team sports industry since its average winning percent is always 0.5. In addition, the domain of inputs is narrow in the professional team sports industry, since the number of workers in a sports team is fixed because of roster restrictions and thus the variation of playing talents depends only on players' quality. These peculiar characteristics should be taken into account in any empirical analysis. In addition to reviewing the literature, this chapter also discusses how to take into account the aforementioned peculiar characteristics in an empirical analysis. It also addresses some further research topics in the literature.

The remainder of the chapter is organized as follows. The next section provides a review of the literature on team sports efficiency estimation. The focus is not the implications of the literature, but the econometric methods for estimating the efficiency of sports teams. The selection of different input variables and the application of different frontier models are discussed. This is followed by an overview of stochastic frontier models. The chapter discusses various methodologies for measuring technical efficiency and allocative efficiency and offers a comparison between established methods of measurements. The final section addresses some issues for empirical analysis of team efficiency with respect to the peculiar economics of the industry as well suggesting research topics yet to be tackled.

Efficiency Estimation of Professional Sports Teams

The seminal work by Scully (1974) offered the first empirical estimation of a sporting production function. The formal representation of a sporting production function is

$$W_{it} = f(X_{it}), \tag{11.1}$$

where W_{it} is the winning percentage for team i in season t and X_{it} is a vector of player talent inputs. This production function allows for player talent inputs (X) to be combined to produce team wins. Scully (1974) applied the production function to Major League Baseball (MLB), and he selected as input variables slugging percentage and strike-out to walk ratio. However, his focus was not on estimating team efficiency, but on analyzing the relationship between wages and marginal revenue product for individual players. Zak, Huang, and Siegfried (1979) provided the first paper to estimate sports team efficiency by applying a frontier production model. They employed a deterministic frontier production function to capture the relationship between wins and a variety of statistics in the National Basketball Association (NBA).

Since then, numerous empirical works have covered Major League Baseball (MLB), the National Basketball Association (NBA), the National Football League (NFL), and the National Hockey League (NHL) in the United States and association football leagues, Rugby League Football, and English country cricket in European countries. Reviews of these works can be found in Dawson, Dobson, and Gerrard (2000a, 2000b) and Lee and Berri (2004). Previous empirical works can be classified according to the econometric models applied and the input variables selected. The classification by the econometric models might be based on the parametric or nonparametric, deterministic or stochastic, and cross-section or panel data specification.

Several different frontier models have been adopted: a deterministic frontier production function model (Zak, Huang, and Siegfried, 1979; Porter and Scully, 1982; Ruggiero, Hadley, and Gustafson, 1996; Hadley et al., 2000), a stochastic frontier model (Ruggiero, Hadley, and Gustafson, 1996; Hofler and Payne, 1997; Dawson, Dobson and Gerrard, 2000a, 2000b; Lee and Berri, 2004), and a data envelopment analysis (DEA) (Fizel and D'itri, 1996; Gustafson, Hadley, and Ruggiero, 1997; Haas, 2003b). Porter and Scully (1982) assumed a deterministic frontier production and applied it to MLB with the same two inputs as Scully (1974). They found a positive correlation between coaching efficiency and tenure, with the contribution of the coach to team performance being comparable to that of an individual star player. Ruggiero, Hadley, and Gustafson (1996) provided an empirical comparison of deterministic and stochastic frontier approaches using data on MLB and found they generate inherently similar results. Hadley et al. (2000) also adopted a deterministic regression approach to NFL data and, interestingly, used the Poisson regression model, which was appropriate given the count nature of the dependent variable. Their empirical results suggested that efficient coaching can account for an additional three to four victories in a given season.

Hofler and Payne (1997) used a stochastic frontier model in the analysis of the NBA. Dawson, Dobson, and Gerrard (2000a, 2000b) are perhaps the first papers to use a panel data model with a stochastic frontier approach for the English Premier League. Their application of stochastic frontier models is noteworthy from the selection of input variables to the estimation methodology, as we will discuss later in this section. The panel data model allowed them to generate both time-invariant and time-varying efficiency estimations. They found that the temporal structure of efficiency and the estimation procedures of the time-varying models produce different results and that managerial efficiency was falling during the sample period. They focused attention on the coach's efficiency rather than team efficiency by treating the individual coach as the unit of analysis, where the subscript i in the production function (1) represents the ith coach, but not the ith team. Therefore, their panel data set must be either extremely unbalanced or not a typical panel data set, which includes cross-section data over time series. Alternatively, the efficiency of coaches can be analyzed if we estimate team efficiency in each season and have coaching tenure information. Later, Lee and Berri (2004) also applied panel data stochastic frontier models to NBA data. Like Dawson, Dobson, and Gerrard, they applied both time-invariant and time-varying efficiency estimation models, but unlike Dawson, Dobson, and Gerrard, their hypothesis test results suggested that team efficiency in the NBA was time-invariant. The selection of a specific time-varying model among various models is critical in the analysis of team or managerial efficiency because of the joint-product nature of wins. The rationale will be discussed extensively in the last section of the chapter.

Fizel and D'itri (1996) used a DEA approach to analyze college basketball team efficiency and their empirical results implied that if coach retention is based on winning percentage rather than coaching efficiency, excellent coaches will be ignored in hiring and firing decisions. Gustafson, Hadley, and Ruggiero (1997) also applied DEA in their analysis of MLB. What distinguishes their work from other empirical works is their interest in the cost function. They established a cost frontier that indicates the minimum cost of attaining any given output amount to measure cost efficiency for MLB teams and found that the more efficient teams are those that are successful in winning and attracting fans. Haas (2003b) analyzed Major League Soccer by using DEA, but his input variable of player wage bill, which is player talent multiplied by its price, is not an input in a physical unit. The legitimacy of his input variable can be sustained only under the assumption of constant wage per talent over time and across teams.

As briefly mentioned above, Dawson, Dobson, and Gerrard (2000a, 2000b) and Lee and Berri (2004) used panel data and panel data models whereas other empirical works used either cross-sectional data or cross-sectional models with panel data. A panel data model has some advantages in econometrics since it can relax a distributional assumption of technical inefficiency and the assumption of no correlation between inputs and technical inefficiency. Furthermore, it allows for estimation of time-varying efficiency.

The selection of team input variables is also a factor classifying previous empirical works into two groups. There has been little deviation in the selection of output, but the selection of inputs varies between the existing production analyses. The selection of player talent inputs seems to be controversial and critical in the empirical analysis of sports teams or managerial efficiency.

Most previous empirical works used *ex post* input variables, whereas another group (Fizel and D'itri, 1996; Dawson, Dobson, and Gerrard, 2000a, 2000b; Lee and Berri, 2004) used *ex ante* variables. Dawson, Dobson, and Gerrard explicitly argued that coaches have both direct and indirect effects on team winning performance; most empirical works in the literature have ignored the indirect effect. The direct effect relates the ability of coaches to convert the available players' talents into team wins through team selection and choice of strategy. On the other hand, coaches also have an indirect effect on team wins through their skill in training and motivating players to improve their playing talent. That is, coaches seek not only to maximize wins given a certain amount of playing inputs, but also to enhance the quality of inputs. Estimation of the indirect effect would require *ex ante* input variables that exclude the performance-enhancing impact of coaches. The *ex post* versus *ex ante* inputs issue is also related to the exogeneity of inputs. In a production function, output is assumed to be endogenous, while inputs are assumed to be exogenous. Thus *ex ante* variables are required for exogeneity.

Another side of the *ex post* versus *ex ante* inputs issue or the exogeneity issue is the input variable selection of player performance statistics versus player talent index. The *ex post* inputs used previously are various choices of player performance statistics and the *ex ante* inputs are player talent measures. Most existing production analyses have used a wide variety of player statistics. For instance, Zak, Huang, and Siegfried (1979) selected ratios of field goal percentage, rebounds, assists, and so on as input variables in their analysis of NBA team efficiency. Porter and Scully (1982) had two inputs— slugging percentage and team strike-out to walk ratio for MLB. On the other hand, Fizel and D'itri (1996) used a talent index of *Hoop Scoop* created by Francis (1983–92), and Dawson, Dobson and Gerrard (2000a, 2000b) developed a player quality measure that they defined as the weighted sum of player variables. Lee and Berri (2004) explicitly discussed this input variable issue. In a manufacturing firm, managers decide how to combine differing quantities of capital, labor, and material to produce a certain amount of output. Likewise, throughout the course of a basketball game, a coach adjusts the composition of the lineup in an effort to produce a win. Although these decisions impact player statistics such as points and rebounds in a game, it is not those statistics the coach is choosing to expand or conserve, rather it is the actual playing talent at different positions that coach must utilize effectively to achieve the team objective of winning. Lee and Berri assumed a basketball team has three different inputs: the playing talents of guards, small forwards, and big men. Using the playing talent index developed by Berri (2004b), they found a unit of big men talent has a greater impact on team wins than a unit of small forwards or guards talent.

This playing talent measure argument is reasonable with respect to the definition of inputs. Suppose a firm minimizes its cost to produce a certain amount of output. There is an isoquant, and a firm chooses a combination of inputs on the isoquant to minimize its cost, given input prices. With player statistics such as rebound and assist, we do not have input price, but with a playing talent measure, we can calculate input price data simply by dividing players' salary by the measure.

Stochastic Frontier Model

The measurement of efficiency has proved difficult and complex, and the literature provides a wide range of methodologies. Schmidt (1986a), Cornwell and Schmidt (1996), Kalirajan and Shand (1999), Kumbhakar and Lovell (2000), and Heshmati (2003) provide a review of the literature.

This section surveys the econometric approach to efficiency estimation, but it does not attempt to provide a comprehensive review of the literature on efficiency estimation. Rather, the section focuses on the selected stochastic frontier models that are considered to be necessary for our discussion of sports team efficiency estimation. Specifically, this section discusses cross-section and panel data models of stochastic frontier production, highlighting the implications of both time-invariant and time-varying models. It then presents a brief overview of estimating allocative and technical efficiency and the impact of exogenous variables on technical efficiency.

The estimation of the stochastic frontier function was independently introduced by Aigner, Lovell, and Schmidt (1977) and Meeusen and van den Broeck (1977). The stochastic frontier production model is defined by

$$y_i = \alpha + x_i \beta + v_i - u_i, \tag{11.2}$$

where i indexes firms or teams, y_i is the dependent variable that represents the logarithm of output for firm i ($i = 1, \ldots, N$), x_i is $1 \times k$ vector of inputs, β is a $k \times 1$ vector of coefficients, and v_i is an $i.i.d.$ $N(0, \sigma^2)$. The variable u_i is the non-negative technical inefficiency error for firm i. Estimating the model and separating technical inefficiency from a statistical noise term requires specific assumptions of the one-sided distribution of technical inefficiency, such as half-normal, exponential, truncated-normal, and so on. Furthermore, inefficiency is assumed to be independent of inputs. The production function can be estimated consistently by maximum likelihood (ML) and corrected ordinary least squares introduced by Aigner, Lovell, and Schmidt (1977) and firm-specific technical inefficiency can be measured by the conditional expectation of u_i, given $v_i - u_i$ derived by Jondrow et al. (1982).

More recent literature examining stochastic frontier models in the context of panel data removes the problem of strong distributional assumptions. Schmidt and Sickles (1984) apply the stochastic frontier production approach to a standard panel data model. Inter-firm differences in time-invariant individual effects are interpreted as measures of technical inefficiency in their model. Therefore, we need neither a specific distributional assumption about technical inefficiency nor the assumption that the levels of inefficiency and other explanatory variables are uncorrelated.

Specifically, the time-invariant stochastic frontier production function is defined by

$$y_{it} = \alpha_0 + x_{it}\,\beta + v_{it} - u_i = x_{it}\,\beta + \alpha_i + v_{it}, \tag{11.3}$$

where $\alpha_i = \alpha_0 - u_i$ is the intercept for firm i. Time-invariant technical efficiency technical inefficiency for firm i can be separated from estimates of α_i as

$$\hat{u}_i = (\hat{\alpha}_0 - \hat{\alpha}_i). \tag{11.4}$$

Equation (11.4) derives a constant term by finding the most efficient firm among all i in which u_i is assumed to be zero. Technical efficiency at each data point is then calculated as

$$TE_i = \exp(-\hat{u}_i). \tag{11.5}$$

The most efficient firm has $\hat{u}_i = 0$ and $TE_i = 1$; then the range for any TE is [0, 1]. The most efficient firm is assumed to be perfectly efficient, and the efficiency of firm i is measured as the efficiency relative to the most efficient firm.

The time-invariant assumption of technical efficiency is restrictive and would be unrealistic in potential applications. Thus the time-varying model has been developed so that the assumption of time-invariance can be relaxed, without losing the benefits of panel data. The so-called first generation of time-varying stochastic frontier models are by Cornwell, Schmidt, and Sickles (1990), Kumbhakar (1990), Battese and Coelli (1992), and Lee and Schmidt (1993). These models can be classified according to the assumption and the specification of temporal pattern of technical inefficiency. The time-varying stochastic frontier model is represented by

$$y_{it} = \alpha_t + x_{it}\,\beta + v_{it} - u_{it} = x_{it}\,\beta + \alpha_{it} + v_{it}, \tag{11.6}$$

where $\alpha_{it} = \alpha_t - u_{it}$ is the intercept for firm i at period t.

With respect to the specification, Cornwell, Schmidt, and Sickles ($\alpha_{it} = \alpha_{i0} + \alpha_{i1}t + \alpha_{i2}t^2$), Kumbhakar ($\alpha_{it} = \theta_t\alpha_i$ and $\theta_t = [1 + \exp(bt+ct^2)]^{-1}$), and Battese and Coelli ($\alpha_{it} = \theta_t\alpha_i$ and $\theta_t = \exp[-\eta\,(t-T)]$) considered specific cases for temporal patterns of technical inefficiency, whereas Lee and Schmidt ($\alpha_{it} = \theta_t\alpha_i$) allowed a flexible temporal pattern.

On the other hand, Kumbhakar, Battese and Coelli, and Lee and Schmidt imposed an identical temporal pattern of technical inefficiency across firms, whereas Cornwell, Schmidt, and Sickles did not. In addition, Kumbhakar and Battese and Coelli assumed a specific distribution of technical inefficiency such as half-normal, and used ML estimation, whereas the others (Cornwell, Schmidt, and Sickles, and Lee and Schmidt) followed traditional panel data models without a distributional assumption, and uncorrelation assumptions between inefficiency and inputs. Later Han, Orea, and Schmidt (2005) imposed Battese and Coelli's parametric function on the Lee and Schmidt model and applied their model of fixed-effect treatment to Spanish savings banks. Certainly, Lee and Schmidt can also be estimated using ML, with a distributional assumption of technical inefficiency. Therefore, the main factor to classify the aforementioned time-varying models is the specification of temporal pattern of technical efficiency.

The so-called second generation of time-varying stochastic frontier models were introduced by Cuesta (2000) and Lee (2004b). These models were intended to relax the assumption of identical temporal pattern without imposing any additional assumptions. Cuesta imposed the specific form of Battese and Coelli on the specification of temporal pattern, but allowed firm-specific temporal variations in inefficiency. Thus, $\theta_t = \exp[-\eta\,(t - T)]$ in Battese and Coelli became $\theta_{it} = \exp[-\eta_i(t - T)]$ and the log-likelihood function was derived. This constitutes a plausible way to extend time-varying models, given the assumption of an identical temporal pattern of inefficiency across firms. However, this model is designed for the analysis of panel data with small N and large T and it still assumes a specific form of temporal pattern. Lee (2004b) introduced the "group-specific" stochastic frontier model that allows for different temporal patterns between firms from different groups, but restricts the same pattern between firms from the same group. This group-specific model partially relaxes the identical temporal pattern assumption without imposing any specific form of temporal pattern. When applied to Indonesian rice farms, the model was shown to be an improvement on the Lee and Schmidt model, and found a wide range of variation on the efficiency rankings of farms over time.

The concept of economic efficiency is decomposed into technical efficiency and allocative efficiency. A firm is allocative inefficient when the marginal rate of technical substitution between any two of its inputs is not equal to the ratio of corresponding input prices. The following discussion highlights aspects of measuring allocative efficiency but is not intended to be exhaustive. Schmidt and Lovell (1979, 1980) incorporated allocative efficiency into the model by attaching error terms to the first-order conditions for cost-minimization, so that both technical inefficiency and allocative inefficiency could be estimated. This leads to the system equations of cost frontier and the first-order conditions. While error terms representing technical inefficiency are always positive in the cost frontier, error terms in the share equations would be positive or negative since they imply over- or underutilization of input. Their models work for Cobb-Douglas production function and cross-sectional data and with some distributional assumptions, they can be estimated by ML. Schmidt (1986b) developed the same model in a panel data context. Like the time-invariant model of Schmidt and Sickles (1984), this model did not assume any distribution of inefficiency terms and uncorrelation between inputs and inefficiency, and derived an estimation method in the traditional panel data model setting.

Kumbhakar (1987) also analyzed estimation of technical and allocative inefficiency under profit maximization. The system equations include production frontier and the first-order conditions of profit maximization and, with the distributional assumptions of inefficiency terms, the relevant parameters can be estimated by ML. Later, Atkinson and Cornwell (1994) generalized the parametric approach introduced by Lau and Yotopoulos (1971) to a panel data setting. In the parametric approach, the firm is assumed to minimize shadow cost. Therefore, input mix may be inefficient in terms of market prices. The firm minimizes actual costs only if the ratio of shadow prices equals the ratio of market prices. Atkinson and Cornwell estimated translog cost systems for the U.S. airline industry by feasible generalized least squares, and their use of panel data allows for joint estimation of cost frontier and firm-specific allocative and technical inefficiency without the restrictions on production technology and the distribution of the errors.

The last topic this section addresses is the effects of exogenous variables on technical efficiency and its incorporation in stochastic frontier model. With the production function (2), (3), or (6), we have an additional regression equation as follows:

$$u = g(z, \gamma) + w, \tag{11.7}$$

where z is a set of exogenous variables that affect technical inefficiency. There are two ways to estimate the effects of exogenous variables on technical inefficiency. A "one-step" model specifies the stochastic frontier by substituting equation (11.7) into production frontier equation (11.2), (11.3) or (11.6), and estimating the frontier equation. A "two-step" model such as that of Pitt and Lee (1981) and Kalirajan (1981), estimates a standard stochastic frontier model in the first step and estimates equation (11.7) in the second step. Recently Wang and Schmidt (2002) provided extensive Monte Carlo evidence that a two-step approach causes biased estimation results.

Kumbhakar, Ghosh, and McGuckin (1991), Reifschneider and Stevenson (1991), and Battese and Coelli (1995) among others presented one-step models. The difference between them hinges mainly on assumptions about $g(z, \gamma)$ and w made so that the technical inefficiency term, u, is positive. Battese and Coelli developed a model within a panel data context that has been applied to various empirical analyses.

Program software for various efficiency estimation methods is available. FRONTIER 4.1, developed by Coelli (1996), covers the ML estimation of various stochastic frontier models from the cross-section model of Aigner, Lovell, and Schmidt (1977) to the panel data model of Battese and Coelli (1995). It can accommodate time-varying (only the Battese and Coelli model) and invariant efficiencies, cost and production functions, and half-normal and truncated normal distributions. The GAUSS code of the time-varying Lee and Schmidt model is also available upon request to Young Hoon Lee. He provides not only the code to estimate production frontiers and technical efficiency by the Lee and Schmidt model, but also the code to test the specifications of Kumbhakar (1990) and Battese and Coelli (1992).

Peculiar Characteristics of the Team Sport Industry and Further Research Topics

Given the review of literature on sport team efficiency and stochastic frontier models, this section discusses some peculiar characteristics of sporting production and future research opportunities. The peculiar characteristics must be taken into account in the empirical analysis of sports team efficiency since they distinguish a sporting production from other industries.

First, the joint-product characteristic of sports teams must be considered in the selection of the time-varying stochastic frontier model. Consider the case where there are two manufacturing firms. Both firms can increase their outputs without change in inputs used if both firms can manage to be more efficient. Therefore, the average efficiency rises in this case. This is impossible in sports teams. Consider a league with two teams. Suppose that the level of playing talent of both teams remains constant over time and Team A can increase its winning percent by improving its efficiency. If this is the case, it is impossible for Team B to raise its winning percent. In fact, Team B loses more and become less efficient, since average winning percent over teams is always 0.5. That is, the rise of Team A's efficiency level implies the fall of Team B's efficiency level and vice versa given that the average efficiency level is always constant over time.

A time-varying stochastic frontier model that allows for estimation of time-specific as well as firm-specific technical inefficiency is useful in many applications. For instance, when we analyze coach retention, we need a time-varying model, since firing decisions are based on recent changes in coaches' efficiency, but not average efficiency over the tenure period. Among the aforementioned time-varying stochastic frontier models, those with identical temporal pattern assumptions (Kumbhakar, Battese and Coelli, and Lee and Schmidt) are not recommended for team efficiency estimation, since an identical temporal pattern of technical inefficiency across teams implies the temporal change in average inefficiency, which is always constant. Note the empirical results in Lee and Berri (2004) as evidence. They applied the Lee and Schmidt model in the analysis of the NBA and found the time-invariant hypothesis is not rejected and their estimates of temporal pattern are extremely constant. Therefore, the recommended time-varying models are Cornwell, Schmidt, and Sickles, Cuesta (2000), and Lee (2004b). With a sample of large N and small T, Lee (2004b) has an advantage over other models with respect to the number of parameters. On the other hand, Cornwell, Schmidt, and Sickles (1990), and Cuesta (2000) have an advantage over Lee (2004b) with sample of small T and large N.

Second, unlike many other industries, in the sports industry firm sizes are identical with respect to the number of players. A narrow range of inputs might distinguish the functional form of a sporting production from other industries. However, previous works have rarely shown any interest in the functional form and they—with the exception of Zak, Huang, and Siegfried (1979) and Lee and Berri (2004)—have assumed either a linear function or a Cobb-Douglas function without verification. Zak, Huang, and Siegfried explicitly addressed the advantage of a Cobb-Douglas function in which the marginal revenue of each input depends on the levels of other inputs, and the coefficients of the Cobb-Douglas form are easy to interpret as input elasticities. Lee and Berri tested the Cobb-Douglas form with a translog form as an alternative and could not reject the null (i.e., the Cobb-Douglas form). In sum, more careful analysis of production functional form (hypothesis testing and adoption of flexible functional forms) seems to be necessary.

Next, we will address a couple of additional research topics. The management of a sports team has two human components: the general manager and the coach. The main role of a general manager is to draw up the team roster and also to allocate the playing talent inputs of the team with the object of cost-minimization. On the other hand, the main role of a coach is to utilize a given roster of players (i.e., a given set of inputs) to achieve more wins. However, the literature has not analyzed the general manager's efficiency, which is a key aspect of team efficiency. Only Gustafson, Hadley, and Ruggiero (1997) have been concerned with cost minimization. They measured cost efficiency by considering cost frontiers, but did not decompose the frontiers into coach efficiency and general manager efficiency. Cost frontier estimation without estimating allocative efficiency overstates technical inefficiency if firms are allocative inefficient.

Technical efficiency has been related to coach efficiency and allocative efficiency can be also related to general manager efficiency. Then, by applying the established stochastic frontier models that allow for both estimation of allocative and technical efficiency, we may estimate the performance of general managers. The disregard of general manager efficiency has been caused by the selection of player statistics as an input variable. The analysis of cost-minimizing input allocation requires input price information, but the prices of player statistics such as shooting percentage are not measurable. However, with player talent measures as an input, we can calculate the input price of a playing talent by dividing salary by the amount of talent. This is another reason *ex ante* player talent measures are preferred as input variables.

Analyzing team factors affecting team efficiency is also an interesting topic since team management can find a way to improve its efficiency by knowing these factors. However, it is surprising that among the numerous empirical works in team or managerial efficiency estimation there have been only a few (Porter and Scully, 1982; Kahane, 2003) that have pursued this topic. As we discussed in the last section, it has been recognized that the two-step method will provide biased estimation results, because the model in the first step is misspecified. One-step methods will solve this bias problem.

The last concern is also with input variables. Consider the case of basketball. Lee and Berri (2004) assumed there are three inputs in a basketball team: guard, small forward, and big men. Suppose Teams A and B each have two guards and their total talents are equal to each other, say 100. In Team A, two guards are equally talented and each of their talent ratings is 50. On the other hand, Team B has a star guard of talent 80 and another of talent 20. Lee and Berri (2004) assumed that Teams A and B have the same amount of guard input, since they take account only the total amount of talent by position. However, the composition might influence winning performance and should be addressed in the future.

12

Econometric Models in Sports Economics

Michael A. Leeds and Barbara Erin McCormick

This chapter has three central purposes. First, it provides theoretical grounding in some important (and, in some cases, commonly used) techniques that we may know only as Limdep or STATA commands. A more thorough understanding of these techniques will allow sports economists to use them more readily and to justify their use more thoroughly. Second, it reinforces the first goal by pointing out both basic source material on the techniques presented as well as representative applications in the sports economics literature. Finally, it offers a wish list of techniques that would allow sports economists to advance the field but which are, for a variety of reasons, underutilized. We assume the reader has a solid background in basic econometrics. Those wishing to refresh their skills should refer to a basic text such as Kmenta (1997) or Greene (2000).

A complete review of econometric applications could fill a textbook. As a result, the techniques presented here are by no means comprehensive. Instead, they represent an idiosyncratic view of the field of sports economics and the needs of the people who work in it. At some risk of oversimplification, we divide this chapter into two segments. The first can be broadly thought of as dealing with specification error in cross-section analyses. It begins with the Heckman correction for self-selection bias. Although most sports economists are familiar with the basic point of the Heckman correction, the justification presented in most econometrics texts is not directly applicable to many situations encountered in sports economics. Thus, in addition to noting what the Heckman correction does, we also provide a more appropriate justification than many sports economists may be familiar with. We then present a completely new way to approach self-selection and related problems, the Differences-in-Differences (DiD) estimator.

Next, we look at another source of bias: simultaneity. We assume the reader is familiar with simultaneous equations estimation, but we point out that many economists use simultaneous equation models based on personal opinion rather than objective econometric tests. We present one such tool, the Hausman test for endogeneity, a method that is not used frequently enough in the sports economics literature.

The final issue in cross-sectional estimation deals with a set of problems that arise when the error term is not normally distributed. Quantile regressions provide a useful, yet underutilized, way of dealing with non-normal error terms. We also point out that quantile regression techniques can be valuable even when the error term is normally distributed. In particular, quantile regressions provide insights into counterfactual situations (what happens if women are treated like men or if free agency was not granted to football players) that OLS estimation cannot provide. Because quantile regressions have often been used in conjunction with the Oaxaca decomposition, we also briefly discuss that older and more familiar technique.

The second portion of the chapter deals with time-series analysis, an area that most sports economists have avoided. Again, we begin by focusing on specification issues. We begin by looking at how one determines the proper order of a time series. We then turn to the problems caused by nonstationarity and the methods that exist for detecting and correcting for it. Finally, we look at a powerful tool in time-series analysis that too few papers in sports economics use, the Granger test for causality.

Specification Tests in Cross-Section Analysis

One of the most common reasons for having a paper rejected by a journal is the referee's complaint that the econometric model used to test the paper's central hypothesis is incorrectly specified. An improperly specified model can lead to inconsistent estimates, miscalculated t-statistics, or results that do not apply to most observations in the sample. In this section we explore several important specification tests and a variety of methods for correcting problems of misspecification.

Selection Bias and the Heckman Correction

Suppose we wish to look at the impact of participation in varsity athletics on later earnings (see, for example, Long and Caudill, 1991, on college athletics; and Ewing, 1995, on high school athletics). In particular, let us specify the simple wage equation:

$$\ln(w_i) = \alpha + \beta'X_i + \gamma A_i + \varepsilon_i, \tag{12.1}$$

where X_i is a vector of personal characteristics and A_i is a dummy variable equal to 1 if the individual participated in varsity athletics. Ideally, if $\hat{\gamma} > 0$ and is statistically significant, then we can conclude that participation in athletics has a positive impact on earnings later in life. Conversely, we can conclude that it does not have a positive impact if $\hat{\gamma}$ is either not positive or not statistically significant. A positive result would confirm one of the central justifications for athletic programs, that they promote self-discipline, teamwork, and other skills that are highly valued in the job market.

However, it is also possible that, rather than conveying those skills, varsity athletics may attract people who already possess them. The dummy variable A_i thus captures both skills that athletics provide and skills that athletes already possess and would possess even if they never played a sport. Because varsity athletics is correlated with the presence of these underlying abilities, it may effectively serve as a proxy for those abilities and return a positive and significant coefficient despite not having any impact on a student's later earning power. If this is the case, then estimating equation (12.1) by OLS could lead to misguided policy prescriptions.

Econometrically speaking, the coefficient on A_i may be biased because one of the assumptions that underlie equation (12.1) may not hold. In particular, in estimating equation (12.1) with OLS we assume that none of the independent variables is correlated with the error term (ε_i). Because one cannot typically measure such intangibles as self-discipline, they are contained in ε_i. If people who participate in athletics are more self-disciplined than people who are not, then the dummy variable will tend to equal 1 when ε_i is large and will tend to be zero when ε_i is small. Because A_i and ε_i are correlated, the coefficient γ will be biased. In this example, the source of the bias is *self-selection*. Individuals who choose to participate in varsity athletics are systematically different from people who do not. In particular, they possess unobservable qualities that are present in the error term.

We can eliminate self-selection bias with a technique known as the *Heckman correction,* first proposed in Heckman (1979). Heckman's article, however, couched the problem in terms of a censored dependent variable. Here, as in many sports settings, the issue is not censored variable bias. Instead, it is closer to simultaneous equation bias, as a supposedly independent variable is correlated with the error term. Fortunately, Willis and Rosen (1979) have shown that the Heckman correction applies in this situation as well.[1] The key to the Willis and Rosen approach is that individuals choose to take part in athletics if participating is more rewarding than not participating. The indicator function is thus

$$z_i = v_{A,i} - v_{NA,i} \; \mu_i \,, \tag{12.2}$$

where $v_{A,i}$ is the value to person i of participating in athletics, $v_{NA,i}$ is the value of not participating, and μ_i is a random error term. Person i participates in athletics if $z_i > 0$ and does not do so if $z_i < 0$. The estimation problem lies in the fact that unobserved characteristics that promote participation in athletics, μ_i in equation (12.2), may be correlated with characteristics that promote high earnings later in life, in equation (12.1).

We can purge the error term of the nonrandom components by treating those nonrandom components as an omitted variable from the regression. It is not hard to show that the expected value of the logarithm of earnings for ex-athletes is:

$$E(\ln(w_i)\big| z_i > 0) = \alpha + \beta X_i + \gamma A_i + \left(\frac{\sigma_{\varepsilon\mu}}{\sigma_\mu}\right)\lambda_i \;. \tag{12.3}$$

In effect, we can eliminate the correlation between A_i and ε_i by adding another variable and coefficient to equation (12.1). The ratio $\frac{\sigma_{\varepsilon\mu}}{\sigma_\mu}$ is the unknown coefficient that we must estimate. We formulate the variable λ_i, known as the *Heckman lambda*, by computing

$$\lambda_i = \frac{\phi(\hat{z}_i)}{(1 - \Phi(\hat{z}_i))}, \tag{12.4}$$

where Φ, ϕ is the density function of a standard normal variate, Φ_i is the cumulative distribution function, and the ratio $\dfrac{\phi(\hat{z}_i)}{(1 - \Phi(\hat{z}_i))}$ is known as the *inverse Mills ratio*. The standard normal variate, $\hat{z}_i$, is the predicted value of z_i in equation (12.2), which we estimate with a probit equation. If we run the probit equation, compute the Heckman lambda, and include the lambda in equation (12.1), we can purge the error term of its non-zero component and obtain unbiased estimates of the coefficients. Fortunately, most econometric packages now allow us to compute the Heckman lambda and include it in the original equation automatically.

Differences in Differences Estimation

A new technique that economists use to account for selection bias is the Differences-in-Differences (DiD) estimator, developed by Card and Sullivan (1988). According to Buckley and Shang (2003), DiD accounts for selection bias because any variable that remains constant over time and is correlated with the selection decision and the outcome will not bias the estimated effect of the selection decision. In effect, DiD creates a control group effect against which we can compare the selection group. More generally, DiD is useful for evaluating a policy change that is designed to affect only members of the treatment group. (See McCormick, 2005, for an application of this technique to sports economics.)

Consider, for example, the impact of a change in NCAA academic standards on the earnings of former athletes.[2] One could estimate the impact of this reform by using a dummy variable for athletes who graduated after the reform. However, this would ignore the possibility that the reform was part of a more general change in academic standards that may have affected athletes and non-athletes alike. The idea behind DiD analysis is that we must compare the impact of the reform—the *difference* in earnings before and after reform—for athletes with the impact on non-athletes—the *difference* in the difference. If there is a statistically significant difference-in-differences, then we can conclude that the policy had the intended effect.

The first difference is found by comparing earnings before and after the reform separately for the treatment group (athletes) and the control group (non-athletes).

$$\Delta_A^1 = (w_A^{NEW} - w_A^{OLD}) \tag{12.5}$$

$$\Delta_N^1 = (w_N^{NEW} - w_N^{OLD}), \tag{12.6}$$

where the subscript A denotes former student athletes, which comprise the treatment group, and N denotes non-athletes (the control group). The superscript NEW indicates that the outcome is for the year following the enactment of the reforms, and OLD indicates that the outcome is for the year prior to the new requirements.

The first difference for the experimental group, Δ_A^1, reveals the change in the earnings for athletes that occurs after the reforms have been put in place.

This tests whether the reforms had a statistically significant impact on the wages of former student athletes. The corresponding first difference for the control group (Δ^1_N) examines whether the educational reforms also had a direct effect on the wages of non-athletes or was part of a broader movement that affected all students and not just athletes. Because the educational reforms were directed specifically at student athletes, they should not have affected the control group, and we would expect Δ^1_N to equal zero.

The second difference—the difference-in-differences—is given by:

$$\Delta^2 = \Delta^1_A - \Delta^1_N. \tag{12.7}$$

The second difference in equation (12.7) shows whether the reactions to the policy change by former student athletes and non-athletes differ. In other words, Δ^2 is used to determine if the reforms affected student athletes more than they affected non-athletes.

In order to estimate the first and second differences, one pools the samples for the two cohorts and runs the regression

$$w_{it} = \alpha_{it} + \gamma_1 A_i + \gamma_2 NEW_i + \gamma_3 (A \times NEW)_{it} + \varepsilon_{it}, \tag{12.8}$$

where w_{it} is the wage for individual i in year t. The indicator variable A_i equals 1 if the individual is a student athlete and 0 if a non-athlete. The indicator variable NEW_i specifies the cohort: it equals 1 if the individual went to school prior to the tighter academic requirements and 0 if not. Finally, the interaction variable $(A \times NEW)_{it} = 1$ indicates that the wage is for student athletes in the later cohort.

We can add a vector of control variables, X_{it}, such as demographic variables or socioeconomic information, to formulate the extended regression model

$$w_{it} = \alpha_{it} + \beta X_{it} + \gamma_1 A_i + \gamma_2 NEW_i + \gamma_3 (A \times NEW)_{it} + \varepsilon_{it}. \tag{12.9}$$

Using the results from estimating equation (12.9), the first difference for student athletes is given by

$$\hat{\gamma}_1 + \hat{\gamma}_2 = E(\overline{w} \mid A_i = 1, NEW_i = 1) - E(w_{it} \mid A_i = 1, NEW_i = 0), \tag{12.10}$$

which expresses the expected change in wages resulting from the new policy.

The corresponding first difference for non-athletes is

$$\hat{\gamma}_2 = E(\overline{w}_{it} \mid A_i = 0, NEW_i = 1) - E(w_{it} \mid A_i = 0, NEW_i = 0), \quad (12.11)$$

which conveys the expected change in wages for non-athletes. The second difference, the DiD estimator, is therefore

$$\hat{\gamma}_3 = \{E(\overline{w}_{it} \mid A_i = 1, NEW_i = 1) - E(w_{it}, A_i = 1, NEW_i = 0)\}, \quad (12.12)$$

which expresses the expected difference in the differences of the average wage for former student athletes versus non-athletes during both pre- and post-policy enactment. Thus, we can formulate a consistent estimate of $\hat{\gamma}_3$ by calculating the difference between the average change in wages in the samples of pre-reform and post-reform cohorts for athletes and non-athletes.

Simultaneity and the Hausman Test

To introduce the Hausman test, let us continue a previous example by assuming that we wish to estimate the impact of varsity athletics on the later earnings of married women. There is an ample literature on the greater complexity of estimating equation (12.1) for women than for men. One of these complexities stems from the fact that women bear a disproportionate share of the responsibilities for childrearing. Because children may take time and energy that would otherwise be devoted to the job, many economists expect that the number of children has a negative effect on the woman's wage. They therefore include the number of children in the family unit (K_i) as an explanatory variable in wage equations like equation (12.1).

$$\ln(w_i) = \alpha + \beta'X_i + \chi A_i + \delta K_i + \varepsilon_i . \quad (12.13)$$

Demographers, however, note that the number of children in the family may itself be a function of a woman's wage, so

$$K_i = a + b\ln(w_i) + c'Z_i + \eta_i, \quad (12.14)$$

where Z_i is a vector of exogenous variables affecting fertility decisions. If this is the case, OLS estimates of (12.13) and (12.14) are subject to the familiar *simultaneity bias*. A researcher may therefore want to estimate the wage equation as part of a simultaneous system using two- or three-stage least squares. Both techniques effectively estimate equation (12.13) after replacing the endogenous variable K_i with the instrumental variable $\hat{K}_i$. Although these techniques are well known, economists often use them without testing whether such estimation is necessary.

At first glance, using $\hat{K}_i$ instead of K_i seems like the safe thing to do, even if it is not necessary. After all, if one chooses the correct set of instruments, $\hat{K}_i$ is a consistent estimator of K_i, and so the resulting estimation will also be consistent even if K_i is truly exogenous. Using instrumental variables unnecessarily, however, does bring a potential cost. Although replacing K_i with $\hat{K}_i$ yields consistent estimates, these estimates of $\hat{K}_i$ will not be efficient if K_i is exogenous. Thus, in addition to being theoretically misleading, mistakenly calling K_i endogenous could lead to erroneous results from hypothesis tests. Fortunately, Hausman (1978) has provided a way to avoid biased or inefficient results by devising a test for endogeneity.[3]

The idea behind the Hausman test rests on the notion that if the variable in question (K_i) is exogenous then it conveys the same information as its instrument, $\hat{K}_i$. Thus, if K_i is exogenous and we run two regressions, one with K_i and the other with $\hat{K}_i$, their coefficients would be statistically indistinguishable. If K_i is endogenous, then its coefficient is biased, and will not be the same as the coefficient on $\hat{K}_i$.

To see this in practice, let us consider the test for equations (12.13) and (12.14) under the simplifying assumption that X_i and Z_i are exogenous scalars (A_i is a scalar by construction). If K_i is endogenous, one can calculate the instrument from the reduced form equation

$$\hat{K}_i = \hat{\mu}_0 + \hat{\mu}_1' X_i + \hat{\mu}_2 A_i + \hat{\mu}_3' Z_i. \tag{12.15}$$

We can thus rewrite equation (12.1) as

$$\ln(w_i) = \alpha + \beta' X_i + \gamma A_i + \delta(\hat{K}_i + u_i) + \varepsilon_i, \tag{12.16}$$

where u_i is the error term from the reduced form regression. Note that equation (12.15) specifies that K_i and u_i have the same coefficient. This holds, however, only if both terms are uncorrelated with ε_i. Although $\hat{K}_i$ is uncorrelated with ε_i by construction, the error term u_i is uncorrelated with ε_i only if K_i is exogenous. If K_i is endogenous, then so is u_i; its coefficient will be distorted by this correlation, and its coefficient will therefore differ from δ. The essence of the Hausman test is thus to test whether the coefficients on $\hat{K}_i$ and u_i are statistically distinguishable. If they are, then we conclude that K_i is endogenous and we should use simultaneous equations methods. If they are not, then K_i is exogenous and the OLS estimator is more efficient. Again, most statistical software can now conduct a Hausman test automatically.

Quantile Regressions

All the empirical analyses described above maintain that the error term (once it is purged of simultaneity or self-selection) is normally distributed with zero mean. The regression line thus provides the mean of the dependent variable given the observed values of the independent variables. This implies that if we were estimating the pay of basketball players based on measures of performance, we would expect a player with performance measures X_i who plays in a city with characteristics Y_j to be paid

$$E\left(S_{ij}\big|X_i,Y_j\right)= \beta'X_i + \gamma'Y_j, \tag{12.17}$$

where S_{ij} is player i's salary (or a transformation of the salary such as its natural logarithm) when he or she plays in city j. The theoretical basis for this specification is that players receive their marginal revenue product (MRP) and that the MRP is captured by the performance variables in X_i and the city-specific variables in Y_j.[4]

McLaughlin (1994) points out that when markets are thin, marginal revenue product is only one factor in determining compensation. In particular, when there are few buyers with specific needs and few sellers with specific skills, rents arise. These rents are distributed among buyers and sellers based on the relative bargaining strengths of the player and the team. It can be very difficult, however, to account for bargaining strength. Sometimes, all we know is that some players are systematically paid more than their marginal revenue products while others are paid less. One way to capture bargaining strength is to analyze the determinants of the salaries of players who make above-average and below-average salaries *conditional on their marginal revenue product*. The italicized term is important, as we must distinguish between highly paid players whose salaries can be explained by observable skills, observations that would appear far out along an OLS regression line, and those who earn more than their skills alone justify, observations that would lie far above the regression line. OLS cannot tell us about players whose salaries lie above or below the conditional mean, but a highly underutilized technique known as quantile regression can.[5] For examples of this use of quantile regressions, see Leeds and Kowalewski (2001) and Kowalewski (2005).

Quantile regression (QR) has existed since the work of Koenker and Bassett

(1978), but it was not used in the economic literature until the work of Buchinsky (1994) and DiNardo, Fortin, Lemieux (1996). QR and OLS differ fundamentally, as QR is based on least absolute deviation of the error terms rather than least squares. That is, QR chooses the regression line that minimizes the sum of the absolute value of the distance between the observed value of S_i and the regression line rather than the sum of the squared distance. The QR estimator for the seventy-fifth quantile of equation (12.17)—those players whose salaries are in the top quarter of the salary distribution *conditional on the independent variables*—chooses $\hat{\beta}$ and $\hat{\gamma}$ to minimize the sum

$$Z_{75} = (0.75) \sum_{S_{ij} \geq \hat{\beta}'X - \hat{\gamma}'Y} \left| S_{ij} - \hat{\beta}'X_i - \hat{\gamma}'Y_j \right| + (0.25) \sum_{S_{ij} < \hat{\beta}'X - \hat{\gamma}'Y} \left| S_{ij} - \hat{\beta}'X_i - \hat{\gamma}'Y_j \right|. \quad (12.18)$$

In effect, the algorithm separates the observations into those above a position in the conditional distribution and those below that position. It then minimizes the weighted sum of the absolute deviations from the regression line. Thus, in this case, the line is chosen so that 75 percent of the sample observations lie below the fitted line and 25 percent lie above it. QR is slowly filtering into statistical packages. To date, only a few, such as STATA, carry it.

Perhaps the most valuable aspect of the QR technique can be illustrated in the area of discrimination in professional sports. Discrimination in professional sports has been examined in a wide variety of ways. However, only a handful of studies have acknowledged that race (or sex or ethnicity) can affect the entire distribution of earnings.[6] For example, racial discrimination in the National Basketball Association may apply less (or more) to superstars such as Tim Duncan and Kevin Garnett than it does to average players or to marginal players. However, OLS can tell us only the impact of race on the conditional mean. QR allows us to build an entire counterfactual distribution. It allows us to see how the impact of discrimination varies across the spectrum of player talents and salaries.

The procedure is actually a generalization of the Oaxaca decomposition, which first tried to simulate counterfactual wages. Oaxaca (1973a) points out that the standard control for discrimination, including a dummy variable that captures race or sex (or whatever potential source of discrimination one wishes to test). In the context of equation (12.17), the inclusion of a dummy variable shifts the regression line up or down without affecting any of the other independent variables. Discrimination, however, can enter in a variety of ways. It may, for example, affect the value a team places on a player's performance. Thus, scoring an additional point per game may bring a lesser (or greater) increase in pay for a black basketball player than for a white one. The Oaxaca decomposition captures the broader impact of discrimination by simulating how a person of one race (or sex) would fare if he or she were treated like a member of the other race (or sex).

To perform an Oaxaca decomposition of the impact of race on pay in the NBA, one first runs separate wage equations for black and white players. (For simplicity, we ignore city effects here.)

$$S_B = \alpha_B + \beta'_B X_B + \varepsilon_B \qquad (12.19a)$$

$$S_W = \alpha_W + \beta'_W X_W + \varepsilon_W, \qquad (12.19b)$$

where B denotes black players and W denotes white players. The average wages for each group are given by:

$$\overline{S}_B = \alpha_B + \beta'_B \overline{X}_B \qquad (12.20a)$$

$$\overline{S}_W = \alpha_W + \beta'_W \overline{X}_W, \qquad (12.20b)$$

where $\overline{X}_B$ and $\overline{X}_W$ are vectors of average performance levels for blacks and whites. We can use equations (12.20a) and (12.20b) to rewrite the difference in the average salaries for black and white players, $\Delta \overline{S} = \overline{S}_B - \overline{S}_W$, as

$$\Delta \overline{S} = \alpha_B + \beta'_B \overline{X}_B - \alpha_W - \beta'_W \overline{X}_W = (\alpha_B - \alpha_W) + (\beta'_B - \beta'_W)\overline{X}_W + \beta'_B (\overline{X}_B - \overline{X}_W) \quad (12.21)$$

The first term on the right side of equation (12.21), $(\alpha_B - \alpha_W)$, indicates the difference in the intercepts for black and white players. This is what standard dummy variable specifications pick up. The second term, $(\beta'_B - \beta'_W)\overline{X}_W$, accounts for differences "in the coefficients." It allows the returns to performance to vary by race so that a player with the skills of the average white player would be compensated differently. The third term, $\beta'_B(\overline{X}_B - \overline{X}_W)$, accounts for differences "in the data." It acknowledges that some of the difference in pay between black and white players could be due to differences in their marginal products, which would not disappear even in a world without discrimination.

Because the sum $D = (\alpha_B - \alpha_W) + (\beta'_B - \beta'_W)\overline{X}_W$ reflects the difference in pay that is not due to differences in market-relevant factors, Oaxaca regards D as the overall impact of discrimination. If $D < 0$, then one can claim that the average white player would be paid less if he or she was treated as a black player. Conversely, if $D > 0$, white players would be paid more if they were treated like blacks, and one could conclude that black players were the beneficiaries of discrimination.

Although a major improvement on previous studies, the Oaxaca decomposition still is limited. It effectively compares individuals with the mean characteristics of each population subgroup and does not allow different effects for people with different abilities. Machado and Mata (2001) have developed a way to create a counterfactual distribution of salaries. The methodology for doing this closely follows Oaxaca's framework.

Again, one begins by running separate regressions for whites and blacks. This time, however, the regressions take the form

$$S_r = \alpha_r + X_r \beta_r^\theta + \varepsilon_i, \tag{12.22}$$

where r (= B, W) indexes race, and θ denotes the θth quantile. Rather than running a single OLS regression, one now runs a series of quantile regressions for different values of θ.[7] One can then use the estimated coefficients to formulate the counterfactual salary for what the ith white player would have earned if he or she were black and in the (conditional) quantile θ:

$$\hat{S}_i^\theta = \hat{\alpha}_B + X_i \hat{\beta}_B^\theta. \tag{12.23}$$

By randomly paring observations with quantiles, one can formulate a counterfactual distribution of salaries that white players would have earned if they experienced the same conditions as black players. One can then compare the hypothetical distribution with the actual distribution to determine the impact of discrimination on the entire population of players and not just on the average player. To date, only a handful of papers (e.g., Hamilton, 1997; and Leeds, Wheaton, and Pistolet, 2002) have used this very powerful tool.

Time Series and Granger Causality

Sports economics is full of chicken-and-egg questions. For example, are the New York Yankees so successful on the field because they have such high revenues and hence can afford the most talented and hence most highly paid players? Or, is the team's high revenue stream a result of its high winning percentage? Given the abundance of such questions of causality, there is surprisingly little research in the area. It is especially puzzling in light of the fact that the tools to analyze such questions have existed and have been used in other areas of economics for a long time. The few sports economics papers that explore issues of causality deal largely with British rugby and soccer leagues (see Davies, Downward, and Jackson, 1995; and Dobson and Goddard, 1998a). This is perhaps fitting, as the most popular tool for testing causality was first posited by the British Nobel laureate Clive Granger (1969). Although the basic idea of Granger causality is relatively easily grasped, its practice involves the use of time-series analysis, a field unfamiliar to many sports economists.[8] In this section, we use Granger causality as a spring-board for discussing larger issues in time-series analysis.[9]

Specification Issues in Time Series

In order to test whether the Yankees' revenue stream causes their record or vice versa, we first must specify the correct form of the Vector Autoregression, or VAR. A VAR is an autoregressive process for a system of variables. In this case, the simplest VAR would be the first-order process, which takes the form:

$$Y_t = AY_{t-1} + \varepsilon_t, \tag{12.24}$$

where $Y_t = \begin{bmatrix} R_t \\ W_t \end{bmatrix}$ (R_t is revenue in year t and W_t is winning percentage in

year t), A is a 2×2 matrix of coefficients, and $\varepsilon_t = \begin{bmatrix} \varepsilon_{1t} \\ \varepsilon_{2t} \end{bmatrix}$ is a white-noise

error term. The vector notation is equivalent to the system of equations

$$R_t = a_{11}R_{t-1} + a_{12}W_{t-1} + e_{1t} \; ; \; W_t = a_{21}R_{t-1} + a_{22}W_{t-1} + e_{2t}. \tag{12.25}$$

More complex autoregressive structures can be expressed as

$$Y_t = A_1Y_{t-1} + A_2Y_{t-2} + ... + A_KY_{t-K} + \varepsilon_t \tag{12.26}$$

Equation (12.25) may also include vectors of contemporaneous and lagged exogenous variables (e.g., variables that control for labor stoppages and league expansion), though, for simplicity, we ignore them for now. Before testing the system for Granger causality, we must first be sure that the equations are correctly specified. The first order of business is to determine the correct order of the autoregressive process. In particular, we must decide whether the process specified in equation (12.25) is better or worse than one based on L lagged values of Y ($L > K$). There are many ways to test which specification is better. Perhaps the easiest way is to see whether including additional lags significantly increases the value of the likelihood function. We can do this by estimating equation (12.25) for both K and L lags. We can then compare the values of the likelihood functions by performing a standard likelihood ratio test. Although this technique is simple to use, it can be cumbersome. If, for example, we find that L

lags significantly improve the likelihood function, then we must continue by running a regression with M lags ($M > L$), and repeating the process.

Once we are satisfied that the VAR has the correct order, we then need to determine whether the autoregressive processes are stationary. Stationarity is one of the more intimidating concepts in time-series econometrics, but it really has an intuitively appealing interpretation. There is also an easy test for whether a process is stationary, and a simple way to make a nonstationary process stationary.

To keep matters simple, suppose that revenue follows a first-order autoregressive process:

$$R_t = \alpha R_{t-1} + \eta_t \, . \tag{12.27}$$

This process is stationary if $|\alpha| < 1$.[10] Stationarity thus means that a random shock to revenue in period t has a decreasing impact on future levels of revenue. If we were to plot values of R_t, we would find that it fluctuates around a fixed value. If $|\alpha| \geq 1$ then the series is nonstationary. A random shock has a lingering effect on future values, and the time series moves in a specific direction.

We worry about nonstationarity because problems can result if we regress one nonstationary series on another. Suppose, for example, that the Yankees' revenues and winning percentage are completely independent of one another but that both are nonstationary series. Suppose further that revenue trends upwards over time while winning percentage trends downwards. These two trends imply that when we regress revenues on winning percentage we are likely to find a significant, negative relationship despite the fact that no relationship actually exists. The reason lies in the nonstationarity that causes one variable to increase at the same time that the other decreases. Thus, regressing one nonstationary process on another often yields "false positives," finding a relationship between two variables when none really exists.

Unfortunately, one cannot test equation (12.27) directly for whether $a \geq 1$ (whether a *unit root* exists). The problem is that if the process is nonstationary, then $\frac{\hat{\alpha}}{\sigma_\alpha}$ does not follow a t-distribution. If that is so, then the critical values for a t-test are no longer valid. Fortunately, a simple alternative test for nonstationarity, the Dickey-Fuller test, exists. Although we shall not go into the specifics of this test, the Dickey-Fuller test does the same thing as a t-test but develops alternative critical values in place of the t-statistics.

One can commonly eliminate nonstationarity by taking first differences, transforming equation (12.27) into

$$\Delta R_t = R_t - R_{t-1} = V_t. \tag{12.28}$$

This new series is stationary if the error term $v_t (= \eta_t - \eta_{t-1})$ is white noise. We can check whether equation (12.28) is stationary by performing yet another Dickey-Fuller test on the transformed process. Only when we have the appropriate order and a stationary process can we finally perform a test for Granger causality.

Granger Causality

The "Granger causality test" is a misnomer, as Granger actually proposed a test that causation does *not* exist. Thus, we cannot say, for example, that revenues cause winning percentage. Instead, we can say that we reject the hypothesis that revenue does not cause winning percentage. In general, a variable does not "Granger cause" another if we can exclude its lagged values from the right-hand side of the regression without worsening the quality of the regression. The Granger test for causality is better regarded as a screen by which we can establish a necessary condition, but *not* a sufficient condition, for causality. Perhaps for this reason, Granger causality is not transitive. That is, it is possible for X_i to Granger cause Y_i and for Y_i to Granger cause Z_i, while X_i does not Granger cause Y_i.

In addition to not being a direct test of causality, the Granger causality test does not give a unique direction of causation. It is possible, for example, that we reject the hypothesis that revenue does not Granger cause winning percentage, and we also reject the hypothesis that winning percentage does not Granger cause revenue. In the context of our simple example, if a_{12} in

$$R_t = a_{11}R_{t-1} + a_{12}W_{t-1} + e_{1t}, \tag{12.29}$$

is statistically insignificant then winning percentage does *not* Granger cause revenue. If a_{12} is statistically significant and if a_{21} is statistically insignificant in the equation

$$W_t = a_{21}R_{t-1} + a_{22}W_{t-1} + e_{2t}, \tag{12.30}$$

then we say that winning percentage Granger causes revenue but revenue does not Granger cause winning percentage. If the both a_{12} and a_{21} are statistically significant then both revenue and winning percentage Granger cause each other.

In a more complex specification, in which equations (12.29) and (12.30) include higher-order lags of the variables, one must do a joint test of whether all the W_{t-j} in equation (12.28) and all R_{t-j} in equation (12.29) ($j \geq 1$) are significant. If so, then one can again reject the hypothesis that winning percentage does not cause revenues. Although Granger causality is relatively easy to run on any statistical package that handles time series, several packages, such as SAS, now include specific commands for a Granger causality test.

Conclusion

Improperly specified econometric models are perhaps the most significant obstacle to publishing academic articles. Although many statistical tools are now at our fingertips, we often do not know how to use them or how to justify our use of them. We hope this essay helps sports economists understand some of the pitfalls of econometric estimation. We also hope that, by presenting such underutilized techniques as Differences-in-Differences, quantile regression, and Granger causality, we encourage new research that makes use of these estimation methods.

Notes

1. See Maddala (1999) for an excellent treatment of the Heckman correction.
2. The NCAA has enacted several policies to make the eligibility requirements for participation in intercollegiate athletics more rigorous, including Propositions 16 and 48. In doing so, the NCAA hopes to motivate higher university graduation rates for student athletes, which would then increase the future earning potential of those student athletes.
3. For an example of the use of this technique, see Fort and Gill (2000).
4. This is used by a wide literature that began with Scully (1974). For a reference that is particularly relevant for this context, see Kahn and Sherer (1988).
5. There are actually many other contexts in which quantile regressions are useful, such as when we have reason to believe that the error structure is not normally distributed, as when we believe that the tails of the distribution are too thick for it to be normal.
6. Specifically, see Hamilton (1997) and Leeds, Wheaton, and Pistolet (2002).
7. One can use a random sample of values for Θ over the interval [0,100], or, as Albrecht, Bjorklund, and Vroman (2003) choose, for all possible values of Θ.
8. For recent examples of studies using time series techniques, see Narayan and Smyth (2004) and Schmidt and Berri (2002 and 2004).
9. A good source for those needing background in time-series econometrics is Hill, Griffiths, and Judge (2001).
10. We can easily expand equation (12.26) to account for the presence of a constant term, control variables, and so on, but that would simply add to the complexity of the problem without shedding additional light on it.

13

The Theory of Contests

Stefan Szymanski

The literature on the economics of sports dates back to the famous article of Simon Rottenberg published in 1956, but since that date there have been relatively few articles that have set out to model sports leagues in a precise way, using the tool kit of calculus and game theory that is now standard in most of the economics literature.

The most natural way to conceive of a sporting contest or tournament (the two words are used interchangeably), theoretically speaking, is within the framework of a Tullock (1980) contest. This chapter sets out how this framework can be applied, the kinds of questions that can be answered, and where the literature stands today and how it might develop in the future.

Tullock Contests

A Tullock contest involves several players competing to win a prize. Each player is assumed to choose independently an input quantity, which might be thought of as effort or as a financial payment toward winning the prize, such that the probability of winning is increasing in this quantity. The most important feature of the Tullock model is that expected payoffs are proportional to the contribution of each player. Thus the simplest framework for thinking about the problem is the case where there is a prize V and there are n contestants. Each contestant supplies effort, and the probability of winning for each player depends on the share of total effort supplied:

$$p_i = \frac{e_i^\gamma}{\sum_{j=1}^n e_j^\gamma}, \qquad (13.1)$$

where the payoff to each player is

$$\pi_i = p_i V - c_i e_i, \tag{13.2}$$

where V is value of the prize and c_i is contestant i's marginal cost of effort/investment. Equation (13.1) is commonly known as the *contest success function,* and is commonly used in this simple logit form, although alternative specifications exist. Note that equation (13.1) incorporates an *adding up con-straint* such that $p_k = 1 - \sum_{j \neq k} p_j$. In the mainstream contest literature attention usually focuses on the symmetric case where the value of the prize is identical for all contestants as are marginal costs ($c_i = c_j$ for all i and j). The parameter γ in the contest success function represents the sensitivity of the probability of success to effort; when $\gamma = 0$, success is independent of effort, as $\gamma \to 0$. Then if one player contributes more effort than the others, that player becomes increasingly certain to win (in the limiting case the contest becomes like an all-pay auction where the highest bidder wins with probability one).

The conventional approach is to search for a pure-strategy Nash equilibrium of the model. The best response function for each player is found by taking the first order condition with respect to effort, holding the choices of all other players as given. This is

$$\frac{\partial \pi_i}{\partial e_i} = \frac{\gamma V e_i^\gamma \sum_{j \neq i} e_j^\gamma}{e_i \left(\sum_{j=1}^{n} e_j^\gamma \right)^2} - c = 0 \cdot \tag{13.3}$$

Equation (13.3) describes the best response of player i to any possible combination of effort choices of all the other players in the game. At the symmetric equilibrium it must be the case that $e_i = e_j$ for all i and j, and hence (13.3) simplifies to

$$e^* = \frac{(n-1)\gamma V}{cn^2} \cdot \tag{13.4}$$

If each player in the contest supplies e^* effort, then every player's choice of action is a best response to the choice of action of every other player, and hence this is a pure-strategy Nash equilibrium. At the Nash equilibrium each player has a probability of winning the prize that is $1/n$ and hence the payoff of each player is

$$\pi^* = \frac{V[n - \gamma(n-1)]}{n^2}.$$

(13.5)

Note that $\gamma < n/(n-1)$ is a necessary condition for profits to be positive at the Nash equilibrium, and hence a pure-strategy Nash equilibrium does not exist for values of γ greater than this (players would prefer not to enter the contest). Intuitively, we know from equation (13.4) that the effort choice is increasing in γ, which measures the power of the contest success function to discriminate between different effort levels. As γ becomes large, a small amount of extra effort produces a near certainty of winning; that is, the marginal return to effort is increasing. This however, can lead to overinvestment in effort, so that the expected return of contestants is negative. It is still the case, however, that a mixed-strategy equilibrium will exist. This involves players randomizing over whether to enter the contest or not, and hence ensures that it is possible that under some realizations of the random choice there are few enough contestants to generate positive profits, to compensate for those realizations where there are too many—and hence expected profits can be zero. Although this interpretation might seem natural in the context of a repeated game, Tullock himself has argued that the mixed-strategy equilibrium is deeply unsatisfactory.

The central question in this literature has been the extent to which competition will eliminate economic rents. Clearly this depends on the number of contestants and the sensitivity of the contest success function to effort. There exists a critical value of γ for each value of n that will ensure that profits are zero at the pure-strategy equilibrium. However, there can be no presumption that the true γ in any given contest will take this value. Moreover, it is questionable within the framework of this model whether rent dissipation is socially beneficial. As stated, the contest is of no intrinsic benefit, and since effort is costly the socially optimal outcome is to cancel the contest and award the prize randomly. There are a number of ways a benefit can be attributed to the contest. For example, it might be supposed that effort produces some output that is socially desirable (such as innovation) and hence a planner's objective might be to maximize total effort. Alternatively, it may be that each contestant is an agent for some principal who values the prize and that effort, since it increases the probability of the prize, generates a reward that is paid by the principal to the agent. This is essentially the team sport interpretation of the contest, where the agent is the owner of the team and fans are the principal.

Sporting Tournaments

The first papers to use a contest/tournament framework were El-Hodiri and Quirk (1971) and Quirk and El-Hodiri (1974). They modeled a team sports league in a dynamic framework where new talent enters a league from year to year and teams can trade talent. The contest element resided in the assumption that revenues were a concave function of the probability of the home team winning (reaching a maximum at some probability greater than one half) and that this probability was increasing in the home team's share of talent playing in the match. These papers used dynamic programming to identify steady state talent share. The model, however, was a cooperative rather than a noncooperative game, in that the necessary conditions for a maximum were taken to be not only that each team should maximize its payoff function in terms of its own talent inventory, but also in terms of the quantity of talent hired by every other team.

Quirk and El-Hodiri (1974) made an important claim, extending Rottenberg's invariance principle to gate revenue sharing. Rottenberg (1956) had claimed that rules over the ownership of talent, such as the reserve clause, would have no impact on the equilibrium distribution of talent. This was a Coasian argument relying on the notion that gains from trade will always be exploited. Thus if the marginal revenue product of a player was higher at one team than at another, that player would move to that team—if the team owned the player's contract, he would be traded, while if the player was a free agent, he would receive a higher wage offer. In either case the player ends up where his marginal contribution is greatest. Note that this argument does not specify the trading mechanism itself. Quirk and El-Hodiri's claim, based on the identification of the steady state given the set-up of their dynamic cooperative game, was that the same applied if the revenue sharing parameter changes, that is, that the distribution of talent would be independent of the amount of revenue sharing operated by the league.

The framework of the El-Hodiri and Quirk model is somewhat different from the conventional Tullock model, being both dynamic and cooperative so that at equilibrium the marginal revenue of an increase in the probability of winning is equalized across all teams (note that this is a condition for joint profit maximization). A more conventional framework is described by Fort and Quirk (1995) and Vrooman (1995). To use the example of Fort and Quirk, they define revenue as a function of win percentage so that team profits are defined as

$$\pi_i = R^i(w^i) - cw^i, \tag{13.6}$$

where c is defined as the marginal cost of a unit of talent (their equation 13). The first order condition is derived by taking the derivative with respect to win percentage so that at equilibrium $MR^i - c = 0$ (their equation 14), and also therefore the marginal revenue of a win is equalized across all teams.

Note again that this is a condition for joint profit maximization. However, this result depends on the derivation of the marginal revenue of a win.

Strictly speaking, teams cannot choose wins (unless they fix matches); instead they choose to invest in talent, which then delivers wins. If as is commonly supposed for North American leagues, the quantity of talent is fixed, teams cannot even choose the quantity of talent independently—there must be some function that relates planned investment to realized talent share. This function, of course, is a contest success function, and it would appear from the literature that sports economists typically have in mind a function such as (13.1). Suppose that each team allocates a budget B to talent investment, and that each team is awarded a share of talent that is proportional to its investment, and that the share of talent in turn determines the share of wins. If we restrict ourselves to the simple two-team case, we can write

$$w_i = \frac{t_i}{t_1 + t_2} = \frac{B_i}{B_1 + B_2}, \tag{13.7}$$

which is strictly analogous to (13.1), with the assumption that $\gamma = 1$. In passing, it is worth observing that restricting ourselves to the two-team case, although frequently considered objectionable, in fact makes little difference to the equilibrium analysis. The reason that the two-team case is often considered unreasonable is that it ignores externalities that may be imposed by one team on another. However, in a noncooperative game such as this, teams impose externalities on each other even when there are only two. For example, Team 1 will choose an investment level to maximize its own profit, ignoring the impact that this choice will have on the profits of Team 2 (which is clearly a negative externality). It remains an interesting question whether the possibility of positive externalities would much affect the nature of the equilibrium in the case of a model with more than two teams, but it is not obvious that the effect would be anything more than second order.

There is a significant practical difficulty involved with modeling more than two teams, which is to define the nature of the asymmetry. The whole interest in modeling a sporting league resides with the asymmetry, due to differences in the ability of teams to generate revenue from different levels of success (or, less plausibly, differences in the ability of clubs to extract different levels of success from a given expenditure on talent). Almost all of the contest literature concentrates on symmetric contests, given its focus on the issue of rent dissipation. The most important question in the sports literature is competitive balance, and the desirability of restrictions agreed to by member teams to increase the competitive balance of the league. To model this requires an asymmetric model. Asymmetry between two teams can be easily modeled, whereas asymmetry between three teams could take many forms, and hence any particular results are likely to be viewed as arbitrary.

From equation (13.7) it should be apparent that there is no need to model the budget choices B_i independently of the choices t_i, even if the sum of talent is fixed. That is because any given share of the aggregate budget will, from (13.6), translate into exactly the same percentage share of talent, and hence we can model the problem as if teams could choose talent directly. We can now write the profit function for each team as

$$\pi_i = R_i\left[w_i(t_i)\right] - ct_i, \tag{13.8}$$

and maximizing this subject to (13.7) generates the first-order condition (or best response function)

$$\frac{\partial \pi_i}{\partial t_i} = \frac{\partial R_i}{\partial w_i}\frac{\partial w_i}{\partial t_i} - c = 0, \tag{13.9}$$

so that the marginal revenue of an additional unit of talent is equal to the marginal revenue of a win multiplied by the marginal effect of a unit of talent on win percentage. Fort and Quirk (explicitly) and Vrooman (implicitly) assume that the marginal effect of a unit of talent on win percentage is a constant. Strictly speaking, this is not possible, given that win percentage can never exceed unity. However, it is possible to understand how this assumption is reached. If we take the derivative of equation (13.7), we obtain

$$\frac{\partial w_i}{\partial t_i} = \frac{t_1 + t_2 - t_i\left(1 + \dfrac{dt_j}{dt_i}\right)}{\left(t_1 + t_2\right)^2}. \tag{13.10}$$

The key quantity is $\dfrac{dt_j}{dt_i}$. If this is equal to -1, then (13.10) reduces to $1/(t_1 + t_2)$, which can be treated as a constant. The quantity $\dfrac{dt_j}{dt_i}$ is typically known as a

conjectural variation. Conjectural variations describe the expected response of one player to the choice of another. In the familiar textbook quantity-setting oligopoly model, a conjectural variation of zero corresponds to the Cournot model, a conjectural variation of -1 corresponds to the Bertrand model, and a conjectural variation of $+1$ corresponds to the joint profit maximizing model. Traditionally it has been argued that the use of different conjectural variations shows how different equilibria can be reached from the same modeling framework. This view, however, is now not widely accepted, since the logic of the textbook oligopoly model, and the contest model described here, is based on the assumption that each player makes a single choice, simultaneously and independently of the choices of others, and that once this choice is made, the corresponding payoffs are distributed and the game ends. Hence there is no opportunity for any reaction by one player in the game to the choice of another, and hence the only conceivable conjec-

tural variation is $\dfrac{dt_j}{dt_i} = 0.$

Although this is true for the model stated here, there has been some confusion in the sports literature because a conjectural variation equal to "–1" does in fact appear to be correct if the supply of talent is fixed, since any increase in the quantity of talent hired by one team necessarily implies that the other team must reduce the quantity it hires by the same amount, assuming talent is fully employed. This confusion is a consequence of the elision, which equates budget choice with talent choice.

The distribution of talent is the same if the choice variable is the budget B_i with $\dfrac{dB_j}{dB_i} = 0$, as it is when the choice variable is the quantity of talent t_i with

$\dfrac{dt_j}{dt_i} = 0.$ In the first case, presumably few would argue that budget choices are anything other than independent, while in the second case, it seems tempting to think that talent choices are interdependent. Strictly speaking, therefore, one should always conceive of the problem as one of choosing budgets, which also happens to be the more realistic assumption. The conjectural varia-

tion $\dfrac{dt_j}{dt_i} = 0$ is typically known as the Nash conjecture, and this is necessary to identify the Nash equilibrium of the model.

With Nash conjectures, the equilibrium condition (13.9) becomes

$$\frac{\partial \pi_i}{\partial t_i} = \frac{\partial R_i}{\partial w_i} \frac{t_j}{(t_1 + t_2)^2} - c = 0, \tag{13.11}$$

so that, taking the ratio of the two first-order conditions, we obtain the result

$$\frac{\dfrac{\partial R_i}{\partial w_i}}{\dfrac{\partial R_j}{\partial w_j}} = \frac{t_i}{t_j}.$$ (13.12)

This is the Nash equilibrium condition. The left hand side of equation (13.12) is the ratio of marginal revenues of a win to team i and team j, and the right hand side is the ratio of talent. The implication of equation (13.12) is that if, in equilibrium, team i is stronger than team j ($t_i > t_j$), then it is also the case that the marginal revenue of a win for team i exceeds the marginal revenue of team j (at equilibrium).

This is a rather striking result. Recall that the earlier work of Quirk and El-Hodiri, Fort and Quirk, and Vrooman claimed that the marginal revenue of a win would be equalized in equilibrium. This is exactly what one would expect in a Coasian world—otherwise it would be profitable to trade talent from a team where its marginal revenue is lower to one where it is higher (given that transferring talent increases win probability). The implication of equation (13.12) is that the Nash equilibrium is inefficient, in that talent is not allocated to its most valuable use. Generally speaking, it is often the case that Nash equilibria are inefficient. For example, the standard classroom example of a game, the prisoner's dilemma, involves identifying a dominant strategy equilibrium (that is also a Nash equilibrium) that is plainly inefficient for the players. The Cournot-Nash equilibrium of the standard quantity setting oligopoly model is also plainly inefficient for the players of the game (collusion increases profits). In either case, there are gains from trade that go unrealized—so that the competitive equilibrium is not Coasian. The same is true of the Nash equilibrium of the sports league model, but it is the direction in which talent must move to realize the gains from trade that is surprising for sports economists. Since the marginal revenue of a win is greater for the team with the greater share of talent, this necessarily implies that total profits for the league can be increased by moving talent *away from* the weaker team *to* the stronger team.

Overwhelmingly the balance of opinion in the sports literature is that unrestrained competition between teams in a league will lead to excessively unbalanced competition. Over and again sports leagues have used this rationale to impose restraints, which in any other industry would be considered anticompetitive. Because competitive balance is generally considered to be in the interest of the fans, teams have escaped antitrust prosecution. The Coasian approach of Rottenberg, El-Hodiri, Quirk, Fort, Vrooman, and others has tended to suggest that such restraints will have no impact on competitive balance, since under any circumstances talent will move to where it is most valuably employed. The competitive model described above suggests that this will not be the case, due to the competitive externality imposed by one team on another. The important feature of this competitive externality is that the externality imposed by the weak team on the strong team is greater than the externality imposed by the strong team on the weak team. This is because a unit increase in talent at the weak team imposes a greater absolute loss of income on the strong team than a unit increase in talent at the strong team imposes on the weak team. In other words, for any given win percentage, the loss of aggregate income when a weak team gets stronger is greater than the loss of income when a strong team gets stronger.

This result, although perfectly standard in the wider economics literature, calls for a serious reexamination of economic policy analysis for sports leagues. Szymanski and Kesenne (2004) and Szymanski (2004a) show that revenue sharing (which moves the teams closer to the joint profit maximizing equilibrium) is more likely to reduce competitive balance than increase it. Szymanski (2004b) provides econometric evidence that a less balanced distribution of results would have increased attendance at Major League Baseball over the last quarter of a century.

Some Misconceptions about Tournaments

Most sports leagues are organized along the lines of a tournament. There appears to be a presumption in some of the sports literature that this form of incentive structure is necessarily efficient. This is unlikely to be the case. For example, the rank-order tournament model of Lazear and Rosen (1981) is often cited as if this proved that contests are efficient. That paper, however, shows that under most plausible circumstances a tournament is no more efficient than an individual incentive contract, and under many circumstances less efficient.

In the Lazear and Rosen setup, a risk-neutral principal wants to design an incentive scheme to maximize total output from two agents, each of whom works individually. The important point about this is that although the effort contribution of each agent is assumed to be unobservable, output is contingent on both effort and luck, but the luck of the agents is correlated, so that a good signal from agent 1 increases the probability that agent 2 was working in a favorable environment too.

In a sports context, it should first be noted that most agents work under conditions where their effort input is quite closely observable, and hence it is possible to design effort schemes that are effort- rather than output-dependent, and these are more efficient. It can be argued that even if effort is observable on the field, it is more difficult to observe off the field (training, etc.), and hence it is not fully observable. However, it is still not clear that the efficient contract should be contingent on relative effort. First, consider the issue of risk aversion. If agents are risk averse, then making their contract dependent on the output of other agents is almost certainly inefficient (as Lazear and Rosen point out) because this just introduces extra noise into the payoff function of the agent, who therefore demands higher aggregate compensation in order to participate in the contract. Generally, an incentive contract based on own output is more efficient. Consider an example in sports: would it be better to award a star batter based on the total number of home runs scored in a season or the rank of the batter? With an own-performance scheme (e.g., $10,000 per home run), the batter has an incentive to go on scoring whatever level has been achieved already. (If it is felt that an income effect will start to influence productivity, the club could increase the marginal reward for higher totals scored.) By contrast, a ranking system may be significantly affected by the productivity of other batters, which itself may be random. For example, suppose the player gets $10,000 for every extra rank in the table of home runs scored, then, if most batters are randomly having a bad season, the batter may start to cruise, being assured of first place and the maximum payment. Likewise, if the other batters have an unexpectedly good season, then the batter may become discouraged, deeming it too difficult to rise in the ranking and therefore not worth the extra effort.

If players are not risk averse, then incentive schemes based on relative performance have no obvious merit. It is well established in the literature that an efficient incentive scheme for risk-neutral agents is to make them residual claimants for their output—in other words to pay them all of their marginal returns. This is akin to selling the club to the players. Although such extreme solutions are not common, it is likely that many of the leading stars would be willing to buy up their clubs—what makes this less likely in general is the distributional issue about who gets the rents, rather than the incentive issue.

Conclusion

The economic theory of tournaments and contests provides a natural framework for thinking about policy issues in the economics of sports. However, few papers have exploited this link systematically. This chapter has attempted to draw out some of the more important connections. For a fuller review, see Szymanski (2003b).

References

Abrevaya, J. 2004. "Fit to be Tied: The Incentive Effects of Overtime Rules in Professional Hockey." *Journal of Sports Economics,* 5: 292–306.

Ahlert, Gerd (2001). "The Economic Effects of the Soccer World Cup 2006 in Germany with Regard to Different Financing." *Economic Systems Research,* 13:1, 109–127.

Ahn, S., and Y.H. Lee. 2003. "The Attendance Demand of Major League Baseball." Paper presented at the 2003 Western Economics Association meetings (Denver, July).

Ahn, S.C., Y.H. Lee, and P. Schmidt. 2001. "GMM Estimation of Linear Panel Data Models with Time-Varying Individual Effects." *Journal of Econometrics,* 101: 219–55.

Aigner, D.J., and G.G. Cain. 1977. "Statistical Theories of Discrimination in Labor Markets." *Industrial and Labor Relations Review,* 30(2), 175–87.

Aigner, D. J., C.A.K. Lovell, and P. Schmidt. 1977. "Formulation and Estimation of Stochastic Frontier Production Function Models." *Journal of Econometrics,* 58(1): 226–39.

Albrecht, J., A. Bjorklund, and S. Vroman. 2003. "Is There a Glass Ceiling in Sweden?" *Journal of Labor Economics,* 21(1): 145–77.

Allen, W.D. 2002. "Crime, Punishment, and Recidivism: Lessons from the National Hockey League." *Journal of Sports Economics,* 3: 39–60.

Anderson, D.J., and J.J. Ceslock. 2004. "Institutional Strategies to Achieve Gender Equity in Intercollegiate Athletics: Does Title IX Harm Male Athletes?" *American Economic Review,* 94: 307–11.

Antonioni, P., and J. Cubbin. 2000. "The Bosman Ruling and the Emergence of a Single Market for Soccer Talent." *European Journal of Law and Economics,* 9(2): 157–73.

Ashenfelter, O. 1987. "Arbitration and the Negotiation Process." *American Economic Review,* 77(May): 342–47.

Ashenfelter, O., and D. Bloom. 1984. "Models of Arbitrator Behavior: Theory and Evidence." *American Economic Review,* 74(Mar.): 111–24.

Ashton, J., B. Gerrard, and R. Hudson. 2003. "Economic Impact of National Sporting Success: Evidence from the London Stock Exchange." *Applied Economics Letters,* 10(12): 783–85.

Atkinson, S.E., and C. Cornwell. 1994. "Parametric Estimation of Technical and Allocative Efficiency with Panel Data." *International Economic Review,* 35(1): 231–43.

Audas, R., S. Dobson, and J. Goddard. 2002. "The Impact of Managerial Change on Team Performance in Professional Sports." *Journal of Economics and Business,* 54: 633–50.

———. 1999. "Organizational Performance and Managerial Turnover." *Managerial and Decision Economics,* 20: 305–18.

Baade, R. 2000. "The Impact of Sports Teams and Facilities on Neighborhood Economies: What Is the Score?" In *The Economics of Sports,* ed. William S. Kern, 21–49. Kalamazoo, MI: W.E. Upjohn Institute for Employment Research.

———. 1996. "Professional Sports as a Catalyst for Metropolitan Economic Development." *Journal of Urban Affairs,* 18(1): 1–17.

Baade, R., and V. Matheson. 2004. "The Quest for the Cup: Assessing the Economic Impact of the World Cup." *Regional Studies,* 38(4): 343–54.

Baade, R., and A. Sanderson. 1997. "The Employment Effects of Teams and Sports Facilities." In *Sports, Jobs, and Taxes,* ed. R. Noll and A. Zimbalist, 92–118. Washington, D.C.: Brookings Institution.

Baade, R.A., and L.J. Tiehen. 1990. "An Analysis of Major League Baseball Attendance, 1969–1987." *Journal of Sport and Social Issues,* 14(Spring): 14–32.

Baimbridge, M., S. Cameron, and P. Dawson. 1996. "Satellite Television and the Demand for Football: A Whole New Ball Game?" *Scottish Journal of Political Economy,* 43(3): 317–33.

Balfour, A., and P. Porter. 1991. "The Reserve Clause in Professional Sports: Legality and Effect on Competitive Balance." *Labor Law Journal,* 42: 8–18.

Banaian, K., and D. Gallagher. 1999. "When a Cap is Not a Cap: Player Mobility and Pay in the NBA." Paper presented at the 1999 Western Economic Association meetings (San Diego, CA, July).

Battese, G., and T. Coelli. 1995. "A Model for Technical Inefficiency Effects in a Stochastic Frontier Production Function for Panel Data." *Empirical Economics,* 20(2): 325–32.

———. 1992. "Frontier Production Functions, Technical Efficiency and Panel Data: With Application to Paddy Farmers in India." *Journal of Productivity Analysis,* 3(2): 153–69.

Baye, M.R., D. Kovenock, and C.G. de Vries. 1996. "The All-Pay Auction with Complete Information." *Economic Theory,* 8: 291–305.

———. 1994. "The Solution to the Tullock Rent-Seeking Game When R > 2: Mixed Strategy Equilibria and Mean Dissipating Rates." *Public Choice,* 81: 363–80.

Becker, B.E., and M.A. Huselid. 1992. "The Incentive Effects of Tournament Compensation Schemes." *Administrative Science Quarterly,* 37: 336–50.

Becker, G. 1971. *The Economics of Discrimination.* 2nd ed. Chicago: University of Chicago Press.

———. 1957. *The Economics of Discrimination.* Chicago: University of Chicago Press.

Bender, P. (no date). *Patricia's Various Basketball Stuff* (Online). Available at www.dfw.net/~patricia.

Bennett, J. (ed.). 1998. *Statistics in Sport.* London: Arnold.

Berri, D.J. 2004a. "Is There a Short Supply of Tall People in the College Game?" In *Economics of Collegiate Sports,* ed. J. Fizel and R. Fort, 211–33. Westport, CT: Praeger.

————. 2004b. "A Simple Measure of Worker Productivity in the National Basketball Association." Unpublished mimeo.

————. 2001. "Mixing the Princes and the Paupers: A Case Study of Worker Productivity and Pay Inequality." Paper presented at the 2001 Western Economic Association meetings (San Francisco, July).

————. 1999. "Who Is Most Valuable? Measuring the Player's Production of Wins in the National Basketball Association." *Managerial and Decision Economics,* 20(8), Fall: 411–27.

Berri, D.J., and S.L. Brook. 1999. "Trading Players in the NBA: For Better or Worse." In *Sports Economics: Current Research,* ed. J.L. Fizel, E. Gustafson, and L. Hadley, 135–51. Westport, CT: Praeger.

Berri, D. J., S. L. Brook, A. Fenn, B. Frick, and R. Vicente-Mayoral. 2005. "The Short Supply of Tall People: Explaining Competitive Imbalance in the National Basketball Association." *Journal of Economics Issues,* forthcoming.

Berri, D.J., S.L. Brook, and M.B. Schmidt. 2004. "Does One Simply Need to Score to Score?" Paper presented at the 2004 Western Economic Association meetings (Vancouver, B.C., July).

Berri, D.J., and E. Eschker. 2004. "Performance When It Counts: Player Productivity and the Playoffs in the NBA." Paper presented at the Western Economic Association meetings (Vancouver, B.C., July).

Berri, D.J., and A. Fenn. 2004. "Is the Sports Media Color Blind?" Paper presented at the 2004 Southern Economic Association meetings (New Orleans, Nov.).

Berri, D.J., and T. Jewell. 2004. "Wage Inequality and Firm Performance: Evidence from Professional Basketball's Natural Experiment." *Atlantic Economic Journal,* 32(2), June: 130–39.

Berri, D.J., and A. Krautmann. 2004. "Shirking on the Court: Testing for the Dis-Incentive Effects of Guaranteed Pay." Paper presented at the 2004 Western Economic Association meetings (Vancouver, B.C., July).

Berri, D.J., and M.B. Schmidt. Forthcoming. "On the Road with the National Basketball Association's Superstar Externality." *Journal of Sports Economics.*

————. 2002. "Instrumental vs. Bounded Rationality: The Case of Major League Baseball and the National Basketball Association." *Journal of Socio-Economics* (formerly *Journal of Behavioral Economics*), 31(3): 191–214.

Berri, D.J., M.B. Schmidt, and S.L. Brook. 2004. "Stars at the Gate: The Impact of Star Power on NBA Gate Revenues." *Journal of Sports Economics,* 5(1): 33–50.

Berry, S.M., C.S. Reese, and P.D. Larkey. 1999. "Bridging Different Eras in Sports." *Journal of the American Statistical Association,* 94: 661–86.

Besanko, D., and D. Simon. 1985. "Resource Allocation in the Baseball Players Labor Market: An Empirical Investigation." *Review of Economics and Statistics,* 21: 71–84.

Bird, P. 1982. "The Demand for League Football." *Applied Economics,* 14: 637–49.

Blass, A.A. 1992. "Does the Baseball Labor Market Contradict the Human Capital Model of Investment?" *Review of Economics and Statistics,* 74(2): 261–68.

Bodvarsson, O.B., and K. Banaian. 1998. "The Value of Arbitration Rights in Major League Baseball: Implications for Salaries and Discrimination." *Quarterly Journal of Business and Economics,* 37(1): 65–80.

Bodvarsson, O.B., and R.T. Brastow. 1999. "A Test of Employer Discrimination in the NBA." *Contemporary Economic Policy,* 17: 243–55.

————. 1998. "Do Employers Pay for Consistent Performance? Evidence from the NBA." *Economic Inquiry,* 36(1): 145–60.

Bodvarsson, O.B., and M.D. Partridge. 2001. "A Supply and Demand Model of Co-Worker, Employer and Customer Discrimination." *Labour Economics,* 8: 389–416.

Boileau, R. 1984. "Les Canadiens français et le hockey professionnel [French Canadians and Professional Hockey]." In *Les activités socio-économiques et les français au Québec,* ed. M. Amyot, 198–206. Quebec City: Editeur officiel du Québec.

Boileau, R., and R. Boulanger. 1982. "Les francophones au hockey professionnel: Compétence limitée ou promotion bloquée?" *Desport,* Sept.: 15–18.

Boucher, M. 1985. "Coûts de transaction et faible nombre relative des Canadiens français dans la LNH [Transactions Costs and the Relatively Small Number of French Canadians in the NHL]." *L'Actualité économique,* 61: 388–93.

———. 1984. "Les Canadiens français dans la Ligue Nationale de Hockey: Une analyse statistique [French Canadians in the National Hockey League: A Statistical Analysis]." *L'Actualité économique,* 60: 308–25.

———. 1983. "Marginal Revenue Products of National Hockey League Players: Some Empirical Results." Working Paper, Cahier 83–03, Groupe de recherché sur l'économie du secteur public, Quebec City.

Brocas, I., and J. Carrillo. 2004. "Do the 'Three-Point Victory' and 'Golden Goal' Rules Make Soccer More Exciting?" *Journal of Sports Economics,* 5(2): 169–85.

Brown, E., R. Spiro, and D. Keenan. 1991. "Wage and Non-wage Discrimination in Professional Basketball: Do Fans Affect It?" *American Journal of Economics and Sociology,* 50(3): 333–45.

Brown. R.W., and R.T. Jewell. 2003. "Is Women's College Basketball a Revenue-Generating Sport? Marginal Revenue Product Estimates and Team Revenues." Unpublished manuscript.

Brown, W.O., and Sauer, R.D. 1993. "Does the Basketball Market Believe in the Hot Hand?" *American Economic Review,* 83: 1377–86.

Bruggink, T.H., and J.W. Eaton. 1996. "Rebuilding Attendance in Major League Baseball: The Demand for Individual Games." In *Baseball Economics: Current Research,* ed. J. Fizel, E. Gustafson, and L. Hadley, 9–31. Westport, CT: Praeger.

Bruggink, T.H., and D. Rose. 1990. "Financial Restraint in the Free Agent Labor Market in Major League Baseball: Players Look at Strike Three." *Southern Economic Journal,* 56(4): 1029–43.

Buchinsky, M. 1994. "Changes in the U.S. Wage Structure, 1963–1987: Application of Quantile Regression." *Econometrica,* 62(2): 405–58.

Buckley, J., and Y. Shang. 2003. "Estimating Policy and Program Effects with Observational Data: The Differences-in-Differences Estimator." *Practical Assessment, Research and Evaluation,* www.pareonline.net/home.htm.

Burdekin, R.C., R.T. Hossfeld, and J.K. Smith. 2005. "Are NBA Fans Becoming Indifferent to Race? Evidence from the 1990s." *Journal of Sports Economics,* 6(2):144–159.

Burdekin, R.C., and T.L. Idson. 1991. "Customer Preferences, Attendance and the Racial Structure of Professional Basketball Teams." *Applied Economics,* 23: 179–86.

Burger, J.D., and S.J.K. Walters. 2003a. "The Behavior of Major League Arbitrators, 1979–2001." Paper presented at the International Western Economic Association (Denver, July).

———. 2003b. "Market Size, Pay and Performance: A General Model and Application to Major League Baseball." *Journal of Sports Economics,* 4(2): 108–25.

Burgess, P., D Marburger, and J. Scoggins. 1996. "Do Baseball Arbitrators Simply Flip a Coin?" In *Baseball Economics: Current Research*, eds. J. Fizel, E101-110–127. Westport, CT: Praeger Publishers.

Burgess, P., and D. Marburger. 1993. "Do Negotiated and Arbitrated Salaries Differ under Final Offer Arbitration?" *Industrial and Labor Relations Review*, 46(Apr.): 548–59.

Burkitt, B., and S. Cameron. 1992. "Impact of League Restructuring on Team Sport Attendances: The Case of Rugby League." *Applied Economics*, 24(Feb.): 265–71.

Butler, M.R. 2002. "Interleague Play and Baseball Attendance." *Journal of Sports Economics*, 3(4): 320–34.

———. 1995. "Competitive Balance in Major League Baseball." *American Economist*, 39(Fall): 46–52.

Cain, M., D. Law, and D. Peel. 2000. "The Favourite-Longshot Bias and Market Efficiency in UK Football Betting." *Scottish Journal of Political Economy*, 47(1): 25–36.

Cairns, J. 1992. "The Demand for Professional Team Sports." *British Review of Economics Issues*, 12(28): 1–20.

———. 1987. "Evaluating Changes in League Structure: The Reorganisation of the Scottish Football League." *Applied Economics*, 19(2): 259–75.

Camerer, C.F., and R.A. Weber. 1999. "The Econometrics and Behavioral Economics of Escalation of Commitment: A Re-Examination of Staw and Hoang's NBA Data." *Journal of Economic Behavior and Organization*, 39: 59–82.

Canes, M.E. 1974. "The Social Benefits of Restrictions on Team Quality." In *Government and the Sports Business*, ed. R.G. Noll, 81–113. Washington, D.C.: Brookings Institution.

Card, D., and D. Sullivan. 1988. "Measuring the Effect of Subsidized Training Programs on Movements In and Out of Employment." *Econometrica*, 56(3): 497–530.

Carlton, D.W, A.S. Frankel, and E.M. Landes. 2004. "The Control of Externalities in Sports Leagues: An Analysis of Restrictions in the National Hockey League." *Journal of Political Economy*, 112: S268–S288.

Carmichael, F., D. Forrest, and R. Simmons. 1999. "The Labour Market in Association Football: Who Gets Transferred and For How Much?" *Bulletin of Economic Research*, 51: 125–50.

Carmichael, F., and D. Thomas. 2000. "Institutional Responses to Uncertainty: Evidence from the Transfer Market." *Economic Issues*, 5(1): 1–19.

———. 1995. "Production and Efficiency in Team Sports: An Investigation of Rugby League Football." *Applied Economics*, 27: 859–69.

———. 1993. "Bargaining in the Transfer Market: Theory and Evidence." *Applied Economics*, 25(12): 1467–76.

Carmichael, F., D. Thomas, and R. Ward. 2001. "Production and Efficiency in Association Football." *Journal of Sports Economics*, 2(3): 228–43.

———. 2000. "Team Performance: The Case of English Premiership Football." *Managerial and Decision Economics*, 21: 31–45.

Carroll, K.A., and B.R. Humphreys. 2000. "Nonprofit Decision Making and Social Regulation: The Intended and Unintended Consequences of Title IX." *Journal of Economic Behavior and Organization*, 43(3): 359–76.

Cassing, J., and R.W. Douglas. 1980. "Implications of the Auction Mechanism in Baseball's Free Agent Draft." *Southern Economic Journal*, 47(July): 110–21.

Caudill, S.B., J.M. Ford, and D.M. Gropper. 1995. "Frontier Estimation and Firm-Specific Inefficiency Measures in the Presence of Heteroskedasticity." *Journal of Business and Economic Statistics*, 13: 105–11.

Caudill, S.B., and F.G. Mixon. 1998. "Television Revenue and the Structure of Athletic Contests: The Case of the National Basketball Association." *Eastern Economic Journal,* 24(1): 43–50.

Chapman, K.S., and Southwick, L. Jr. 1991. "Testing the Matching Hypothesis: The Case of Major League Baseball." *American Economic Review,* 81: 1352–60.

Chiappori, P., S. Levitt, and T. Groseclose. 2002. "Testing Mixed-Strategy Equilibria When Players Are Heterogeneous: The Case of Penalty Kicks in Soccer." *American Economic Review,* 92(4): 1138–51.

Cincinnati Reds. 1996. *The Effects of the Construction, Operation and Financing of New Sports Stadia on Cincinnati's Economic Growth.* Prepared by Center for Economic Education, University of Cincinnati, Jan.

Clement, R.C., and R.E. McCormick. 1990. "Coaching Team Production." In *Sportometrics,* ed. B.L. Goff and R.D. Tollison, 75–92. College Station, TX: Texas A&M Press.

———. 1989. "Coaching Team Production," *Economic Inquiry,* 27: 287–304.

Coase, R. 1960. "The Problem of Social Cost." *Journal of Law and Economics,* 3: 1–44.

Coate, D., and D. Robbins. 2001. "The Tournament Careers of Top-Ranked Men and Women Tennis Professionals: Are the Gentlemen More Committed Than the Ladies?" *Journal of Labor Research,* 22(1): 185–92.

Coates, D. 2004. "Final Offer Arbitration: A Time-Series Analysis." Paper presented at the Southern Economic Association annual meeting (New Orleans, Nov.).

Cocco, A., and J.C.H. Jones. 1997. "On Going South: The Economics of Survival and Relocation of Small Market NHL Franchises in Canada." *Applied Economics,* 29: 1537–52.

Coelli, T.J. 1996. "A Guide to FRONTIER Version 4.1: A Computer Program for Stochastic Frontier Production and Cost Function Estimation." CEPA Working Paper 96/7, Department of Econometrics, University of New England, Armidale, NSW, Australia.

Coffin, D.A. 1996. "If You Build It, Will They Come? Attendance and New Stadium Construction." In *Baseball Economics: Current Research,* ed. J. Fizel, E. Gustafson, and L. Hadley, 33–46. Westport, CT: Praeger.

Colburn, K., Jr. 1985. "Honor, Ritual and Violence in Ice Hockey." *Canadian Journal of Sociology,* 10: 153–70.

Cornwell, C., and P. Schmidt. 1996. "Production Frontiers and Efficiency Measurement." In *The Econometrics of Panel Data,* ed. L. Matyas and P. Sevestre, 845–75. Norwell, MA: Kluwer Academic.

Cornwell, C., P. Schmidt, and R.C. Sickles. 1990. "Production Frontiers with Cross-Sectional and Time-Series Variation in Efficiency Levels." *Journal of Econometrics,* 46(1/2): 185–200.

Coulombe, S., and M. Lavoie. 1985a. "Les francophones dans la Ligue Nationale de Hockey: Une analyse économique de la discrimination [Francophones in the National Hockey League: An Economic Analysis of Discrimination]." *L'Actualité économique,* 61: 73–92.

———. 1985b. "Discrimination à l'Embauche et performance supérieure des Franco-Québécois dans la LHN: Une mise au point." *L'Actualité économique,* 61: 527–30.

Cuesta, R.A. 2000. "A Production Model with Firm-Specific Temporal Variation in Technical Inefficiency: With Application to Spanish Dairy Farms." *Journal of Productivity Analysis,* 13: 139–49.

Cunningham, G.B., and M. Sagas. 2002. "The Differential Effects of Human Capital for Male and Female Division I Basketball Coaches." *Research Quarterly for Exercise and Sport,* 73(4): 489–95.

Curme, M.A., and G.M. Daugherty. 2004. "Competition and Pay for National Hockey League Players Born in Québec." *Journal of Sports Economics,* 5: 186–205.

Curtis, J.E., and J.W. Loy. 1978. "Race/Ethnicity and Relative Centrality of Playing Positions in Team-Sports." *Exercise and Sport Sciences Reviews,* 6: 285–313.

Cymrot, D. 1983. "Migration Trends and Earnings of Free Agents in Major League Baseball, 1976–1979." *Economic Inquiry,* 21(4) 545–56.

Daly, G. 1981. "Externalities, Property Rights, and the Allocation of Resources in Major League Baseball." *Economic Inquiry,* 19: 77–95.

Daly, G., and Moore, W.J. (1981) "Externalities, Property, Rights, and the Allocation of Resources in Major League Baseball." *Economic Inquiry* 19: 77–95.

Davies, B., P. Downward, and I. Jackson. 1995. "The Demand for Rugby League: Evidence from Causality Tests." *Applied Economics,* 27(10): 1003–7.

Dawson, P., and S. Dobson. 2002. "Managerial Efficiency and Human Capital: An Application to English Association Football." *Managerial and Decision Economics,* 23: 471–86.

Dawson, P., S. Dobson, and B. Gerrard. 2000a. "Stochastic Frontiers and the Temporal Structure of Managerial Efficiency in English Soccer." *Journal of Sports Economics,* 1(4): 341–62.

———. 2000b. "Estimating Coaching Efficiency in Professional Team Sports: Evidence from English Association Football." *Scottish Journal of Political Economy,* 47(4): 399–421.

DeBrock, L., W. Hendricks, and R. Koenker. 1996. "The Economics of Persistence: Graduation Rates of Athletes as Labor Market Choice." *Journal of Human Resources,* 31(3): 513–39.

DeGennaro, R. 2003. "The Utility of Sport and Returns to Ownership." *Journal of Sports Economics,* 4(2): 145–53.

Demmert, H. 1973. *The Economics of Professional Sports.* Lexington, MA: Lexington Books.

Depken, C.A., and D.P. Wilson. 2004a. "The Efficiency of the NASCAR Racing System: Initial Empirical Evidence." *Journal of Sports Economics,* 5(4): 371–86.

———. 2004b. "Wherein Lies the Benefit of the Second Referee in the NHL?" *Review of Industrial Organization,* 24: 51–72.

De Ruyter, K., and M. Wetzels. 2000. "With a Little Help From My Fans: Extending Models of Pro-social Behavior to Explain Supporters' Intentions to Buy Soccer Club Shares." *Journal of Economic Psychology,* 21: 387–409.

Dey, M.S. 1997. "Racial Differences in National Basketball Association Players' Salaries." *American Economist,* 41(Fall): 84–90.

Dilger, A. 2001. "The Ericson Case." *Journal of Sports Economics,* 2(2): 194–200.

DiNardo, J., N.M. Fortin, and T. Lemieux. 1996. "Labor Market Institutions and the Distribution of Wages, 1973–1992: A Semiparametric Approach." *Econometrica,* 64(5): 1001–44.

Dixit, A. 1987. "Strategic Behavior in Contests." *American Economic Review,* 77: 891–98.

Dobson, S., and J. Goddard. 1998a. "Performance and Revenue in Professional League Football: Evidence from Granger Causality Tests." *Applied Econometrics,* 30(12): 1641–51.

————. 1996. "The Demand of Football in the Regions of England and Wales." *Regional Studies*, 30(5): 443–54.

————. 1995. "The Demand for Professional League Football in England and Wales, 1925–92." *Journal of the Royal Statistical Society Series D, The Statistician*, 44(2): 259–77.

————. 1992. "The Demand for Standing and Seated Viewing Accommodation in the English Football League." *Applied Economics*, 24(10): 1155–63.

Dobson, S., J. Goddard, and C. Ramlogan. 2001. "Revenue Convergence in the English Soccer League." *Journal of Sports Economics*, 2(3): 257–74.

Domazlicky, B.R., and P.M. Kerr. 1990. "Baseball Attendance and the Designated Hitter." *American Economist*, 34: 62–68.

Duggan, M., and S.D. Levitt. 2002. "Winning Isn't Everything: Corruption in Sumo Wrestling." *American Economic Review*, 92: 1594–1605.

Dworkin, J. 1986. "Salary Arbitration in Baseball: An Impartial Assessment after Ten Years." *Arbitration Journal*, 41(Mar.): 63–69.

————. 1981. *Owners Versus Players: Baseball and Collective Bargaining*. Boston: Auburn House.

Eastman, B.D. 1981. "The Labor Economics of the National Hockey League." *Atlantic Economic Journal*, 9: 100–110.

Eckard, E.W. 2003. "The ANOVA-Based Competitive Balance Measure: A Defense." *Journal of Sports Economics*, 4(1): 74–80

————. 2001a. "Baseball's Blue Ribbon Economic Report: Solutions in Search of a Problem." *Journal of Sports Economics*, 2(3): 213–27.

————. 2001b. "Free Agency, Competitive Balance, and Diminishing Returns to Pennant Contention." *Economic Inquiry*, 39(July): 430–43.

Ehrenberg, R.G., and M.L. Bognanno. 1990a. "Do Tournaments Have Incentive Effects?" *Journal of Political Economy*, 98(6): 1307–24.

————. 1990b "The Incentive Effects of Tournaments Revisited: Evidence from the European PGA Tour." *Industrial and Labor Relations Review*, 43(special issue, Feb.): 74-S–88-S.

El-Hodiri, M., and J. Quirk. 1971. "The Economic Theory of a Professional Sports League." *Journal of Political Economy*, 79(Nov.–Dec.): 1302–19.

Engelhardt, G.M. 1995. "Fighting Behavior and Winning National Hockey League Games: A Paradox." *Perceptual and Motor Skills*, 80: 416–18.

Ericson, T. 2000. "The Bosman Case: Effects of the Abolition of the Transfer Fee." *Journal of Sports Economics*, 1(3): 203–18.

Eschker, E., S.J. Perez, and M.V. Siegler. 2004. "The NBA and the Influx of International Basketball Players." *Applied Economics*, 36: 1009–20.

Esteller-Moré, A., and M. Eres-García. 2002. "A Note on Consistent Players' Valuation." *Journal of Sports Economics*, 3(4): 354–60.

Etzioni, Amitai. 1988. *The Moral Dimension: Toward a New Economics*. New York: Macmillan.

Ewing, B. 1995. "High School Athletics and the Wages of Black Males." *Review of Black Political Economy*, 24(1): 67–80.

Farber, H.S. 1980. "An Analysis of Final-Offer Arbitration." *Journal of Conflict Resolution*, 24: 683–705.

Farber, H.S., and M.S. Bazerman. 1986. "The General Basis of Arbitrator Behavior: An Empirical Analysis of Conventional and Final-Offer Arbitration." *Econometrica*, 54: 819–44.

Farrell, M.J. 1957. "The Measurement of Productive Efficiency." *Journal of the Royal Statistical Society Series A, General,* 120: 253–81.

Faurot, D. 2004. "Low Settlements before Arbitration in Major League Baseball." Paper presented at the 2004 International Western Economic Association meetings (Vancouver, B.C., July).

Faurot, D., and S. McAllister. 1992. "Salary Arbitration and Pre-Arbitration Negotiation in Major League Baseball." *Industrial and Labor Relations Review,* 15(4): 697–710.

Feess, E., and G. Mühlheusser. 2003a. "The Impact of Transfer Fees on Professional Sports: An Analysis of the New Transfer System for European Football." *Scandinavian Journal of Economics,* 105(1): 139–54.

———. 2003b. "Transfer Fee Regulations in European Football." *European Economic Review,* 47(4): 645–68.

———. 2002. "Economic Consequences of Transfer Fee Regulations in European Football." *European Journal of Law and Economics,* 13: 221–37.

Ferguson, D., K. Stewart, J.C.H. Jones, and A. Le Dressay. 1991. "The Pricing of Sports Events: Do Teams Maximize Profit?" *Journal of Industrial Economics,* 39: 297–310.

Financial World Magazine, various editions, 1991–96.

Fizel, J. 2004. "Major League Baseball Arbitration Decisions: Preliminary Comparisons of Individual Arbitrators vs. Arbitrator Panels." Paper presented at Southern Economic Association meeting (New Orleans, Nov.).

———. 1997. "Free Agency and Competitive Balance." In *Stee-rike Four! What's Wrong with the Business of Baseball?* ed. D.R. Marburger, 61–72. Westport, CT: Praeger.

———. 1996. "Is There Bias in Major League Baseball Arbitration?" In *Baseball Economics: Current Research,* ed. J. Fizel, E. Gustafson, and L. Hadley, 111–27. Westport, CT: Praeger.

———. 1994. "Play Ball: Baseball Arbitration after 20 Years." *Dispute Resolution Journal,* 49(2): 42–47.

Fizel, J., and M. D'itri. 1996. "Estimating Managerial Efficiency: The Case of College Basketball Coaches." *Journal of Sport Management,* 10: 435–45.

Fizel, J., and R. Fort (ed.). 2004. *Economics of College Sports.* Westport, CT: Praeger.

Fizel, J., E. Gustafson, and L. Hadley (ed.) 1996. *Baseball Economics: Current Research.* Westport, CT: Praeger.

Fizel, J., A. Krautmann, and L. Hadley. 2002. "Equity and Arbitration in Major League Baseball." *Managerial and Decision Economics,* 23: 427–35.

Fleisher, A.A. III, B.L. Goff, and R.D. Tollison. 1992. *The National Collegiate Athletic Association: A Study in Cartel Behavior.* Chicago: University of Chicago Press.

Forrest, D., and R. Simmons. 2000. "Forecasting Sport: The Behavior and Performance of Football Tipsters." *International Journal of Forecasting,* 16: 317–31.

Forrest, D., R. Simmons, and P. Feehan. 2002. "A Spatial Cross-sectional Analysis of the Elasticity of Demand for Soccer." *Scottish Journal of Political Economy,* 49(3): 336–55.

Fort, R. 2004a. "Subsidies as Incentive Mechanisms in Sports." *Managerial and Decision Economics,* 25: 95–102.

———. 2004b. "Inelastic Sports Pricing." *Managerial and Decision Economics,* 25: 87–94.

———. 2003. *Sports Economics.* Upper Saddle River, NJ: Prentice Hall.

———. 2001. "Revenue Disparity and Competitive Balance in Major League Baseball." In *Baseball's Revenue Gap: Pennant for Sale?* Hearings before the Subcommittee on Antitrust, Business Rights, and Competition of the Committee on the Judiciary (42–52), U.S. Senate, 106th Congress, Second Session, Nov., 21.

Fort, R., and A. Gill. 2000. "Race and Baseball Card Markets." *Journal of Sports Economics,* 1(1): 21–38.

Fort, R.D., and J. Maxcy. 2003. "Competitive Balance in Sports Leagues: An Introduction." *Journal of Sports Economics,* 4(2): 154–60.

Fort, R., and J. Quirk. 1995. "Cross-Subsidization, Incentives, and Outcomes in Professional Team Sports Leagues." *Journal of Economic Literature,* 33(3): 1265–99.

Fort, R., and R. Rosenman. 1999. "Streak Management." In *Sports Economics: Current Research,* ed. J. Fizel, E. Gustafson, and L. Hadley, 119–33. Westport, CT: Praeger.

———. 1998. "Winning and Managing for Streaks in Baseball." *American Statistical Association, 1998 Proceedings of the Section on Statistics in Sports.* Alexandria, VA: American Statistical Association.

Francis, C. 1983–92. *Hoop Scoop.* Louisville, KY: Hoop Scoop.

Frederick, D., W. Kaempfer, M. Ross, and R. Wobbekind. 1996. "Race, Risk and Repeated Arbitration." In *Baseball Economics: Current Research,* ed. J. Fizel, E. Gustafson, and L. Hadley, 129–41. Westport, CT: Praeger.

Frederick, D., W. Kaempfer, and R. Wobbekind. 1992. "Salary Arbitration as a Market Substitute." In *Diamonds Are Forever: The Business of Baseball,* ed. P. Sommers, 29–49. Washington, D.C.: Brookings Institution.

Freedman, E. 2002. "Who Is Shyam Das?" *Baseball Primer, 2001,* posted online Oct. 24, 2002, www.baseballprimer.com/articles/eugene_freedman_2001–11–19_0.shtml.

Frick, B., J. Prinz, and K. Winkelmann. 2003. "Pay Inequalities and Team Performance: Empirical Evidence from the North American Major Leagues." *International Journal of Manpower,* 24(4): 472–88.

Fullerton, R.L., and R.P. McAfee. 1999. "Auctioning Entry into Tournaments." *Journal of Political Economy,* 107(3): 573–605.

Gaal, J., M.S. Glazier, and T. Evans, 2002, "Gender Based Pay Disparities in Intercollegiate Coaching: The Legal Issues."*Journal of College and University Law* 28(3): 519–568.

García, J., and P. Rodrígues. 2002. "The Determinants of Football Match Attendance Revisited." *Journal of Sports Economics,* 3(1): 18–38.

Gaviria, A. 2000. "Is Soccer Dying? A Time Series Approach." *Applied Economics Letters,* 7: 275–78.

Geddert, R.L., and R.K. Semple. 1987. "A National Hockey League Franchise: The Modified Threshold Concept in Central Place Theory." *Leisure Sciences,* 9: 1–13.

Gerrard, B., and S. Dobson. 2000. "Testing for Monopoly Rents in the Market for Playing Talent." *Journal of Economic Studies,* 27(3): 142–64.

Gius, M., and T. Hylan. 1999. "Testing for the Effect of Arbitration on the Salaries of Hitters in Major League Baseball: Evidence from Panel Data." *Pennsylvania Economic Review,* 7(1): 28–35.

Gius, M., and D. Johnson. 1998. "An Empirical Investigation of Wage Discrimination in Professional Basketball." *Applied Economics Letters,* 5: 703–5.

Gneezy, U., M. Niederle, and A. Rustichini. 2003. "Performance in Competitive Environments: Gender Differences." *Quarterly Journal of Economics,* 118(3): 1049–74.

Goddard, J., and I. Asimakopoulos. 2004. "Forecasting Football Results and the Efficiency of Fixed-Odds Betting." *Journal of Forecasting,* 23(1): 51–66.

Goff, B.L., and R.D. Tollison (eds.). 1990. *Sportometrics.* College Station, TX: Texas A&M Press.

Goff, B.L., R.E. McCormick, and R.D. Tollison. 2002. "Racial Integration as an Innovation: Empirical Evidence from Sports Leagues." *American Economic Review,* 92: 16–26.

Graham, H., and J. Perry. 1993. "Interest Arbitration in Ohio: The Narcotic Effect Revisited." *Journal of Collective Negotiations,* 22(4): 323–26.

Granger, C. 1969. "Investigating Causal Relationships by Econometric Methods and Spectral Analysis." *Econometrica,* 37: 424–38.

Greene, W. 2000. *Econometric Analysis.* Upper Saddle River, NJ: Prentice Hall.

Grenier, G., and M. Lavoie. 1988. "Francophones in the National Hockey League: Tests of Entry and Salary Discrimination." University of Ottawa, Department of Economics Research Working Paper 8805.

Grier, K.B., and R.D. Tollison. 1990. "Arbitrage in a Basketball Economy." *Kyklos,* 43(4): 611–24.

Gruneau, R., and D. Whitson. 1993. *Hockey Night in Canada.* Toronto: Garamond Press.

Guedes, J.C. and F.S. Machado. 2002. "Changing Rewards in Contests: Has the Three-Point Rule in Soccer Brought More Offense to Soccer?" *Empirical Economics,* 27:607–630.

Gustafson, E., and L. Hadley. 2004. "Revenue, Population, and Competitive Balance in Major League Baseball." Working paper, University of Dayton, Aug.

Gustafson, E., and Lawrence Hadley. 1995. "Arbitration and Salary Gaps in Major League Baseball." *Quarterly Journal of Business and Economics,* 34:32–46.

Gustafson, E., L. Hadley, and J. Ruggiero. 1997. "Cost Efficiency in Major League Baseball." Paper presented at the 1997 Western Economics Association meeting, (Seattle, July).

Gwartney, J., and C. Haworth. 1974. "Employer Costs and Discrimination: The Case of Baseball." *Journal of Political Economy,* 82: 873–81.

Haas, D. 2003a. "Productive Efficiency of English Football Teams: A Data Envelopment Analysis Approach." *Managerial and Decision Economics,* 24(5): 403–10.

———. 2003b. "Technical Efficiency in the Major League Soccer." *Journal of Sports Economics,* 4(3): 203–15.

Hadley, L., and E. Gustafson. 1991. "Major League Baseball Salaries: The Impacts of Arbitration and Free Agency." *Journal of Sport Management,* 5(2): 111–27.

Hadley, L., M. Poitras, J. Ruggiero, and S. Knowles. 2000. "Performance Evaluation of National Football League Teams." *Managerial and Decision Economics,* 21: 63–70.

Hadley, L., and J. Ruggiero. Forthcoming. "Final-Offer Arbitration in Major League Baseball: A Nonparametric Analysis." *Annals of Operations Research.*

Hall, S., S. Szymanski, and A. Zimbalist. 2002. "Testing Causality between Team Performance and Payroll: The Cases of Major League Baseball and English Soccer." *Journal of Sports Economics,* 3(2): 149–68.

Hamilton, B.H. 1997. "Racial Discrimination and Professional Basketball Salaries in the 1990s." *Applied Economics,* 29: 287–96.

Han, C., L. Orea, and P. Schmidt. 2005. "Estimation of a Panel Data Model with Parametric Temporal Variation in Individual Effects." *Journal of Econometrics,* June (126) 2: 241.

Hart, R., J. Hutton, and T. Sharot. 1975. "A Statistical Analysis of Association Football Attendance." *Journal of the Royal Statistical Society, Series C,* 24: 17–27.

Haugen, K., and A. Hervik. 2002. "Estimating the Value of the Premier League or the World's Most Profitable Investment Project." *Applied Economics Letters,* 9: 117–20.

Hausman, J.A. 1978. "Specific Tests in Econometrics," *Econometrica,* 46:1251–1271.

Hausman, J.A., and G.K. Leonard. 1997. "Superstars in the National Basketball Association: Economic Value and Policy." *Journal of Labor Economics,* 15(4): 586–624.

Heckelman, J.C., and A.J. Yates. 2003. "And a Hockey Game Broke Out: Crime and Punishment in the NHL." *Economic Inquiry,* 41: 705–12.

Heckman, J. 1979. "Sample Selection Bias as a Specification Error." *Econometrica,* 47(1): 153–61.

Heshmati, A. 2003. "Productivity Growth, Efficiency and Outsourcing in Manufacturing and Service Industries." *Journal of Economic Surveys,* 17: 79–112.

Hill, J.R. 1985. "The Threat of Free Agency and Exploitation in Professional Baseball: 1976–1979." *Quarterly Review of Economics and Business,* 25(4): 68–82.

Hill, J.R., and P.A. Groothuis. 2001. "The New NBA Collective Bargaining Agreement, the Median Voter Model, and a Robin Hood Rent Redistribution." *Journal of Sports Economics,* 2(2): 131–44.

Hill, J.R., J. Madura, and R.A. Zuber. 1982. "The Short Run Demand for Major League Baseball." *Atlantic Economic Journal,* 10(July): 31–35.

Hill, J.R., and W. Spellman. 1983. "Professional Baseball: The Reserve Clause and Salary Structure." *Industrial Relations,* 22(1): 1–19.

Hill, R., W. Griffiths, and G. Judge. 2001. *Undergraduate Econometrics.* New York: John Wiley & Sons.

Hoang, H., and D. Rascher. 1999. "The NBA, Exit Discrimination, and Career Earnings." *Industrial Relations,* 38(1): 69–91.

Hoehn, T., and S. Szymanski. 1999. "European Football: The Structure of Leagues and Revenue Sharing." *Economic Policy,* Apr.: 204–33.

Hoffman, R., C. Lee, V. Matheson, and B. Ramasamy. 2003. "The Socio-economic Determinants of Women's International Soccer Performance." Working paper.

Hoffman, R., C. Lee, and B. Ramasamy. 2002. "The Socio-economic Determinants of International Soccer Performance." *Journal of Applied Economics,* 5(2): 253–72.

Hofler, R.A., and J.E. Payne. 1997. "Measuring Efficiency in the National Basketball Association." *Economic Letters,* 55: 293–99.

Hollinger, J. 2003. *Pro Basketball Prospectus: 2003–04.* Washington, D.C.: Brassey's.

Hood, B., and M. Townsend. 1999. *The Good of the Game: Recapturing Hockey's Greatness.* Toronto: Stoddart.

Houston, R., and D. Wilson. 2002. "Income, Leisure, and Proficiency: An Economic Study of Football Performance." *Applied Economics Letters,* 9: 939–43.

Howard, D.R. 1999. "The Changing Fanscape for Big-League Sports: Implications for Sport Managers." *Journal of Sport Management,* 13: 78–91.

Humphreys, B.R. 2003. "The ANOVA-Based Competitive Balance Measure: A Reply." *Journal of Sports Economics,* 4(1): 81–82.

———. 2002. "Alternative Measures of Competitive Balance in Sports Leagues." *Journal of Sports Economics* 3(2): 133–48.

———. 2000. "Equal Pay on the Hardwood: The Earnings Gap between Male and Female NCAA Division I Basketball Coaches." *Journal of Sports Economics,* 1(3): 299–307.

Hunt, J.W., and K.A. Lewis. 1976. "Dominance, Recontracting, and the Reserve Clause: Major League Baseball." *American Economic Review,* 66(Dec.): 936–43.

Hylan, T., M. Lage, and M. Treglia. 1996. "The Coase Theorem, Free Agency and Major League Baseball: A Panel Study of Pitcher Mobility from 1961–1992." *Southern Economic Journal,* 62: 1029–42.

Idson, T.L., and L.H. Kahane. 2000. "Team Effects on Compensation: An Application to Salary Determination in the National Hockey League." *Economic Inquiry,* 38: 345–57.

James, E., N. Alsalam, J.C. Conaty, and D. To. 1989. "College Quality and Future Earnings: Where Should You Send Your Child to College?" *American Economic Review Papers and Proceedings,* 79(2): 247–52.

Jenkins, J.A. 1996. "A Reexamination of Salary Discrimination in Professional Basketball." *Social Science Quarterly,* 77(3): 594–608.

Jennett, N. 1984. "Attendances, Uncertainty of Outcome and Policy in Scottish League Football." *Scottish Journal of Political Economy,* 31(2): 176–98.

Johnson, B.K., P.A. Groothuis, and J.C. Whitehead. 2001. "The Value of Public Goods Generated by a Major League Sports Team: A CVM Approach." *Journal of Sports Economics,* 2: 6–21.

Johnstone, S., A. Southern, and R. Taylor. 2000. "The Midweek Match: Premiership Football and the Urban Economy." *Local Economy,* 15(3): 198–213.

Jondrow, J., C.A.K. Lovell, I.S. Materov, and P. Schmidt. 1982. "On the Estimation of Technical Inefficiency in the Stochastic Frontier Production Function Model." *Journal of Econometrics,* 19: 233–38.

Jones, E.B., and J.D. Jackson. 1990. "College Grades and Labor Market Rewards." *Journal of Human Resources,* 25(2): 253–66.

Jones, J.C.H. 1984. "Winners, Losers, and Hosers: Demand and Survival in the National Hockey League." *Atlantic Economic Journal,* 12(3): 1–10.

———. 1976. "The Economics of the N.H.L. Revisited: A Postscript on Structural Change, Behaviour and Government Policy." In *Canadian Sport, Sociological Perspectives,* ed. R.S. Gruneau and J.G. Albinson, 249–58. Don Mills, Ontario, Canada: Addison-Wesley.

———. 1969. "The Economics of the National Hockey League." *Canadian Journal of Economics,* 2(1): 1–20.

Jones, J.C.H., and D.K. Davies. 1978. "Not Even Semitough: Professional Sport and Canadian Antitrust." *Antitrust Bulletin,* 23: 713–42.

Jones, J.C.H., and D.G. Ferguson. 1988. "Location and Survival in the National Hockey League." *Journal of Industrial Economics,* 36: 443–57.

Jones, J.C.H., D.G. Ferguson, and K.G. Stewart. 1993. "Blood Sports and Cherry Pie: Some Economics of Violence in the National Hockey League." *American Journal of Economics and Sociology,* 52: 63–78.

Jones, J.C.H., S. Nadeau, and W.D. Walsh. 1999. "Ethnicity, Productivity and Salary: Player Compensation and Discrimination in the National Hockey League." *Applied Economics,* 31: 593–608.

———. 1997. "The Wages of Sin: Employment and Salary Effects of Violence in the National Hockey League." *Atlantic Economic Journal,* 25(2): 191–206.

Jones, J.C.H., J.A. Schofield, and D.E.A Giles. 2000. "Our Fans in the North: The Demand for British Rugby League." *Applied Economics,* 32: 1877–87.

Jones, J.C.H., and K.G. Stewart. 2002. "Hit Somebody: Hockey Violence, Economics, the Law, and the Twist and McSorley Decisions." *Seton Hall Journal of Sport Law,* 12: 165–98.

Jones, J.C.H., K.G. Stewart, and R. Sunderman. 1996. "From the Arena into the Streets: Hockey Violence, Economic Incentives and Public Policy." *American Journal of Economics and Sociology,* 55: 231–43.

Jones, J.C.H., and W.D. Walsh. 1988. "Salary Determination in the National Hockey League: The Effects of Skills, Franchise Characteristics, and Discrimination." *Industrial and Labor Relations Review,* 41: 592–604.

———. 1987. "The World Hockey Association and Player Exploitation in the National Hockey League." *Quarterly Review of Economics and Business,* 27(2): 87–101

Jovanovic, B. 1979. "Job Matching and the Theory of Turnover." *Journal of Political Economy,* 87: 972–90.

Jullien, B., and B. Salanie. 2000. "Estimating Preferences under Risk: The Case of Racetrack Bettors." *Journal of Political Economy,* 108: 503–30.

Kahane, L.H. 2004. "Race, Management and Production in the NBA." Paper presented at the Western Economic Association meetings (Vancouver, B.C., July).

———. 2003. "Production Efficiency and Discriminating Hiring Practices in the National Hockey League: A Stochastic Frontier Approach." Unpublished paper.

———. 2001. "Team and Player Effects on NHL Player Salaries: A Hierarchical Linear Model Approach." *Applied Economics Letters,* 8: 629–32.

Kahane, L.H., T.L. Idson, and P.D. Staudohar. 2000. "Introducing a New Journal." *Journal of Sports Economics* 1: 3–10.

Kahane, L., and S. Shmanske. 1997. "Team Roster Turnover and Attendance in Major League Baseball." *Applied Economics,* 29(Apr.): 425–31.

Kahn, L.M. 2000. "The Sports Business as a Labor Market Laboratory." *Journal of Economic Perspectives,* 14(3): 75–94.

———. 1993. "Managerial Quality, Team Success, and Individual Player Performance in Major League Baseball." *Industrial and Labor Relations Review,* 46(3): 531–47.

———. 1991. "Discrimination in Professional Sports: A Survey of the Literature." *Industrial Labor Relations Review,* 44(Apr.) 1: 395–418.

Kahn, L.M., and P.D. Sherer. 1988. "Racial Differences in Professional Basketball Players' Compensation." *Journal of Labor Economics,* 6(1): 40–61.

Kalirajan, K.P. 1981. "An Econometric Analysis of Yield Variability in Paddy Production." *Canadian Journal of Agricultural Economics,* 29:283–294.

Kalirajan, K.P., and R.T. Shand. 1999. "Frontier Productions and Technical Efficiency Measures." *Journal of Economic Surveys,* 13(2): 149–72.

Kanazawa, M.T., and J.P. Funk. 2001. "Racial Discrimination in Professional Basketball: Evidence from Nielsen Ratings." *Economic Inquiry,* 39(4): 599–608.

Klaassen, J.G.M., and J.R. Magnus. 2001. "Are the Points in Tennis Independent and Identically Distributed? Evidence from a Dynamic Binary Panel Data Model." *Journal of the American Statistical Association,* 96(454): 500–509.

Kmenta, J. 1997. *Elements of Econometrics.* Ann Arbor: University of Michigan Press.

Knowles, G., K. Sherony, and M. Haupert. 1992. "The Demand for Major League

Baseball: A Test of the Uncertainty of Outcome Hypothesis." *American Economist,* 36(Fall): 72–80.

Koch, J.V., and C.W. Vander Hill. 1988. "Is There Discrimination in the Black Man's Game?" *Social Science Quarterly,* 69(1): 83–94.

Koenker, R., and G. Bassett, Jr. 1978. "Regression Quantiles." *Econometrica,* 46(1): 33–50.

Koning, R. 2003. "An Econometric Evaluation of the Effect of Firing a Coach on Team Performance." *Applied Economics,* 35(5): 555–64.

Kowalewski, S. 2005. "An Investigation of Salary Determination in the National Football League." Unpublished doctoral dissertation, Temple University.

Krashinsky, M. 1989. "Do Hockey Teams Discriminate against French Canadians? A Comment on Discrimination and Performance Differentials in the National Hockey League." *Canadian Public Policy (Analyse de Politiques),* 15: 94–97.

Krashinsky, M., and H.A. Krashinsky. 1997. "Do English Canadian Hockey Teams Discriminate against French Canadian Players?" *Canadian Public Policy (Analyse de Politiques),* 23: 212–16.

Krautmann, A. 1999. "What's Wrong with Scully—Estimates of a Player's Marginal Revenue Product." *Economic Inquiry,* 37: 369–81.

Krautmann, A., and D. Berri. 2004. "Can We Find It at the Concessions? Understanding Price Elasticity in Professional Sports." Working paper, DePaul University, Aug.

Krautmann, A., and L. Hadley. 2004. "Dynasties Versus Pennant Races: Competitive Balance in Major League Baseball." Working paper, DePaul University, Aug.

Krautmann, A., E. Gustafson, and L. Hadley. 2000. "Who Pays for Minor League Training Costs?" *Contemporary Economic Policy,* 18(1): 37–47.

Krautmann, A., and M. Oppenheimer. 1996. "Training in Major League Baseball: Are Players Exploited?" In *Baseball Economics: Current Research,* ed. J. Fizel, E. Gustafson, and L. Hadley, 85–97. Westport, CT: Praeger.

Kumbhakar, S.C. 1990. "Production Frontiers, Panel Data, and Time-Varying Technical Inefficiency." *Journal of Econometrics,* 46(1/2): 201–11.

———. 1987. "The Specification of Technical and Allocative Inefficiency in Stochastic Production and Profit Frontiers." *Journal of Econometrics,* 34: 335–48.

Kumbhakar, S.C., S. Ghosh, and J.T. McGuckin. 1991. "A Generalized Production Approach for Estimating Determinants of Inefficiency in U.S. Dairy Farms." *Journal of Business and Economic Statistics,* 9: 279–86.

Kumbhakar, S.C., and C.A.K. Lovell. 2000. *Stochastic Frontier Analysis.* New York: Cambridge University Press.

Kurscheidt, M., and B. Rahmann. 2002. "The Soccer World Cup 2006 in Germany: Choosing Match Locations by Applying a Modified Cost-Benefit Model." In *Transatlantic Sport: The Comparative Economics of North American and European Sports,* ed. C. Barros, M. Ibrahim, and S. Szymanski, 171–203. Northampton, MA: Edward Elgar.

———. 1999. "Local Investment and National Impact: The Case of the Football World Cup 2006 in Germany." In *The Economic Impact of Sport Events,* ed. C. Jeanrenaud, 79–108. Neuchatel, Switzerland: Editions CIES.

Kuypers, T. 2000. "Information and Efficiency: An Empirical Study of a Fixed Odds Betting Market." *Applied Economics,* 32(11): 1353–63.

Lang, E.L., and R.J. Rossi. 1991. "Understanding Academic Performance: 1987–1988 National Study of Intercollegiate Athletes." Paper presented at the American Education Research Association annual meeting (Chicago, Apr.). ERIC Document ED331880.

Lau, L.J., and P.A. Yotopoulos. 1971. "A Test for Relative Efficiency and Application to Indian Agriculture." *American Economic Review,* 61: 94–109.

Lavoie, M. 2003. "The Entry Draft in the National Hockey League: Discrimination, Style of Play, and Team Location." *American Journal of Economics and Sociology,* 62: 383–405.

———. 2000. "The Location of Pay Discrimination in the National Hockey League." *Journal of Sports Economics,* 1: 401–11.

———. 1989. "Stacking, Performance Differentials, and Salary Discrimination in Professional Ice Hockey: A Survey of the Evidence." *Sociology of Sport Journal,* 6: 17–35.

Lavoie, M., and G. Grenier. 1992. "Discrimination and Salary Determination in the National Hockey League: 1977 and 1989 Compared." In *Advances in the Economics of Sport,* vol. 1, ed. Gerald Scully, 151–75. Greenwich, CT: JAI Press.

Lavoie, M., G. Grenier, and S. Coulombe. 1992. "Performance Differentials in the National Hockey League: Discrimination Versus Style-of-Play Thesis." *Canadian Public Policy (Analyse de Politiques),* 18: 461–69.

———. 1989. "Discrimination Versus English Proficiency in the National Hockey League: A Reply." *Canadian Public Policy (Analyse de Politiques),* 15: 98–101.

———. 1987. "Discrimination and Performance Differentials in the National Hockey League." *Canadian Public Policy (Analyse de Politiques),* 13: 407–22.

Lazear, E.P. 1989. "Pay and Equality in Industrial Politics." *Journal of Political Economy,* 97(3): 561–80.

Lazear, E.P., and S. Rosen. 1981. "Rank-Order Tournaments as Optimal Labor Contracts." *Journal of Political Economy,* 89(5): 841–64.

Lee, Y.H. 2004a. "Competitive Balance and Attendance in Japanese, Korean and U.S. Professional Baseball Leagues." In *International Sports Economics Comparisons,* ed. R. Fort and J. Fizel, 281–92. Westport, CT: Praeger.

———. 2004b. "A Stochastic Production Frontier Model with Group-Specific Temporal Variation in Technical Efficiency." Unpublished working paper.

Lee, Y.H., and D. Berri. 2004. "A Re-examination of Production Functions and Efficiency Estimates for the National Basketball Association." Paper presented at the 2004 Western Economics Association meeting (Vancouver, British Columbia, July).

Lee, Y.H., and R. Fort. 2005. "Structural Change in Baseball's Competitive Balance: The Great Depression, Team Location, and Racial Integration." *Economic Inquiry,* 43(Jan.): 158–69

Lee, Y.H., and P. Schmidt. 1993. "A Production Frontier Model with Temporal Variation in Technical Efficiency." In *The Measurement of Productive Efficiency: Techniques and Applications,* ed. H.O. Fried, C.A.K. Lovell, and S. Schmidt, 237–55. New York: Oxford University Press.

Leeds, Michael. 2004. "Has the Impact of New Ballparks Declined with Time?" Working paper, Temple University.

Leeds, M., and S. Kowalewski. 2001. "Winner Take All in the NFL: The Effect of the Salary Cap and Free Agency on the Compensation of Skill Position Players." *Journal of Sports Economics,* 2(3): 244–56.

Leeds, M.A., Y. Suris, and J. Durkin. 2004. "College Football and Title IX." In *Economics of College Sports,* ed. J. Fizel and R. Fort, 137–52. Westport, CT: Praeger.

Leeds, M., E. Wheaton, and I. Pistolet. 2002. "Racial Discrimination in the NBA: A Quantile Regression Approach." Unpublished manuscript.

Leonard, W.M. III, and T. Ellman. 1994. "The Influence of Race/Ethnicity in Salary Arbitration." *Journal of Sport Behavior,* 17(3): 166–69.

Levitt, S.D. 2002. "Testing the Economic Model of Crime: The National Hockey League's Two-Referee Experiment." *Contributions to Economic Analysis and Policy,* 1(1): 1–19.

Long, J.E., and S.B. Caudill. 1991. "The Impact of Participation in Intercollegiate Athletics on Income and Graduation." *Review of Economics and Statistics,* 73(3): 525–31.

Longley, N. 2003. "Measuring Employer-Based Discrimination Versus Customer-Based Discrimination: The Case of French Canadians in the National Hockey League." *American Journal of Economics and Sociology,* 62: 365–82.

———. 2000. "The Underrepresentation of French Canadians on English Canadian Teams: Evidence from 1943 to 1998." *Journal of Sports Economics,* 1: 236–56.

———. 1997. "Do English Canadian Hockey Teams Discriminate against French Canadian Players: A Reply." *Canadian Public Policy (Analyse de Politiques),* 23: 217–20.

———. 1995. "Salary Discrimination in the National Hockey League: The Effects of Team Location." *Canadian Public Policy (Analyse de Politiques),* 21: 413–22.

Lucifora, C., and R. Simmons. 2003. "Superstar Effects in Sport: Evidence from Italian Soccer." *Journal of Sports Economics,* 4(1): 35–55.

Lynch, J.G., and J.S. Zax. 2000. "The Rewards to Running: Prize Structure and Performance in Professional Road Racing." *Journal of Sports Economics,* 1(4): 323–40.

Machado, J., and J. Mata. 2001. "Earnings Functions in Portugal, 1982–1994: Evidence from Quantile Regressions." *Empirical Economics,* 26(1): 115–34.

Maddala, G. 1999. *Limited-Dependent and Qualitative Variables in Econometrics.* New York: Cambridge University Press.

Magnus, J.R., and J.G.M. Klaassen. 2001. "Forecasting the Winner of a Tennis Match." Working paper.

———. 1999. "The Final Set in a Tennis Match: Four Years at Wimbledon." *Journal of Applied Statistics,* 26(4): 461–68.

———. 1996. "Testing Some Common Tennis Hypotheses: Four Years at Wimbledon." Working paper.

Major League Baseball. 2000. *The Report of the Independent Members of the Commissioner's Blue Ribbon Panel on Baseball Economics.* New York: Major League Baseball.

Maloney, M.T., and R.E. McCormick. 2000. "The Response of Workers to Wages in Tournaments." *Journal of Sports Economics,* 1(2): 99–123.

———. 1993. "An Examination of the Role That Intercollegiate Athletic Participation Plays in Academic Achievement: Athletes' Feats in the Classroom." *Journal of Human Resources,* 28(3): 555–70.

Maloney, M.T., and K. Terkun. 2002. "Road Warrior Booty: Prize Structures in Motorcycle Racing." *Contributions to Economic Analysis and Policy,* 1(1): 1–16.

Marburger, D. 2004. "Arbitrator Compromise in Final Offer Arbitration: Evidence from Major League Baseball." *Economic Inquiry,* 42(1): 60–68.

——— (ed.). 1997. *Stee-rike Four: What's Wrong with the Business of Baseball?* Westport, CT: Praeger.

———. 1996. "A Comparison of Salary Determination in the Free Agent and Salary Arbitration Markets." In *Baseball Economics: Current Research,* ed. J. Fizel, E. Gustafson, and L. Hadley, 67–76. Westport, CT: Praeger.

———. 1994. "Bargaining Power and the Structure of Salaries in Major League Baseball." *Managerial and Decision Economics,* 15(5): 433–41.

————. 1993. "Exchangeable Arbitrator Behavior: A Closer Look." *Economic Letters,* 43: 219–20.

Marburger, D., and D. Scoggins. 1996. "Risk and Final Offer Usage Rates: Evidence from Major League Baseball." *Journal of Labor Research,* 17(4): 735–45.

Marcum, J.P., and T.N. Greenstein. 1985. "Factors Affecting Attendance of Major League Baseball: Within-Season Analysis." *Sociology of Sport Journal,* 2(Dec.): 314–22.

Marple, D.P. 1975. "Analyse de la discrimination que subissent les Canadiens français au hockey professionnel [Analysis of Discrimination against French Canadian Professional Hockey Players]." *Mouvement,* 10(1): 7–13.

Marple, D.P., and P. Pirie. 1977. "The French Canadian Ice Hockey Player: A Review of Evidence and Suggestions for Future Research." Paper presented to the 1997 Canadian Sociological and Anthropological Association meeting (Fredericton, New Brunswick, June).

Mason, D.S., and T. Slack. 2001. "Industry Factors and the Changing Dynamics of the Player-Agent Relationship in Professional Ice Hockey." *Sport Management Review,* 4: 165–91.

Matheson, V. 2004. "Does Familiarity Breed Contempt in Soccer Officiating?" Working paper.

Matheson, Victor, and Robert Baade. 2004."Mega-Sporting Events in Developing Nations: Playing the Way to Prosperity?" Working Papers 0404, College of the Holy Cross.

Matheson, V., and R. Baade. 2003. "Playing the Way to Prosperity? Mega-Events in Developing Nations." *South African Journal of Economics,* December 72 (5):1084.

Maxcy, J. 2002. "Rethinking Restrictions on Player Mobility in Major League Baseball." *Contemporary Economic Policy,* 20(2): 145–59.

McBride, D.K., L.L. Worcester, and S.L. Tennyson. 1999. "Women's Athletics and the Elimination of Men's Sports Programs: A Reevaluation." *Cato Journal,* 19(2): 323–30.

McCormick, B. 2004. "The Impact of Intercollegiate Athletic Participation on Graduation Rates." Unpublished manuscript.

McCormick, R.E., and R.C. Clement. 1992. "Intrafirm Profit Opportunities and Managerial Slack: Evidence from Professional Basketball." In *Advances in the Economics of Sports,* ed. Gerald W. Scully, 13–35. Greenwich, CT: JAI Press.

McCormick, R.E., and R.D. Tollison. 2001. "Why Do Black Basketball Players Work More for Less Money?" *Journal of Economic Behavior and Organization,* 44(2): 201–19.

————. 1984. "Crime on the Court." *Journal of Political Economy,* 92: 223–35.

McKenzie, R.B., and E.T. Sullivan. 1987. "Does the NCAA Exploit College Athletes? An Economic and Legal Interpretation." *Antitrust Bulletin,* 32(2): 373–99.

McLaughlin, K. 1994. "Rent Sharing in an Equilibrium Model of Matching and Turnover." *Journal of Labor Economics,* 12(4): 499–523.

McLean, R.C., and M.R. Veall. 1992. "Performance and Salary Differentials in the National Hockey League." *Canadian Public Policy (Analyse de Politiques),* 18: 470–75.

Medoff, M.H. 1976. "On Monopsonistic Exploitation in Professional Baseball." *Quarterly Review of Economics and Business,* 16: 113–21.

Meeusen, W., and J. van den Broeck. 1977. "Efficiency Estimation from Cobb-Douglas Production Functions with Composed Error." *International Economic Review,* 18(2): 435–44.

Miceli, T. 2004. "A Principal-Agent Model of Contracting in Major League Baseball." *Journal of Sports Economics,* 5(2), 213–20.

Miller, P. 2003. "Does Team Financial Condition Matter in Baseball's Arbitration System?" Unpublished mimeo.

———. 2000a. "An Analysis of Final Offers Chosen in Baseball's Arbitration System: The Effect of Pre-Arbitration Negotiation on the Choice of Final Offers." *Journal of Sports Economics,* 1(1): 39–55.

———. 2000b. "A Theoretical and Empirical Comparison of Free Agent and Arbitration-Eligible Salaries Negotiated in Major League Baseball." *Southern Economic Journal,* 67(1): 87–104.

Moldovanu, B., and A. Sela. 2001. "Optimal Prizes in Contests." *American Economic Review,* 91(3): 542–58.

Mulligan, J.G. 2001. "The Pricing of a Round of Golf: Inefficiency of Membership Fees Revisited." *Journal of Sports Economics,* 2(4): 328–40.

Mullin, C., and L. Dunn. 2002. "Using Baseball Card Prices to Measure Star Quality and Monopsony." *Economic Inquiry,* 40(4): 620–32.

Munasinghe, L., B. O'Flaherty, and S. Danninger. 2001. "Globalization and the Rate of Technological Progress: What Track and Field Records Show." *Journal of Political Economy,* 109(5):1132–49.

Nalebuff, B.J., and J.E. Stiglitz. 1983. "Prizes and Incentives: Towards a General Theory of Compensation and Competition." *Bell Journal of Economics,* 14(Spring): 21–43.

Narayan, P., and R. Smyth. 2004. "The Race That Stops a Nation: The Demand for the Melbourne Cup." *Economic Record,* 80(249): 193–207.

Neale, W.C. 1964. "The Peculiar Economics of Professional Sports." *Quarterly Journal of Economics,* 78(1): 1–14.

Noll, R.G. 2002. "The Economics of Promotion and Relegation in Sports Leagues: The Case of English Football." *Journal of Sports Economics,* 3(2): 169–203.

———. 1988. "Professional Basketball." Stanford University Studies in Industrial Economics Paper no. 144.

———. 1974. "Attendance and Price Setting." In *Government and the Sports Business,* ed. R.G. Noll, 115–57. Washington, D.C.: Brookings Institution.

Noll, R.G., and A. Zimbalist (eds.). 1997. *Sports, Jobs and Taxes: The Economic Impact of Sports Teams and Stadiums.* Washington, D.C.: Brookings Institution Press.

North, Douglass. 1994. "Economic Performance through Time." *American Economic Review,* 84(3): 359–68.

Oaxaca, R. 1973a. "Male-Female Differentials in Urban Labor Markets." *International Economic Review,* 14: 693–709.

———. 1973b. "Sex Discrimination in Wages." In *Discrimination in Labor Markets,* ed. O. Ashenfelter and A. Rees, 124–51. Princeton, NJ: Princeton University Press.

O'Keefe, Mary W., Kip Viscusi, and Richard Zeckhauser. 1984. "Economic Contests: Comparative Reward Schemes." *Journal of Labor Economics* 2(1):27–56.

Oliver, D. 2004. *Basketball on Paper.* Washington, D.C.: Brassey's.

Oorlog, D.R. 1995. "Marginal Revenue and Labor Strife in Major League Baseball." *Journal of Labor Research,* 16(1): 25–42.

Orszag, J.M. 1994. "A New Look at Incentive Effects and Golf Tournaments." *Economic Letters,* 46(1):77–88.

Palacios-Huerta, I. 2003. "Professionals Play Minimax." *Review of Economic Studies,* 70(2): 395–415.

Palomino, F., L. Rigotti, and A. Rustichini. 1999. "Skill, Strategy, and Passion: An Empirical Analysis of Soccer." Working paper.

Paul, R.J. 2003. "Variations in NHL Attendance: The Impact of Violence, Scoring, and Regional Rivalries." *American Journal of Economics and Sociology,* 62: 345–64.

Peel, D., and D. Thomas. 1992. "The Demand for Football: Some Evidence on Outcome Uncertainty." *Empirical Economics,* 17: 323–31.

———. 1988. "Outcome Uncertainty and the Demand for Football: An Analysis of Match Attendance in the English Football League." *Scottish Journal of Political Economy,* 35(3): 242–49.

Pitt, M.M., and L.F. Lee. 1981. "The Measurement and Sources of Technical Inefficiency in the Indonesian Weaving Industry." *Journal of Development Economics,* 9:43–64.

Poitras, M., and L. Hadley. 2005. "Do New Major League Ballparks Pay for Themselves?" *Journal of Business,* forthcoming.

Pope, P., and D. Peel. 1989. "Information, Prices and Efficiency in a Fixed-Odds Betting Market." *Economica,* 56: 323–41.

Porter, P.K., and G.W. Scully. 1982. "Measuring Managerial Efficiency: The Case of Baseball." *Southern Economic Journal,* 48: 642–50.

Preston, I., and S. Szymanski. 2000. "Racial Discrimination in English Football." *Scottish Journal of Political Economy,* 47(4): 342–63.

Public Policy Forum. 1999. *The National Hockey League in Canada.* Ottawa (October).

Quinn, K., and D. Surdam. 2004. "The Dog That Didn't Bark? Attendance Effects of Team Relocation and League Expansion in Major League Baseball, 1950–1975." Paper presented at Illinois Economics Association meetings (Chicago, October).

Quirk, J., and M. El-Hodiri. 1974. "The Economic Theory of a Professional Sports League." In *Government and the Sports Business,* ed. R. Noll, 33–80. Washington, D.C.: Brookings Institution.

Quirk, J., and R.D. Fort. 1992. *Pay Dirt: The Business of Professional Team Sports.* Princeton, NJ: Princeton University Press.

Raimondo, H.J. 1983. "Free Agents' Impact on the Labor Market for Baseball Players." *Journal of Labor Research,* 4(Spring): 183–93.

Rascher, D. 1999. "A Test of the Optimal Positive Production Network Externality in Major League Baseball." In *Sports Economics: Current Research,* ed. J. Fizel, E. Gustafson, and L. Hadley, 33–45. Westport, CT: Praeger.

Ray, M.A., and P.W. Grimes. 1993. "Jockeying for Position: Winnings and Gender Discrimination on the Thoroughbred Racetrack." *Social Science Quarterly,* 74(1): 46–61.

Reifschneider, D., and R. Stevenson. 1991. "Systematic Departures from the Frontier: A Framework for the Analysis of Firm Inefficiency." *International Economic Review,* 32(3): 715–23.

Reilly, B., and R. Witt. 1995. "English League Transfer Prices: Is There a Racial Dimension?" *Applied Economics Letters,* 2: 220–22.

Richardson, D.H. 2000. "Pay, Performance, and Competitive Balance in the National Hockey League." *Eastern Economic Journal,* 26: 393–417.

Ridder, G., J. Cramer, and P. Hopstaken. 1994. "Down to Ten: Estimating the Effect of a Red Card in Soccer." *Journal of the American Statistical Association,* 89(427): 1124–27.

Rishe, P.J. 2001. "Differing Rates of Return to Performance." *Journal of Sports Economics,* 2(3): 285–96.

———. 1999. "Gender Gaps and Profitability of College Football." *Social Science Quarterly,* 80(4): 702–17.

Robinson, Joan. 1972. *The Economics of Imperfect Competition.* 2nd ed. London: St. Martin's Press.

Robst, J., and J. Kiel. 2000. "The Relationship between Athletic Participation and Academic Performance: Evidence from NCAA Division III." *Applied Economics,* 32(5): 547–58.

Rosen, S. 1986. "Prizes and Incentives in Elimination Tournaments." *American Economic Review,* 76(4): 701–15.

———. 1981. "The Economics of Superstars." *American Economic Review,* 71(5): 845–58.

Rottenberg, S. 1956. "The Baseball Players' Labor Market." *Journal of Political Economy,* 64: 242–58.

Ruggiero, J., L. Hadley, and E. Gustafson. 1996. "Technical Efficiency in Major League Baseball." In *Baseball Economics: Current Research,* ed. J. Fizel, E. Gustafson, and L. Hadley, 191–200. Westport, CT: Praeger.

Sabo, D. 1998. "Women's Athletics and the Elimination of Men's Sports Programs." *Journal of Sport and Social Issues,* 22(1): 27–31.

Sahota, G.S., and C.K. Sahota. 1984. "A Theory of Human Investment in Physical Skills and Its Application to Achievement in Tennis." *Southern Economic Journal,* 50(3): 642–64.

Sample, B. 1992. "A Case in Point: No Regrets Despite Loss." *USA Today Baseball Weekly,* Jan. 29–Feb. 1: 38.

San Francisco Giants. 1994. *Economic and Fiscal Impacts of the Giants Franchise on San Francisco.* Prepared by Economics Research Associates, Jan. 13.

Schmidt, M.B. 2001. "Competition in Major League Baseball: The Impact of Expansion." *Applied Economic Letters,* 8: 21–26.

Schmidt, M.B., and D.J. Berri. 2004. "The Impact of Labor Strikes on Consumer Demand: An Application to Professional Sports." *American Economic Review,* 94(1): 344–57.

———. 2003. "On the Evolution of Competitive Balance: The Impact of an Increasing Global Search." *Economic Inquiry,* 41: 692–704.

———. 2002. "The Impact of the 1981 and 1994–1995 Strikes on Major League Baseball Attendance: A Time-Series Analysis." *Applied Economics,* 34: 471–78.

———. 2001. "Competitive Balance and Attendance: The Case of Major League Baseball." *Journal of Sports Economics,* 2(2): 145–67.

———. 1986a. "Frontier Production Functions." *Econometric Reviews,* 4: 289–328.

———. 1986b. "Estimation of a Fixed-Effect Cobb-Douglas System Using Panel Data." *Journal of Econometrics,* 37: 361–80.

Schmidt, P., and C.A.K. Lovell. 1980. "Estimating Stochastic Production and Cost Frontiers When Technical and Allocative Inefficiency Are Correlated." *Journal of Econometrics,* 13: 83–100.

———. 1979. "Estimating Technical and Allocative Inefficiency Relative to Stochastic Production and Cost Frontiers." *Journal of Econometrics,* 9: 343–66.

Schmidt, P., and R. Sickles. 1984. "Production Frontiers and Panel Data." *Journal of Business and Economic Studies,* 2(4): 367–74.

Schofield, J.A. 1988. "Production Functions in the Sports Industry: An Empirical Analysis of Professional Cricket." *Applied Economics,* 20: 177–93.

Scott, F., Jr., J. Long, and K. Sompii. 1985. "Salary vs. Marginal Revenue Product

Under Monopsony and Competition: The Case of Professional Basketball." *Atlantic Economic Journal,* 13(3): 50–59.

Scully, G.W. 2002. "The Distribution of Performance and Earnings in a Prize Economy." *Journal of Sports Economics,* 3(3): 235–45.

———. 2000. "Diminishing Returns and the Limit of Athletic Performance." *Scottish Journal of Political Economy,* 47(4): 456–70.

———. 1995. *The Market Structure of Sports.* Chicago: University of Chicago Press.

———. 1994. "Managerial Efficiency and Survivability in Professional Team Sports." *Managerial and Decision Economics,* 15: 403–11.

———. 1989a. *The Business of Major League Baseball.* Chicago: University of Chicago Press.

———. 1989b. "The Fans Demand for Winning." In *The Business of Major League Baseball,* ed. G.W. Scully, 101–116. Chicago: University of Chicago Press.

———. 1978. "Binding Salary Arbitration in Major League Baseball." *American Behavioral Scientist,* 21: 431–50.

———. 1974. "Pay and Performance in Major League Baseball." *American Economic Review,* 64(6): 915–30.

Seredynski, G., J.C.H. Jones, and D.G. Ferguson. 1994. "On Team Relocation, League Expansion, and Public Policy: Or, Where Do We Put This Hockey Franchise and Why Would You Care?" *Seton Hall Journal of Sport Law,* 4: 663–700.

Sherony, K., M. Haupert, and G. Knowles. 2001. "Competitive Balance in Major League Baseball: Back to the Future." *Nine: A Journal of Baseball History and Social Policy Perspectives,* 9(2): 225–36.

Shmanske, S. 2004. *Golfonomics.* River Edge, NJ: World Scientific.

———. 2001. "Price Discrimination at the Links." *Contemporary Economic Policy,* 16(3): 368–78.

———. 2000. "Gender, Skill and Earnings in Professional Golf." *Journal of Sports Economics,* 1(4): 385–400.

Siegfried, J.J., and J.D. Eisenberg. 1980. "The Demand for Minor League Baseball." *Atlantic Economic Journal,* 8(July): 59–69.

Siegfried, J.J. and A. Zimbalist. 2000. "A Note on the Local Economic Impact of Sports Expenditures," *Journal of Sports Economics* 3(4) November: 361–366.

Siegfried, J.J., J.D. Eisenberg, and A. Zimbalist. 2000. "The Economics of Sports Facilities and Their Communities." *Journal of Economic Perspectives,* 14(3): 95–114.

Sigelman, L., and P.J. Wahlbeck. 1999. "Gender Proportionality in Intercollegiate Athletics: The Mathematics of Title IX Compliance." *Social Science Quarterly,* 80(3): 518–38.

Simmons, R. 1997. "Implications of the Bosman Ruling for Football Transfer Markets." *Economic Affairs,* 17: 13–18.

——— 1996. "The Demand for English League Football: A Club-Level Analysis." *Applied Economics,* 28: 139–55.

Sloane, P.J. 1976a. "Restrictions on Competition in Professional Team Sports." *Bulletin of Economic Research,* 28(1): 3–22.

———. 1976b. "Sporting Equality: A Comment." *Journal of Industrial Relations,* 18: 79–84.

———. 1971. "The Economics of Professional Football: The Football Club as a Utility Maximiser." *Scottish Journal of Political Economy,* 17: 121–46.

———. 1969. "The Labour Market in Professional Football." *British Journal of Industrial Relations,* 7: 181–99.

Smith, M.D. 1979. "Hockey Violence: A Test of the Violent Sub-culture Hypothesis." *Social Problems,* 27: 235–47.

Solow, J., and A.C. Krautmann. 2004. "Leveling the Playing Field or Just Lowering Salaries?" Working paper, DePaul University, Oct.

Sommers, P.M., and N. Quinton. 1982. "Pay and Performance in Baseball: The Case of the First Family of Free Agents." *Journal of Human Resources,* 17: 426–36.

Speight, A., and D. Thomas. 1997a. "Arbitrator Decision-Making in the Transfer Market: An Empirical Analysis." *Scottish Journal of Political Economy,* 44: 198–215.

———. 1997b. "Conventional Arbitration in the Professional Footballers Labour Market: An Assessment of the FLAC Experience." *Industrial Relations Journal,* 28: 221–35.

———. 1997c. "Football League Transfers: A Comparison of Negotiated Fees with Arbitration Settlements." *Applied Economics Letters,* 4: 41–44.

Spitzer, M., and E. Hoffman. 1980. "A Reply to Consumption Theory, Production Theory, and Ideology in the Coase Theorem." *Southern California Law Review,* 53: 1187–1214.

Sporting News: Official NBA Guide. Annual. Saint Louis: Sporting News.

Staw, B.M., and Hoang, H. 1995. "Sunk Costs in the NBA: Why Draft Order Affects Playing Time and Survival in Professional Basketball." *Administrative Science Quarterly,* 40(3): 474–94.

Stewart, K.G., D.G. Ferguson, and J.C.H. Jones. 1992. "On Violence in Professional Team Sport as the Endogenous Result of Profit Maximization." *Atlantic Economic Journal,* 20: 55–64.

Sutter, M., and M. Kocher. 2004. "Favoritism of Agents: The Case of Referees' Home Bias." *Journal of Economic Psychology,* 25(4): 461–69.

Szymanski, S. 2004a. "Professional Team Sports Are Only a Game: The Walrasian Fixed-Supply Conjecture Model, Contest-Nash, and the Invariance Principle." *Journal of Sports Economics,* 5(2): 111–26.

———. 2004b. "Tilting the Playing Field: Why a Sports League Planner Would Choose *Less,* Not More, Competitive Balance." Unpublished mimeo., Tanaka Business School, Imperial College, London.

———. 2003a. "The Assessment: Economics of Sport." *Oxford Review of Economic Policy,* 19(3): 467–77

———. 2003b. "The Economic Design of Sporting Contests." *Journal of Economic Literature,* 41(4): 1137–87.

———. 2001. "Income Inequality, Competitive Balance and the Attractiveness of Team Sports: Some Evidence and a Natural Experiment from English Soccer." *Economic Journal,* 111: F69–F84.

———. 2000. "A Market Test of Discrimination in the English Soccer Leagues." *Journal of Political Economy,* 108: 590–603.

Szymanski, S., and T. Hoehn. 1999. "European Football: The Structure of Leagues and Revenue Sharing." *Economic Policy,* Apr.: 205–33.

Szymanski, S., and S. Kesenne. 2004. "Competitive Balance and Gate Revenue Sharing in Team Sports." *Journal of Industrial Economics,* 52(1): 165–77.

Szymanski, S., and T. Kuypers. 1999. *Winners and Losers: The Business Strategy of Football.* London: Viking Press.

Szymanski, S., and S. Ross. 2003. "The Law and Economics of Optimal Sports League Design." Working paper.

Szymanski, S., and R. Smith. 2002. "Equality of Opportunity and Equality of Outcome: Static and Dynamic Competitive Balance in European and North American Sports Leagues." In *Transatlantic Sport: The Comparative Economics of North American and European Sports,* ed. C. Barros, M. Ibrahim, and S. Szymanski, 109–26. Northampton, MA: Edward Elgar.

———. 1997. "The English Football Industry: Performance, Profit and Industrial Structure." *International Review of Applied Economics,* 11(2): 135–54.

Szymanski, S., and T.M. Valletti. 2004. "First and Second Prizes in Imperfectly Discriminating Tournaments." Unpublished manuscript.

———. 2003. "Promotion and Relegation in Sporting Contests." Working paper.

Taylor, B.A., and J.B. Trogdon. 2002. "Losing to Win: Tournament Incentives and the Draft Lottery in the National Basketball Association." *Journal of Labor Economics,* 20(1): 23–41.

Team Marketing Report. 1991–96. Various years. Chicago. http://teammarketing.com.

Telser, L. 1995. "The Ultimatum Game and the Law of Demand." *Economic Journal,* 105: 1519–23.

Torgler, B. 2004. "The Economics of the FIFA Football World Cup." *Kyklos,* 57(2): 287–300.

Tullock, G. 1980. "Efficient Rent Seeking." In *Toward a Theory of Rent Seeking,* ed. J. Buchanan, R. Tollison, and G. Tullock, 97–112. College Station, TX: Texas A&M University Press.

Upthegrove, T.R., J.V. Roscigno, and C. Charles. 1999. "Big Money Collegiate Sports: Racial Concentration, Contradictory Pressures, and Academic Performance." *Social Science Quarterly,* 80(4): 718–37.

Utt, J., and R. Fort. 2002. "Pitfalls to Measuring Competitive Balance with Gini Coefficients." *Journal of Sports Economics,* 3(4): 367–73.

von Allmen, P. 2001. "Is the Reward System in NASCAR Efficient?" *Journal of Sports Economics,* 2(1): 62–79.

Voyer, D., and E.F. Wright. 1998. "Predictors of Performance in the National Hockey League." *Journal of Sport Behavior,* 21: 456–74.

Vrooman, J. 1995. "A General Theory of Professional Sports Leagues." *Southern Economic Journal,* 61(4): 971–90

Walker, M., and Wooders, J. 2001. "Minimax Play at Wimbledon." *American Economic Review,* 91: 1521–38.

Wallace, M. 1988. "Labor Market Structure and Salary Determination among Professional Basketball Players." *Work and Occupations,* 15(3): 294–312.

Walsh, W.D. 1992. "The Entry Problem of Francophones in the National Hockey League: A Systemic Interpretation." *Canadian Public Policy (Analyse de Politiques),* 18: 443–60.

Wang, H.J., and P. Schmidt. 2002. "One-Step and Two-Step Estimation of the Effects of Exogenous Variables on Technical Efficiency Levels." *Journal of Productivity Analysis,* 18: 129–44.

Weitzman, M. 1965. "Utility Analysis and Group Behavior: An Empirical Study." *Journal of Political Economy,* 73: 18–26.

Welki, A.M., and T.J. Zlatoper. 1994. "U.S. Professional Football: The Demand for Game-Day Attendance in 1991." *Managerial and Decision Economics,* 15: 489–95.

Whisenant, W.A., P.M. Pederson, and B.L. Obenour. 2002. "Success and Gender: Determining the Rate of Advancement for Intercollegiate Athletic Directors." *Sex Roles,* 47(9/10): 485–91.

White, P.G., and W.G. McTeer. 1991. "The Effect on Performance of Being Traded during the Season: The Case of the National Hockey League." *Journal of Sport Behavior,* 14(3): 201–10.

Whitney, J.D. 1988. "Winning Games Versus Winning Championships: The Economics of Fan Interest and Team Performance." *Economic Inquiry,* 26(Oct.): 703–24.

Widmeyer, W.N., and J.S. Birch. 1984. "Aggression in Professional Ice Hockey: A Strategy for Success or a Reaction to Failure?" *Journal of Psychology,* 104(1): 77–84.

Williams, B. 1994. "Performance Indices for On-Ice Hockey Statistics." *1994 Proceedings of the Section on Statistics in Sports.* American Statistical Association, 50–54.

Williams, B., and D. Williams. 1998. "Performance Indices for Multivariate Ice Hockey Statistics." In *Statistics in Sport,* ed. J. Bennett, 141–55. London: Arnold.

———. 1997. "Are Salaries in the National Hockey League Related to Nationality?" *Chance,* 10(3): 20–24.

Willis, R., and S. Rosen. 1979. "Education and Self-selection. " *Journal of Political Economy,* 87(5, part 2): 507–36.

Wilson, D., and Y. Ying. 2003. "Nationality Preferences for Labour in the International Football Industry." *Applied Economics,* 35(14): 1551–59.

Wittman, D. 1982. "Efficient Rules in Highway Safety and Sports Activity." *American Economic Review,* 72: 78–90.

Zak, T.A., C.J. Huang, and J.J. Siegfried. 1979. "Production Efficiency: The Case of Professional Basketball." *Journal of Business,* 52: 379–92.

Zimbalist, A. 2003a. "Competitive Balance Conundrums: Response to Fort and Maxcy." *Journal of Sports Economics,* 4(2): 154–60.

———. 2003b. *May the Best Team Win: Baseball Economics and Public Policy.* Washington, D.C.: Brookings Institution.

——— 2002. "Competitive Balance in Sports Leagues: An Introduction." *Journal of Sports Economics* 3(2): 111–21.

———. 2001. "Salaries and Performance: Beyond the Scully Model." In *The Economics of Sport, International Library of Critical Writings in Economics,* ed. Andrew Zimbalist, vol. 135, 311–35. Cheltenham, UK: Elgar.

———. 1999. *Unpaid Professionals.* Princeton, NJ: Princeton University Press.

———. 1997. "Gender Equity and the Economics of College Sports." In *Advances in the Economics of Sport,* vol. 2, ed. W. Hendricks, 203–23. Greenwich, CT: JAI.

———. 1992a. *Baseball and Billions.* New York: Basic Books.

———. 1992b. "Salaries and Performance: Beyond the Scully Model." In *Diamonds are Forever: The Business of Baseball,* ed. P. Sommers, 109–133. Washington, D.C.: Brookings Institution.

About the Editor and Contributors

David J. Berri is an Associate Professor of Economics at California State University–Bakersfield. His career began in the field of international trade, but today he focuses almost exclusively on the economics of sports. Within this topic he has published sixteen papers in such journals as the *American Economic Review, Economic Inquiry,* and the *Journal of Sports Economics.* These papers have examined such topics as competitive balance in sports, the impact of labor strikes upon consumer demand, the measurement of worker productivity in professional basketball, and the rationality of decision-makers.

John Fizel is the Director of Penn State University's online MBA program, the *iMBA.* He coedited *International Sports Economics Comparisons* and *Economics of College Sports* (each with Rodney Fort), *Baseball Economics* and *Sports Economics* (each with Elizabeth Gustafson and Lawrence Hadley). He has also contributed a chapter on competitive balance in *Stee-rike Four! What's Wrong with the Business of Baseball?* and a chapter (with Randall Bennett) on college sports in *The Structure of American Industry*, while publishing papers on a variety of sports economics topics.

Rodney Fort, Professor of Economics at Washington State University, is the author of dozens of articles and monographs on sports economics and serves on the editorial board of the *Journal of Sports Economics* and the newly founded *International Journal of Sport Finance.* He is a regular speaker and panel participant on sports issues around the world. His *Sports Economics* (Prentice Hall, 2003) is rapidly becoming the leading textbook in the area. Professor Fort also has testified before the U.S. Senate on competitive balance issues and often renders expert opinion in legal cases in the United States.

Lawrence Hadley is Associate Professor of Economics at the University of Dayton. His primary research interest is the economics of the labor market for Major League Baseball. He is coeditor of *Baseball Economics: Current*

Research and *Sports Economics: Current Research.* He also serves on the editorial board of the *Journal of Sports Economics.*

Brad R. Humphreys is an Associate Professor in the Department of Recreation, Sport and Tourism at the University of Illinois at Urbana-Champaign. His research interests include the economics of sports and the economics of higher education. His research has been published in a number of economics and public policy journals, including the *Journal of Policy Analysis and Management*, the *Southern Economic Journal*, the *Journal of Economic Behavior and Organization*, the *Journal of Sports Economics*, *Regional Science and Urban Economics*, and *Public Choice.*

R. Todd Jewell received a Ph.D. in economics from the University of California at Santa Barbara in 1992, and is currently an Associate Professor at the University of North Texas. He has also taught at UC Santa Barbara, Clarion University of Pennsylvania, and the University of Texas at Dallas. During the fall semester of 2004, he was a visiting researcher at the Universidad de la República in Montevideo, Uruguay. In addition to the economics of college sports, his research interests include immigration from Mexico to the United States and health issues in Latin America.

Anthony Krautmann has been at DePaul University since 1985 where he is currently Professor of Economics. His areas of interests range from the economics of nuclear power, to the demand for state-run lotteries, to the economics of sports. He has published numerous articles on these topics, including in the *Southern Economic Journal*, *Economic Inquiry*, *Journal of Sports Economics*, and *Managerial and Decision Economics.*

John C. Leadley is Professor of Economics at Western Oregon University. He received his Ph.D. from the University of Wisconsin–Madison in 1985 and previously taught at Illinois State University. His specialization is industrial organization, with research interests in the economics of professional sports and health economics.

Young Hoon Lee is Professor of Economics at Hansung University, Korea. His research interests are in sports economics and econometrics (panel data models and stochastic frontier production models). He has published in a wide range of scholarly journals, including *Journal of Econometrics*, *Economic Inquiry*, *Contemporary Economic Policy*, *Journal of Sports Economics*, *Japanese Economic Review*, *Seoul Journal of Economics* and *Journal of Economic Theory and Econometrics.*

Michael A. Leeds is Associate Professor of Economics in the Fox School of Business at Temple University. He has published articles in the areas of labor economics, public finance, and the economics of sports. He and Peter von Allmen are coauthors of *The Economics of Sports.*

Victor A. Matheson is an Assistant Professor in the Department of Economics at the College of the Holy Cross. He earned his Ph.D. in economics from the University of Minnesota. His research interests focus on the economic impact of stadiums, franchises, and large sporting events on local economies. He also works as a professional and intercollegiate soccer referee for Major League Soccer and several NCAA Division I athletic conferences.

Barbara Erin McCormick is a Ph.D. candidate in economics at Temple University in Philadelphia, where she has been employed as an adjunct instructor and graduate assistant since 2000. She is currently completing her dissertation on the impact of athletic participation on the graduation rates of men and women. Her fields of interest include the economics of sports, labor economics, and applied econometrics.

Stefan Szymanski is Professor of Economics and Strategy at Tanaka Business School, Imperial College London. His books include *Winners and Losers: The Business Strategy of Football* (1999), *Il Business del Calcio* (2004), and *National Pastime: How Americans Play Baseball and the Rest of the World Plays Soccer* (2005). He has published numerous scholarly articles on sport economics, including team finance and performance, competitive balance, and international comparisons of sporting institutions.

Peter von Allmen is Associate Professor of Economics at Moravian College in Bethlehem, Pennsylvania. He received his B.A. from the College of Wooster and Ph.D. from Temple University. His research interests include sports economics, family labor supply models, and pedagogy. Within sports economics, his primary interest is in the relationship between pay, performance, and incentives. He is the coauthor (with Michael Leeds) of *The Economics of Sports.*

Zenon X. Zygmont is Associate Professor of Economics at Western Oregon University in Monmouth, Oregon. He received his Ph.D. from George Mason University in 1994 and taught at George Mason and Reed College. His research interests include the economics of collegiate and professional sports, economic education, and the transition of the former Soviet-type economies. He is a Detroit Tigers fan.

Index